ACCESS YOUR ONLINE RESOURCES

Becoming a Sensory Aware School is accompanied by a number of printable online materials, designed to ensure this resource best supports your professional needs.

Go to https://resourcecentre.routledge.com/speechmark and click on the cover of this book.

Answer the question prompt using your copy of the book to gain access to the online content.

"This is an absolutely fantastic resource; I was entranced by all of the amazing activities and how incredibly useful they are. I love the visuals, and the cat food session had me squirming! I think this toolkit will make such a difference in raising awareness and understanding as well as making necessary changes to sensory wellbeing in schools."

Jane De Ste Croix, *Principal Educational Psychologist, Bath and North East Somerset*

"*Becoming a Sensory Aware School* offers practical strategies and compassionate approaches to create a more inclusive and effective learning space for all students. This book provides educators with the tools they need to support every student's sensory journey. From understanding sensory processing to implementing sensory-friendly classroom designs and lesson plans to support students' sensory understanding, it covers all essential aspects. Additionally, it challenges you to reflect on your own sensory preferences and wellbeing. Perfect for teachers and teaching assistants, *Becoming a Sensory Aware School* is a must-read for anyone committed to fostering an environment where all students can thrive."

Beth Smithson, *Sensory Inclusive Schools, Sensory Integration Education*

BECOMING A SENSORY AWARE SCHOOL

Sensory needs are often misunderstood and, as a result, neglected across many schools. Yet sensory needs are universal foundational building blocks at the base of both human and learning needs. This practical book covers everything schools need to know and consider about the sensory needs of all students and staff within the school environment. By focusing on all sensory needs in a holistic way, this leads to a deeper understanding of one another and is a truly inclusive approach to benefit all.

Sensory Aware Schools have the potential for happier and more productive learning environments, with reduced potential for disruption as well as improvements in how school communities work and learn together. Chapters look at the sensory aware student and teacher and the sensory aware classroom and school, setting out the roadmap for working from sensory awareness to sensory inclusion and towards sensory wellbeing.

The book:

- Sets out the core and quality standards for Sensory Aware Schools
- Provides a clear introduction to sensory systems and sensory awareness, discussing a variety of different models and approaches
- Contains audit tools to help the reader to reflect on sensory needs, as well as a wealth of best practice tips, reflective questions and case studies
- Develops staff skills in recognising and responding to sensory needs
- Offers easy-to-implement, practical strategies for effective, short-term adjustments as well as long-term improvements to the sensory school environment
- Includes an extensive sensory curriculum for students.

This accessible book equips the reader with a multitude of strategies and resources and illustrates how adopting a whole school approach to sensory wellbeing will benefit everyone. It is essential reading for school leaders, Special Educational Needs and Disabilities Co-ordinators (SENDCOs) and primary and secondary teachers in mainstream or specialist provision, who are keen to develop an ethos of supporting sensory needs.

Alice Hoyle is a wellbeing education consultant specialising in Relationships, Health and Sex Education (RSHE). She is a neurodivergent (ND) mum supporting varying levels of sensory needs in her ND family. Having worked in schools as a teacher, Personal Social and Health Education (PSHE) lead, Youth Worker and Local Education Authority (LEA) Education Adviser for two decades, she is very aware how sensory needs are hugely misunderstood and neglected across many mainstream schools.

Tessa Hyde is an Occupational Therapist with nearly 40 years of experience working in the UK National Health Service (NHS) and independent sector. She works with schools and families to assess, identify and support the sensory and physical motor co-ordination needs of school aged children. Tessa has a wealth of knowledge and strategies to support co-ordination and sensory needs at home and at school.

Alice and Tessa were neighbours for 10 years. This book was created after Tessa led a successful assessment on one of Alice's daughters, where the suggested strategies were transformative.

BECOMING A SENSORY AWARE SCHOOL

A Toolkit to Develop a Whole School Approach for Sensory Wellbeing

Alice Hoyle and Tessa Hyde

Designed cover image: © Dani Pasteau

First published 2025
by Routledge
4 Park Square, Milton Park, Abingdon, Oxon OX14 4RN

and by Routledge
605 Third Avenue, New York, NY 10158

Routledge is an imprint of the Taylor & Francis Group, an informa business

© 2025 Alice Hoyle and Tessa Hyde

Figures in this book have been created by Alice Hoyle using Canva

The right of Alice Hoyle and Tessa Hyde to be identified as authors of this work has been asserted in accordance with sections 77 and 78 of the Copyright, Designs and Patents Act 1988.

All rights reserved. The purchase of this copyright material confers the right on the purchasing institution to photocopy or download pages which bear the support material icon and a copyright line at the bottom of the page. No other parts of this book may be reprinted or reproduced or utilised in any form or by any electronic, mechanical, or other means, now known or hereafter invented, including photocopying and recording, or in any information storage or retrieval system, without permission in writing from the publishers.

Trademark notice: Product or corporate names may be trademarks or registered trademarks, and are used only for identification and explanation without intent to infringe.

British Library Cataloguing-in-Publication Data
A catalogue record for this book is available from the British Library

ISBN: 9781032529097 (hbk)
ISBN: 9781032529073 (pbk)
ISBN: 9781003409106 (ebk)

DOI: 10.4324/9781003409106

Typeset in Helvetica Neue LT Std
by Newgen Publishing UK

Access the Support Material: https://resourcecentre.routledge.com/speechmark

This book is dedicated to the brilliant and hilarious batgirl that is Iris Hoyle. Without her being the awesome sensory soul that she is, this book wouldn't exist.

This book is also dedicated to the memory of Barbara Hyde 1929–2024 and her catchphrase "Are you having a nice time with Alice?" during the writing process, which made us smile even when we weren't!

CONTENTS

Acknowledgements		xix
one	**Introduction**	**1**
	How this book came about	1
	We are all 'sensory'	2
	Sensory inputs and their impact	3
	Sensory: A foundational building block	4
	A note on terminology around neurodivergence and sensory processing	5
	Definitions for Sensory Aware Schools	8
	What is sensory wellbeing and welldoing?	8
	What is sensory informed practice?	9
	How to use this toolkit	9
two	**What is a Sensory Aware School?**	**13**
	The [School Name] Sensory Aware Schools Charter	14
	What is the sensory school ecosystem?	16
	The Assess Plan Do Review Cycle	18
	An initial step in assessing your school for sensory awareness: The Self Assessment Tool	19
	Setting the standards for Sensory Aware Schools – A Self Assessment Tool: Core and Quality Standards	20
	Recognising your Sensory Aware School status	24
	Sensory Aware School: Core Standard summary	24
	Sensory Aware School: Quality Standard summary	24
	Reflection questions for Chapter 2	25
three	**Understanding our sensory world**	**27**
	The Eight Sensory Systems	29
	The auditory system	30
	The visual system	31
	The gustatory system	32
	The olfactory system	33
	The tactile system	35

Contents

The proprioceptive system	36
The vestibular system	38
The interoception system	39
Motor skills and co-ordination	40
Sensory thresholds	41
Sensory discrimination	42
Sensory modulation and regulation	43
Sensory input throughout the school day: The bottle of pop analogy	44
Responding to dysregulation: Think about Dan Siegel's Hand Model – flipping the lid	45
Other available models for understanding Our Sensory States	46
Our Sensory States	48
The window of tolerance	49
A note on trauma informed practice	51
Some definitions of terms used in the context of sensory processing	51
Reflection questions for Chapter 3	54

four You are a sensory individual — 55

Why is understanding our senses important?	55
Finding our sensory wellbeing through sensory welldoing	55
Starting point: Tuning into our senses	55
A Sensory Snapshot	56
Assessing your own sensory identity in more detail	58
The Sensory Me Audit	59
Sensory Spider Web	63
The Sensory Spectrum	65
Our Sensory States	66
Sensory triggers, sensory glimmers and sensory strategies	67
Wider Sensory Questionnaires/Checklists Available	72
W.E.L.L.D.O.I.N.G: Nine easy tips to build sensory joy in your life	75
Reflection questions for Chapter 4	76

five Recognising and responding to sensory needs — 77

Factors that can affect sensory behaviours	80
What sensory behaviours can you spot? You need to be a sensory detective	81

How to recognise the following behaviours		86
Recognising different sensory states		*86*
Recognising masking		*86*
Recognising stimming		*87*
Recognising sensory overwhelm		*89*
Recognising discharge behaviour		*90*
Recognising shutdowns		*91*
Recognising the under-responsive student		*91*
How reasonable is a reasonable adjustment?		94
Sensory Strategies make things better		*96*
Reasonable adjustments that may be simple to implement		*97*
Responding: Universal strategies		98
Top tips for teachers to create sensory-friendly classrooms		*99*
Importance of ergonomics		*100*
Utilising multisensory learning approaches		*100*
Sensory activities and accommodations		*103*
Managing transitions effectively		*104*
Supporting self regulation strategies through understanding bodily sensations		*104*
Responding: Targeted strategies		105
How targeted strategies can make a difference		*105*
Managing behaviour through co-regulation		*105*
Sensory tools		*106*
General classroom strategies for all students		*114*
Exam concessions		*115*
Specialist strategies		*116*
Reflection questions for Chapter 5		119
six	**Developing your sensory curriculum**	**121**
The eight key learning objectives for sensory awareness, sensory inclusion and sensory wellbeing		123
Principles for sensory welldoing		*124*
A sample group agreement for sensory sessions		*125*
Part 1: Learning more about our sensory selves		126
Sensory continuums/spectrums		*126*
Sensory dice		*129*
A sensory body scan		*133*
Our nervous and sensory systems: Research and presentation		*135*

    Sensation stations   136
    Activities to help explain our proprioceptive and vestibular sense   138
    Activities to explain interoception   141
    HALT for interoception awareness!   144
    Sensory stars   146
    Cat food: Experiencing and explaining sensory triggers   149
    Sensory spiders: A traffic light tool to explain sensory triggers   152
    My sensory body   154
    Sensory me   157
    Sensory Jenga   160
Part 2: Understanding sensory regulation   163
    Our changing sensory states   163
    Sensory states: My own analogy   168
    Stand up, sit down, flop   169
    Further activities to explore sensory needs and regulation   170
    Sensory icebergs   173
    The Sensory Flower: A Situation and Solutions Analysis   175
Part 3: Recognising, responding and respecting sensory differences   178
    A sensory audit of a school day   178
    My personal space: Too close for comfort   180
    Overloaded! The last sensory straw that overloaded the camel's back   182
    Budgeting our sensory spoons   186
    Sensory scenarios   188
Part 4: Embracing sensory wellbeing for ourselves and others   191
    Sensory me: Strategies, glimmers and triggers   191
    My personal window of tolerance   195
    My sensory wellbeing toolkit   196
    Sensory wellbeing sprites   198
    Sensory wellbeing ambassadors   199
    Core messages for sensory awareness, sensory inclusion and sensory wellbeing   200
Reflection questions for Chapter 6   201

seven	**The Sensory Aware School environment**	**203**
	Thinking about initial school design	203
	Sensory experiences around the school	204
	The dining hall	*204*
	The assembly hall	*204*
	Drama/dance studios	*205*
	The sports hall	*205*
	School corridors	*205*
	Classrooms	*205*
	The playground	*206*
	School toilets and changing rooms	*206*
	Features to consider in the school environment	206
	Lighting	*206*
	Visual ambience	*207*
	Sound	*207*
	Temperature	*207*
	Smell and ventilation	*207*
	Your school's unique sensory environment	207
	Carrying out a whole school sensory audit	*208*
	School Space Sensory Audit	*210*
	Classroom Sensory Audit	*213*
	The bare minimum audit	*217*
	A Student-led School Sensory Survey	*217*
	Ideas to improve sensory spaces across the school	220
	Dining halls	*220*
	Assembly halls	*220*
	Drama/dance studios	*221*
	The sports hall	*221*
	Classrooms	*221*
	Corridors	*222*
	Playgrounds	*222*
	An important note about the school bell	*222*
	School toilets	*223*
	Considerations for including a School Sensory Room	226
	Sensory Room resources	*227*

Contents

Quick wins and planned investment to improve the school sensory environment	229
Action Feasibility Assessment	232
Reflection questions for Chapter 7	234

eight — Whole school approach to becoming a Sensory Aware School — 235

The importance of a whole school approach	235
Revisiting the Self Assessment Tool	238
School values and ethos	238
Leadership and management for Sensory Aware Schools	239
Policy development	240
Budgeting and resourcing	243
The school day	243
Uniform	244
Staff role and responsibilities	251
Behavioural approaches	252
Staff training and development	252
Supporting staff sensory needs – staff sensory wellbeing	255
Student voice	256
Parents and carers	257
A Home/School Partnership for Meeting [Student name]'s Sensory Needs	258
Wider partnerships	259
Reflection questions for Chapter 8	262

nine — Conclusion and next steps — 263

Live a life of sensory welldoing	263
Now you have read the book: What is your action plan?	264
Sensory Informed People and Practice	265
The six pillars of Sensory Aware Schools	266
Roadmap for Becoming a Sensory Aware School	268
The 12 Principles of Sensory Aware Schools	269
Action planning for Sensory Aware Schools	270
Final words	272

Further reading and resources — 273

ACKNOWLEDGEMENTS

Alice

First, I need to thank Tessa who foolishly let herself be whisked along by my newfound passion for all things sensory and agreed to write this book with me. With her incredible knowledge and expertise and my education background and somewhat exhausting 'force of nature' personality and creative tangents (ADHD brain), we do make a dream team! I'd also like to thank my long-suffering husband Ben who always gets the right spoon in the right cup for the right drink, and knows never to whistle around me. He calmly supports my hyperfocus work episodes and sensory overload crashes. Finally, I would like to thank my incredible daughters Elsa, Iris and Ada whose dinnertime chatter tangents and resultant communication chaos, alongside the wrong spoon trolling and family catchphrase of "sensory!" (as an excuse to get out of the less pleasant jobs) always make me smile despite the resultant eye twitches this can trigger!

Tessa

This book would not be here without Alice whose energy, enthusiasm, knowledge and motivation are infectious. Working together has been fun, energising and great for learning and exploring new things, with both of us becoming increasingly aware of our sensory wellbeing. I would not be writing this without the many, many children and families who have shared their lives and taught me so much over the years – thank you all. I'd like to also thank my family who have been hugely supportive of me as always, Mum for a lifetime of support, Julia and Jonathan for wonderful food and down time, Georgie and Will for encouragement, thoughts and humouring me with my sensory needs such as being barefoot as much as possible. Finally, my friend Alice Done who has given no end of support, encouragement, reflection and a listening ear whenever I need it, as well as giving invaluable feedback on the manuscript.

Together

We would like to thank Clare Ashworth for commissioning this book, her thoughtful support during development, and all her really helpful comments on all of our draft chapters. Beth Smithson of Sensory Integration Education and Sensory Inclusive

Acknowledgements

Schools gave up hours of her time to help us discuss language choices that best suit a teaching rather than an occupational therapy community and reviewed our key 'occupational therapy' chapters to help us add additional OT perspectives into the mix.

We would also like to thank Alex Bacon, SENDCO and the Junior Leadership Team at Newbridge Primary School who trialled activities and audit tools and gave extensive feedback. Alex especially has been so helpful championing the project from the outset. He helped us to refine the Self Assessment Tool and fed back positively on a chapter we had really been struggling with, giving us the much needed encouragement that we were actually on the right lines!

We'd like to also thank Monica Parry and her Sensory Working Group of students at a large secondary school who trialled activities within Chapter 6 and gave really useful feedback to tweak certain activities for the better; Kate Truscott and students at Eclipse Education for their trialling and feedback on Chapter 6 from their perspective as a specialist education provider; Katherine Jubb, Head of House at Norton Hill School and Sian Gunton, Assistant Head at a large rural secondary school for embracing sensory awareness for their respective schools' activities weeks – they invited Alice to lead some fabulous end of term activities on sensory wellbeing that everyone enjoyed. We thank Heather Pottow for her valuable time, observations, suggestions and encouragement and Rachel Hale for her enthusiasm about the book and phenomenal knowledge of Special Educational Needs and Disabilities (SEND), particularly neurodivergent girls. We are also grateful to Jane De Ste Croix, Principal Educational Psychologist, Bath and North East Somerset for her praise and enthusiasm about Chapter 6.

A special mention is reserved for Emma Bolt, who on the last Sunday before book submission came round with a huge bag of treats (a lovely mix of sweet, crunchy, healthy and yummy, and some sensory joy in a hand lotion) to help us keep going. It was such a massive boost to us. Emma is an amazing SEND campaigner and advocate and partners with Alice on a madcap adventure to set up an independent specialist school in the local area. When we finally get this school set up, we hope it will be one of the most sensory-friendly schools in the UK! Finally, we would like to thank Alice's new kittens Nugget and Bean who have provided endless entertainment and quiet sleepy support next to us during our writing marathons. The sensory wellbeing value in stroking and sitting peacefully with a sleeping cat should never be underestimated.

Chapter one

INTRODUCTION

How this book came about

Alice and Tessa lived on the same street for 10 years. Alice works in schools and across local authorities supporting teachers, parents and students with all aspects of wellbeing education including Relationships, Sex and Health Education (RSHE). Tessa is an experienced Occupational Therapist with almost 40 years' experience of working in the NHS and the independent sector, working with schools and families, to assess, identify and support the sensory and physical motor co-ordination needs of school aged children. Alice and her family have various neurodivergent diagnoses including significant sensory processing needs. In 2022, Tessa led a very successful sensory assessment on one of Alice's daughters where the suggested sensory interventions had a hugely positive impact.

From these conversations about individual sensory needs and adjustments, we got talking about how schools approach understanding sensory needs, based on our experiences of working across many different schools in different capacities as an Occupational Therapist and RSHE Adviser respectively. We realised that much of the literature was focused either on the classroom or on the neurodivergent individuals. It was clear that what was missing was an accessible, easy to read (and hopefully to implement!) toolkit offering resources for a whole school approach to sensory awareness. A toolkit that provides audits for self and environment and sets the standards for Sensory Aware Schools. This approach recognises that every single individual in the school will have sensory needs and offers a range of ideas and strategies to recognise, educate, mitigate and respond to these for the benefit of the whole school community.

We are all 'sensory'

Take a moment to think about the things that make you shudder, clench your teeth or actively avoid them. What are they? Between us (the authors) we cannot tolerate the feeling of wearing tights, woollen or silky things or anything that generates static; the taste and textures of bananas, cheese, fish; having foods touching; watching someone eat with wooden utensils; flickering fluorescent lights; the sound of someone whistling, filing nails, using drills; or going on a roundabout.

What about the things that excite you or soothe and relax you? Those sensations you actively seek? Between us we love the smell after the rain (petrichor); the sensation of clean sheets after a bath; an elasticated waistband; a particular floral shower gel; swimming in the sea and listening to waves on the beach; a hot milky morning coffee; walking barefoot in the garden; the feel of soft cosy clothing; the combination of crunch and chew in a particular caramel biscuit; gummy sweets; a hammock swing to read in; bright colours and maximalist cluttered environments (until a threshold is reached and order needs to be restored!). To assess your sensory preferences in more detail, see Chapter 4.

The wide variety of sensory inputs (see diagram on the opposite page) we receive over the course of a day has the power to regulate us (calm or soothe us or pep up our nervous systems to make us more alert/engaged/awake) or dysregulate us (overexcite, overwhelm or overload our nervous systems) so we go into a state of anxious or possibly angry overload which for some people may lead to meltdowns or shutdowns. Thus, our varied sensory inputs can significantly impact on our mood, behaviour, energy and focus. There may also be neurodevelopmental differences which mean that some sensory thresholds (our tolerance level for a particular sensory input) are much higher or lower than others. We explore and explain this further in Chapter 3.

Our point is that each and every one of us are sensory individuals with different sensory needs. By recognising and accommodating our individual sensory needs as much as possible across the school environment, we can make schools much more pleasant, calm and safe places for *everyone* to work in and to learn. Adopting this inclusive approach to sensory wellbeing could be game changing for the staff and students at your school.

SENSORY INPUTS AND THEIR IMPACT

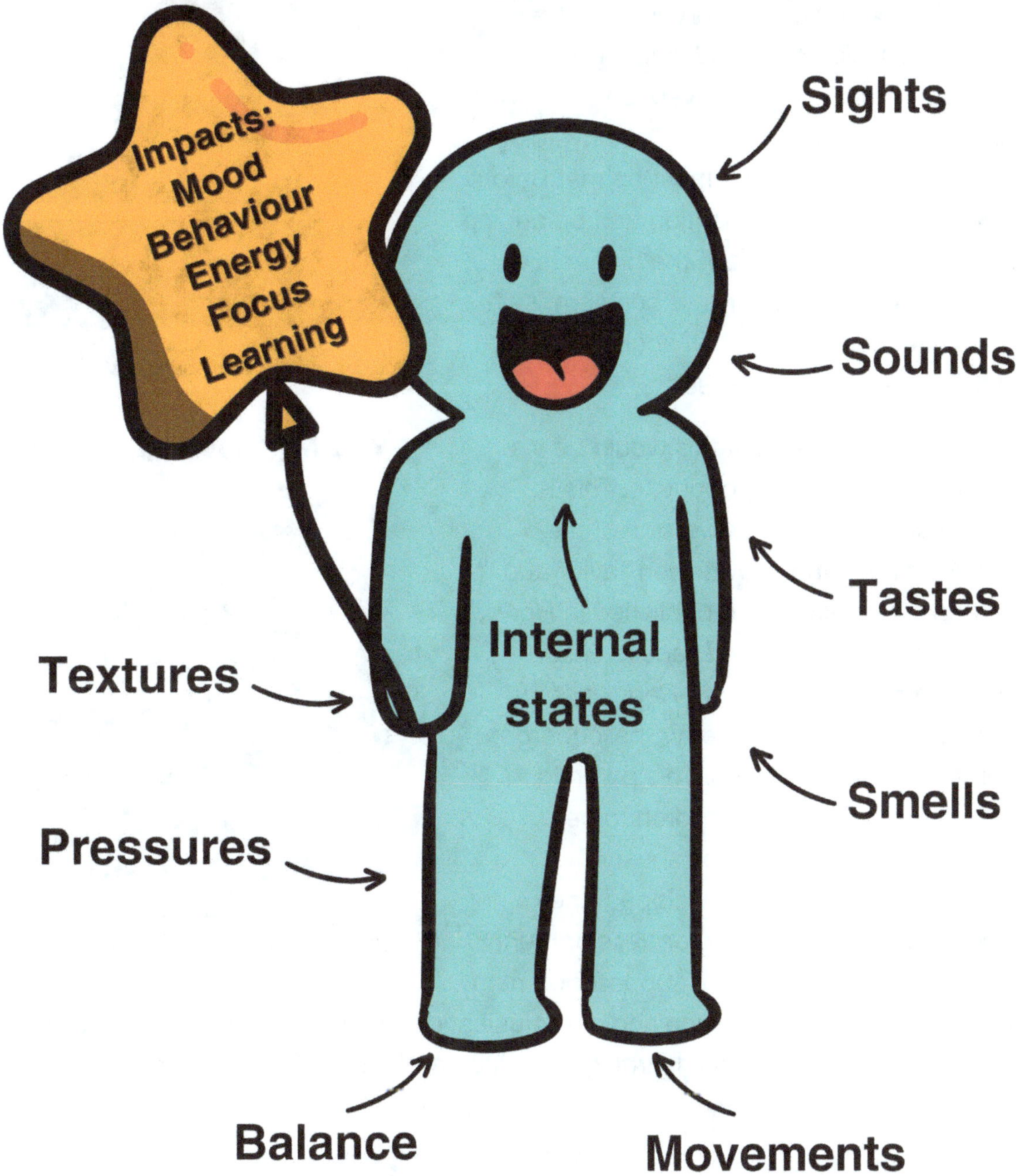

Impacts:
Mood
Behaviour
Energy
Focus
Learning

- Sights
- Sounds
- Tastes
- Smells
- Movements
- Balance
- Pressures
- Textures
- Internal states

Sensory: A foundational building block

Sensory needs, development and integration should be considered foundational building blocks at the base of both human and learning needs. For example, 'sensory' should be seen alongside physiological and safety needs in this adapted and simplified version of Maslow's Hierarchy of Needs opposite. Our physiological, sensory and safety needs must be met before we can address our connection and belonging needs, and ultimately reach the pinnacle of self actualisation (including self esteem, self respect, self confidence, self acceptance and ultimately being your best self).

Another way of looking at this would be via the Pyramid of Learning opposite. This is an adapted and simplified version of the Pyramid of Learning by Kathleen Taylor and Maryann Trott (1991), also published in *How Does Your Engine Run? A Leader's Guide to The Alert Program for Self-Regulation* by Mary Sue Williams and Sherry Shellenberger (TherapyWorks, Inc., 1996). This pyramid explains that in order for children to be able to learn and thrive, their sensory systems need to be fully developed, their sensory, perceptual and motor development supported, which will in turn support optimum development of their language and communication, behaviour and daily living skills and ultimately underpin their learning, cognition and intellectual development.

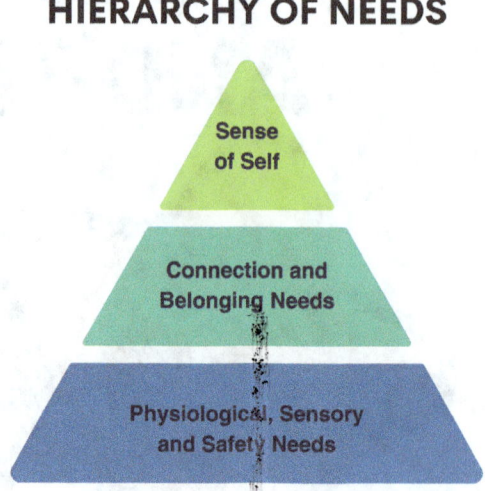

Source: Adapted from Abraham Maslow (1943).

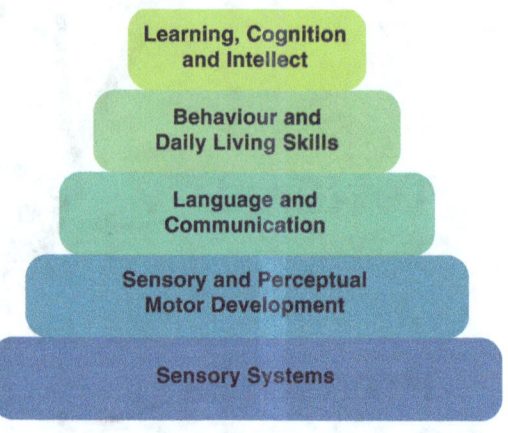

Source: Adapted from Kathleen Taylor and Maryann Trott (1991).

Sensory needs are increasing but sensory awareness is weak

We know that the global COVID-19 pandemic has also hugely increased sensory issues in the classroom. Children spent significant time at home in their comfortable clothes in potentially quieter and more predictable safer environments, and for many children, it has been a shock to the system returning to the 'normality' of school uniform and busy noisy schools. The rates of school non-attendance for anxiety or other mental health reasons have increased exponentially since this time, indicating significant challenges with now attending and learning in school environments. At the same time there has also been a huge increase in neurodivergent diagnoses such as Autism or Attention Deficit Hyperactivity Disorder (ADHD) with corresponding sensory needs.

We also note that screen time is rising. In an increasingly digital world, there can be a disconnect between our sensory experiences and our virtual interactions. For example, we might find ourselves so engrossed in screens that we ignore our bodily cues, such as postponing a trip to the toilet until the last possible moment. This sensory/virtual disconnect can deprive us of the tactile, olfactory and kinesthetic sensations we would typically experience in face-to-face interactions. While screens can bring benefits in decompression and regulation for some people, we must also consider how the reduction in sensory interactions over time may result in a gradual desensitisation, potentially making us less attuned to our own senses.

A note on terminology around neurodivergence and sensory processing

Autism and Autism Spectrum: some people use acronyms such as Autism Spectrum Disorder (ASD), also known as Autism Spectrum Condition (ASC); this book will use the 'Autism' and 'Autism Spectrum' as terms widely accepted by autistic people and their families. See the comment below about 'disorder'.

Attention Deficit Hyperactivity Disorder (ADHD) (which now includes diagnoses of **Attention Deficit Disorder [ADD]**): this book will use ADHD in absence of a better term, although we would prefer the D to stand for 'differences' rather than 'disorder', as disorder has more negative connotations.

Sensory Processing Disorder (SPD): this book does not use the term 'Sensory Processing Disorder' (SPD), as it is not currently recognised as an independent diagnosis within the *Diagnostic and Statistical Manual of Mental Disorders* (DSM–5; APA, 2013); however, it is increasingly used to describe severe sensory processing differences.

The terms on the previous page can be examples of neurodivergence – where individuals have differences in how their brains process information.

What is neurodiversity?

Neurodiversity is the range of variation in human brains; for example, in cognition and learning, attention, mood, memory, sociability. While no two brains will be the same, there is an average or expected neurotype – that is 'neurotypical' and those brains that differentiate away from the mean are sometimes described as neurodivergent. Around 15–20% of brains are thought to be neurodivergent and conditions under the neurodivergent umbrella include Autism, ADHD, Dyslexia, Developmental Co-ordination Disorder (DCD; also known as Dyspraxia), Dyscalculia, Tourette's Syndrome, Obsessive Compulsive Disorder (OCD).

Neurodiversity and sensory processing

It is really common for neurodivergent individuals to also have significant sensory processing needs where their sensory systems can easily get overloaded by certain stimuli, causing meltdowns and shutdowns (for more information, see definitions in Chapter 3 on page 51). Autistic burnout (a pervasive, long-term exhaustion – typically lasting 3+ months) leads to loss of function, and reduced tolerance to sensory stimulus, caused by lifetime stresses of navigating the predominantly neurotypical world without any reasonable adjustments. These consequences are often also caused by masking (where an individual hides their own needs to fit in), where the internal pressures to conform to societal expectations become too much.

Person-first vs. Identity-first language

This book acknowledges both person-first language (for example "child with ADHD") and identity-first language (for example "autistic student"). Some prefer person-first to emphasise the individual, while others see their neurodivergence as central to their identity. The aim should be to respect personal preferences, recognising that language can evolve and vary across individuals and communities.

Sensory needs have been historically misunderstood

We have found that sensory needs have been hugely misunderstood and neglected across many schools (particularly mainstream ones) and indeed by society. At the time of writing, schools currently still have to follow the *SEND Code of Practice* (Department of Education/Department of Health and Social Care, 2014; last updated April 2020) which has Physical and/or Sensory Needs as one of the four main areas of SEND (special educational needs and disability). However, closer reading reveals generally that the UK government meant this to be understood as having a sensory impairment such as having visual or hearing impairments, although there does appear to be a very limited understanding of autistic pupils "having sensory requirements" (paragraph 6.27, p. 98).

In March 2023, the UK government published the *Special Educational Needs and Disabilities (SEND) and Alternative Provision (AP) Improvement Plan: Right Support, Right Place, Right Time*. This set out an intention to publish national standards on how nurseries, schools and colleges must adapt the physical and sensory environment of the setting to enable children and young people with SEND to learn alongside their peers and the role of the local authority in supporting this. More recently we have noticed local authorities publishing their own guidance documents which include reference to responding to general sensory processing needs through modifications to the physical and sensory environment.

Some schools, particularly special schools and/or Special Educational Needs and Disabilities Co-ordinators (SENDCOs), have done excellent work in developing the understanding of individual sensory needs in their school; however, this is yet to filter into national best practice. Our vision would be for all schools to be aware of how our senses uniquely process our world and make the link that our sensory responses can affect our wellbeing, and that this is not necessarily unique to individuals with identified SEND.

This book is a timely sensory intervention for all schools

Our core objective is to provide schools with essential knowledge about the sensory needs of both students and staff. This toolkit emphasises that every individual in the school, including teaching and support staff, will have individual responses to the sensory environment. By adopting this holistic approach, rather than solely focusing on the sensory needs of children with special educational needs such as Autism and ADHD, we can create happier and more productive learning environments with less potential for conflict and disruption. This will build deeper understanding and inclusivity throughout the entire school community. It's also important to note here that the suggestions and strategies aimed at neurodivergent children are not exclusive and can often benefit many other children and staff in the school environment. This approach complements and enhances the mental health and emotional wellbeing agendas, safeguarding and personal development.

The intended audience for this book is school leaders, especially the Inclusion leads, SENDCOs and all educators (teachers and teaching assistants) with an interest in meeting sensory needs. It is a book that can be used in mainstream primary and secondary and specialist schools. As the intended readers are educational professionals rather than those from health backgrounds, we have deliberately chosen where possible to keep our language less medical, with clear explanations to try and make it more accessible for all. At the time of writing, sensory awareness and the language around it continues to evolve, so in wider reading you may see different terminology used; however, the underlying principles remain the same.

Definitions for Sensory Aware Schools

A **Sensory Aware School** is one that recognises we all have sensory needs, and is aiming to become **sensory inclusive** through offering sensory accommodations, an adjusted environment, and having a **sensory informed** and skilled workforce. It is one that acknowledges the sensory differences within the school community and works together with the aim of supporting **sensory wellbeing** through **sensory welldoing**. Some areas may use the term 'Sensory Inclusive School'; this is broadly the same thing.

What is sensory wellbeing and welldoing?

Sensory wellbeing refers to the state of feeling comfortable and balanced in relation to our sensory environment. This is achieved through **sensory welldoing*** which is a deliberate and conscious effort to actively use personalised sensory strategies for your own wellbeing.

---

* The concept of 'welldoing' and a 'common sensory approach' were first developed by Abby Osbourne, Karen Angus-Cole and Loti Venables from their 2024 book *From Wellbeing to Welldoing: How to Think, Learn and Be Well* (SAGE); we have adapted it here for education professionals to think about how they respond to sensory needs in their practice.

What is sensory informed practice?

Sensory informed practice is using your knowledge of the eight sensory systems and the differences between individual sensory profiles. It requires you to recognise the impact of the senses on mood, behaviour, focus, attention and learning, and implement learning opportunities and environmental adjustments that benefit your learners. The smallest and easiest practical changes you can make using your common sense combined with your increased knowledge of sensory needs is known as a **common sensory approach**.* This means not getting overwhelmed or feeling like it's too much and too hard to even start, but trying to make small practical sensory steps to help the students in your classroom and school.

A focus on sensory wellbeing will benefit everyone.

How to use this toolkit

Chapter 2: What is a Sensory Aware School? (Page 13)

This chapter starts by explaining what a sensory aware school is, it explores the sensory school system and a charter for sensory aware schools. It explains how to start to develop an Assess Plan Do Review Cycle. It provides a Self Assessment Tool with an easy to use RAG (Red, Amber, Green) rating for both Core success criteria (the basic minimum for schools), as well as Quality success criteria for schools that have gone the extra mile to be a truly Sensory Aware School. Start here to understand the principles of Sensory Aware Schools.

Chapter 3: Understanding our sensory world (Page 27)

This chapter explains our eight sensory systems. Most people are familiar with the first five, visual (sight), auditory (sound), tactile (touch), gustatory (taste), olfactory (smell); many readers may be less familiar with the remaining three – vestibular (balance), proprioception (movement) and interoception (internal senses; for example, hunger, body temperature, toileting). Each sense is explained in detail along with examples of activities within that sensory modality that people may seek or avoid. The chapter goes on to explore understandings of sensory modulation, regulation and discrimination and explains a variety of different models for helping us understand sensory regulation. Use this chapter to further understand sensory processing.

Chapter 4: You are a sensory individual (Page 55)

This chapter defines what sensory wellbeing and welldoing are, and explores how each of us is a sensory individual. It will help you identify your unique sensory identity for better understanding of sensory wellbeing using activities and reflection questions. The chapter explains concepts such as sensory glimmers and sensory triggers and starts to think about sensory strategies. Commercially and freely available sensory measures are also discussed. Explore this chapter to find out more about your own sensory needs.

Chapter 5: Recognising and responding to sensory needs (Page 77)

This chapter considers the how and why of responding to sensory needs. It details how we can recognise and respond to different sensory needs. It urges the reader to become a sensory detective and to "see behaviour – consider sensory". It considers difficulties in recognising needs caused by factors such as 'masking'. It also considers universal and targeted sensory strategies and resources for students and considers how reasonable is a reasonable adjustment. This chapter is essential reading to build your understanding of school-based strategies to meet sensory needs.

Chapter 6: Developing your sensory curriculum (Page 121)

This chapter sets out what the key learning objectives are for sensory awareness, sensory inclusion and sensory wellbeing. It explores how to establish a safe learning environment to do this work. The chapter is divided into four parts: (1) Learning more about our sensory selves; (2) Understanding our sensory regulation; (3) Recognising, responding and respecting sensory differences; (4) Embracing sensory wellbeing for ourselves and others. Use this chapter to teach your students about their own sensory needs and help them build understanding on how to embrace their sensory selves and support their peers.

Chapter 7: The Sensory Aware School environment (Page 203)

The chapter includes whole school and classroom sensory audits with an option for pupil-led audits. It includes practical strategies for low-cost short-term improvements and longer-term more expensive improvements to the Sensory Aware School environment. The chapter also includes an Action Feasibility Assessment and important points to note around school toilets. This chapter is vital in identifying strengths and weaknesses in your school's sensory environment and action planning for change.

Chapter 8: Whole school approach to becoming a Sensory Aware School (Page 235)

This chapter expands on all the key focus areas from the Self Assessment Tool from Chapter 2 that haven't already been discussed elsewhere in the book. This chapter gives the reader practical ideas and asks reflective questions to help develop a whole school approach to sensory awareness. Use this chapter to help you develop your school ethos and values; policies such as uniform and home/school partnerships; and teacher training and staff development.

Chapter 9: Conclusion and next steps (Page 263)

This chapter pulls the whole book together and sets out the six pillars of Sensory Aware Schools (place, people, participation, practice, provision and policy). It sets out the Roadmap for Sensory Wellbeing, the 12 Principles of Sensory Aware Schools and a blank Action Planning Tool. Use this chapter if you struggle with attention and want to skip to the summary endpoint faster; it obviously will contain spoilers for the rest of the book, but for some people, starting with the end in mind can help you kickstart change!

Further reading and resources (Page 273)

This section provides some further reading and a padlet link for wider resources. Visit this chapter to find wider information on this topic.

We have really enjoyed writing this book and experimenting with our own sensory wellbeing during the process. We did find at times our hyperfocus on all things 'sensory' did make us a little more 'sensitive'. We discuss this observation further in Chapter 4: 'The Seagull Caveat' on page 76.

We really hope that you find this toolkit useful and it creates meaningful change in your school settings. We would love to hear from you about how it goes!

Alice and Tessa

Chapter two

WHAT IS A SENSORY AWARE SCHOOL?

A Sensory Aware School is a nurturing and inclusive environment that recognises and respects the diverse sensory needs of all students and staff and champions sensory wellbeing through sensory welldoing. Sensory schools ideally offer gentle lighting, calming colours and softened acoustics in several, if not all, areas of the school. Sensory Aware Schools have tactile (touch), vestibular (balance and movement) and proprioceptive (body awareness) experiences available, and there's a thoughtful balance between stimulating and calmer areas or opportunities.

This sensory aware approach not only supports students with sensory processing differences, such as those who are neurodivergent, but also creates a more inclusive and comfortable learning atmosphere for everyone. Therefore, Sensory Aware Schools ensure that every child can thrive in a setting that acknowledges the significant impact of our sensory experiences on learning and wellbeing.

Do not panic, this does not require rebuilding schools from the ground up with sensory specifics built into the architect's planning and design! By considering and reflecting on your own school's unique sensory ecosystem, you can add in modifications to make improvements. This process of building in, embracing and embedding sensory awareness means your school can become a Sensory Aware School.

We provide a sample charter on the next page for you to start thinking about what this could look like. You could use this in conjunction with the Sensory Informed People and Practice box on page 265 of Chapter 9 and The 12 Principles of Sensory Aware Schools box on page 269 of Chapter 9 which could offer alternative statements to help you develop this further.

The [School Name] Sensory Aware Schools Charter

At [School Name] we recognise:

- **We all have an individual sensory profile/identity.** Every individual in our school will have unique responses to the sensory environment; this isn't just limited to pupils with SEND.
- **Understanding our sensory worlds and identity is essential.** From visual, auditory, tactile inputs, tastes and smells to movement (proprioception and vestibular) to interoception, there is so much we can learn about our sensory selves to help all of us live our best lives.
- **Sensory welldoing leads to more harmonious and productive learning environment**s. By recognising and working within our sensory needs we can create a happier and more productive learning environment with less potential for conflicts and disruption.

Therefore, we commit to:

- **Supporting our school community to understand and articulate each of our own sensory needs.** We will enable our learners and staff to support and develop their understanding of their needs, and learn in ways that are most appropriate to them.
- **Providing a sensory awareness curriculum** – that enables our learners to support and continue to develop their understanding of their needs, and learn in ways that are most appropriate to them.
- **Undertaking regular sensory audits of the environment and individuals** – to give new insights and help develop plans and policy.
- **Adopting sensory informed practice.** We will support all staff with resources and training – to develop their knowledge, understanding and skills for a sensory skilled workforce.
- **Embracing change** – we need a cultural shift in understanding sensory wellbeing, we may need to make physical changes to improve environments and we remain open and curious to possibilities.
- **Collaborating and disseminating** – we will aim to build supportive networks and disseminate best practice to enhance sensory wellbeing for all.

Whilst being mindful that:

- **This is nothing new, different or difficult.** This approach complements existing agendas around mental health and wellbeing and personal development by supporting individual and collective growth and understanding about our bodies and their needs.
- **It's not going to be perfect.** It's impossible to meet all sensory needs for everyone, all of the time, but through adopting a sensory aware approach, over the course of the school day, sensory regulation and wellbeing on the whole will broadly improve across the school.
- **We will start with the quick wins.** There are so many different ways we can improve the sensory experience of our setting for the benefits of all our students and staff. Some are easy and some are harder and require investment. Small changes can have a big impact, so we will start there.

Point to note

You may wish to just include the "we recognise" and "we commit to" points but do be aware of the "being mindful points" as these can help this work feel less overwhelming for schools and staff.

What is the sensory school ecosystem?

Schools are unique sensory environments, where the sensory ecosystem is made up of a range of factors as depicted below.

- **Individual sensory needs**

    - **Auditory** – sounds; for example, noise level, room acoustics, background noise, hand dryers in the toilets, school bells, fire alarms, whistles in PE, chairs scraping, clicking pens.
    - **Visual** – sights; for example, displays, wall colours, crowds, natural light levels, artificial lighting, screens, amount of visual clutter.
    - **Olfactory and Gustatory** – smells and tastes; for example, perfume, cleaning fluids, classroom subject-specific smells like smoke and gases in science, and food in cookery, snacks at break time and school dinners.
    - **Vestibular** – balance and movement; for example, activity playground equipment or office chairs, climbing stairs, physical education, dance and drama lessons.
    - **Proprioception** – body awareness and movement; for example, carrying heavy books or bags, sitting on the carpet, queuing in the canteen, pushing open a door.
    - **Tactile** – touch; for example, clothing and uniform, paper, pens, surfaces (walls, carpet, tabletops), fidget toys.
    - **Interoception** – awareness of own body; for example, hunger, thirst, toileting, temperature, tiredness, emotional feelings.

We are all unique, we may seek some sensory input and avoid others and our thresholds for registering each sensory input, whether it is low or high, will be different for each of us and can change depending on the environment and other factors. This is explained further in Chapter 3.

- **Interaction of the humans with each other and the school space** – the number of people in a room; how people move (run/walk) about the spaces both indoors and outdoors; queues; crunch points at lesson changeover times – will all have an impact on the sensory feel of a particular space. This will cause variations in levels of noise, temperature, scent, comfortable proximity (spacious/crowded) and so on.

What is a Sensory Aware School?

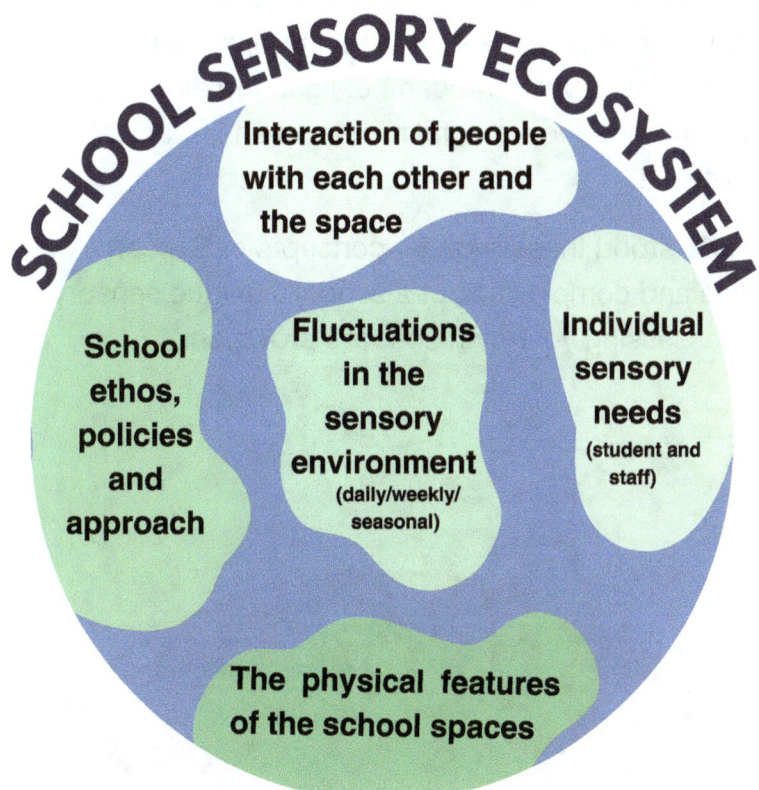

- **Fluctuations in the sensory environment (daily, weekly, seasonally)** – sensory environments in schools can vary significantly from day to day, throughout the week, and across seasons, reflecting changes in activities, routines and even weather. For example, seasonal uniform changes, a difference in classroom heating, the smell of fish on "fishy Fridays" in the canteen, variation in natural lighting in summer versus winter. These fluctuations can impact the sensory experience of individuals.
- **School ethos policy and approach** – school rules and expectations such as lining up for lessons or lunch, one-way systems to move classes through busy corridors, wearing a particular school uniform, sitting still and facing the front while learning, seating plans, will all impact on individuals' sensory processing and needs.

- **The physical features of the school spaces –** some schools are in old buildings and others are new and purpose-built. Therefore, spaces such as corridors, classrooms, halls, toilets vary and can be: light and airy, large but echoey, small and cluttered, tight for space, all of which have an impact on the people working and learning within it.

Once you have understood these broader concepts of Sensory Aware Schools as well as the varieties and complexities of a school's unique sensory ecosystem, it is important to start assessing your own school's provision.

The Assess Plan Do Review Cycle

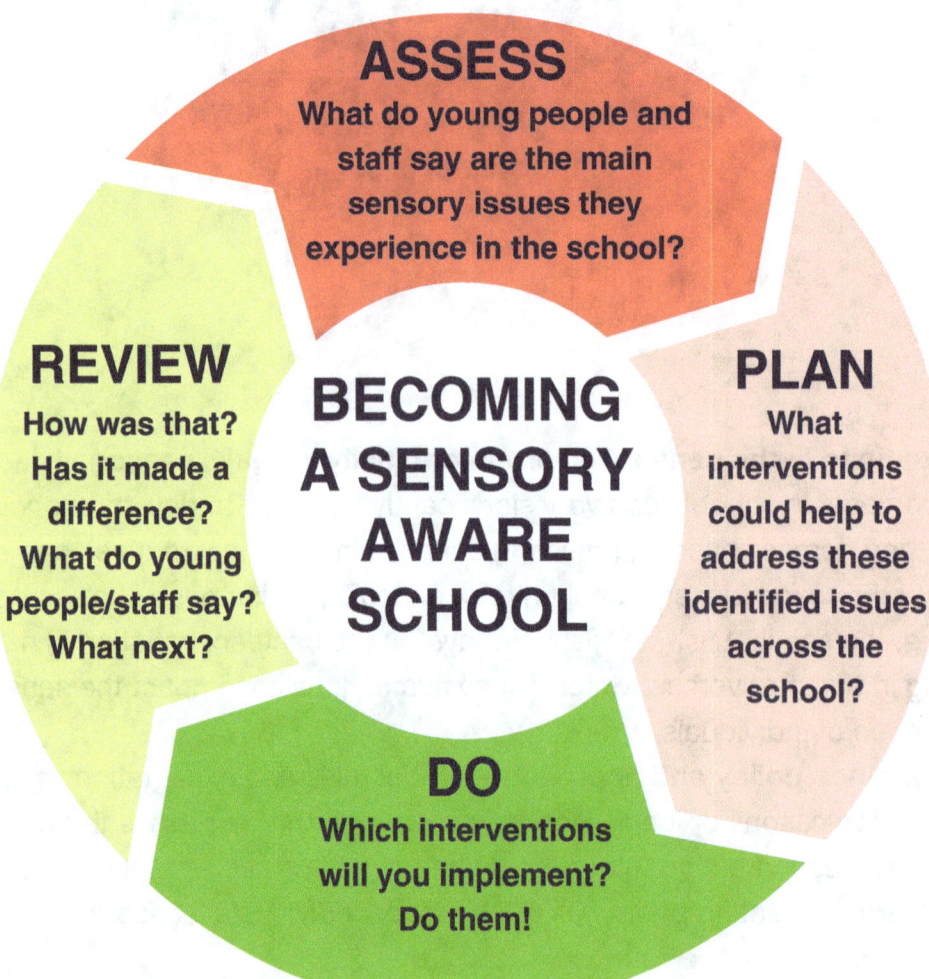

The classic Assess Plan Do Review Cycle can be utilised here to help your school become a Sensory Aware School.

Stage 1 Assess: The rest of this chapter and the audit tools found in Chapter 4 and Chapter 7 can help you assess what is going on in your school.

Stage 2 Plan: This whole book aims to help you develop a plan to become a Sensory Aware School. There are planning tools in Chapter 7 and Chapter 9.

Stage 3 Do: Chapter 5 and Chapter 6 will help you with the strategies and curriculum for this work.

Stage 4 Review: The reflection questions at the end of each chapter and Chapter 9 will help you with this.

An initial step in assessing your school for sensory awareness: The Self Assessment Tool

This tool sets out the standards for Sensory Aware Schools. This was written to enable schools to rapidly identify what they need to consider, as well as what they are doing well and what they need to improve on. The tool is divided into Core Standards – these are the basics all schools could be expected to meet; and Quality Standards – these reflect best practice in sensory awareness.

Setting the standards for Sensory Aware Schools – A Self Assessment Tool: Core and Quality Standards

Go through each of the success criteria marking with a tick where you think your school is for each Area of Focus. If you are just starting out with sensory awareness, you should focus on the Core Standards and only move onto the Quality Standards once you are in green on the Core Standards. Use the completed form to identify areas to work on. Revisit on an annual basis to check progress. Use the Notes/Evidence column to record your evidence and notes for action.

The Self Assessment Tool

Area of Focus	Core Success Criteria Rating Red = Not at all evident Amber = Emerging evidence Green = Consistently evident		Quality Success Criteria (The school meets the Core Standard and the Quality Standard) Rating Red = Not at all evident Amber = Emerging evidence Green= Consistently evident	Notes/Evidence
School Values and Ethos	Sensory awareness is mentioned somewhere in the school's ethos/values/mission statement/policies/ website.	🔴 🟡 🟢	The school ensures that sensory awareness and sensory wellbeing are embedded across the school's ethos, values and mission statement. It is clearly mentioned in policies and on the school website.	🔴 🟡 🟢
Leadership and Management	The Head, senior leaders and Governors are aware of the value of sensory awareness and sensory wellbeing in schools and are starting to develop their approach.	🔴 🟡 🟢	School leaders are embracing sensory aware approaches within the school and actively lead on sensory wellbeing. There is a designated Sensory Wellbeing Champion in the school who is adequately trained, supported by senior leadership and advocates for sensory wellbeing across the school.	🔴 🟡 🟢
Policy Development	The school has a section on sensory awareness in a relevant school policy such as behaviour policy, SEND policy, disability, accessibility and equalities policies.	🔴 🟡 🟢	The school has a Sensory Wellbeing School Policy which is developed in consultation with staff, students and parents and the content aligns with all other school policies. This policy is regularly reviewed and updated.	🔴 🟡 🟢
Planning and Implementation	The school includes sensory awareness in its development plans and goals. Sensory awareness is in the process of being implemented across the school.	🔴 🟡 🟢	The school has a sensory awareness Assess Plan Do Review Cycle – revisited every 2 years as a minimum. Sensory awareness and sensory wellbeing are embedded across the school. Sensory informed practice is adopted by staff.	🔴 🟡 🟢

Copyright material from Alice Hoyle and Tessa Hyde (2025), *Becoming a Sensory Aware School*, Routledge

Category	Description (developing)		Description (established)	
Budgeting and Resourcing	There is a budget allocated to sensory awareness for specific resources for identified children. Sensory resources are regularly checked and evaluated for effectiveness.	🟠🟡🟢	There is adequate resourcing for sensory awareness and sensory wellbeing across the school, with a ringfenced budget which includes allocated additional preparation and planning time, a training budget and funding for purchasing of sensory resources. Sensory resources are carefully selected for their suitability and reviewed for effectiveness once in use.	🟠🟡🟢
Sensory Audits of the Environment.	The school audited some spaces for their sensory characteristics and has considered some reasonable adjustments to help named students cope in those spaces.	🟠🟡🟢	The school has audited all the spaces in the school for the sensory characteristics and made a whole school action plan for implementing any necessary improvements for all students and staff.	🟠🟡🟢
A Sensory-friendly School Environment	The school has at least two different spaces in the environment that are designated 'sensory-friendly' for staff and students to access. Development plans are in place for further sensory improvements.	🟠🟡🟢	The school has several different spaces across the environment that are designated 'sensory-friendly' for staff and students to access. This should include a bookable Sensory Room, as well as at least one open access space for designated students to use as needed. Development plans are clearly in place for further sensory improvements with timeline and budget allocated. Sensory wellbeing is embedded in any future new building work at the school.	🟠🟡🟢
Sensory Audits of Staff and Students	The school offers some staff and students the option of sensory checklists and/or other tools to help identify their own sensory profile.	🟠🟡🟢	The school offers all staff and students the opportunity to identify their own sensory profiles.	🟠🟡🟢
Curriculum and Learning Opportunities	Sensory awareness appears somewhere in the school curriculum. Students are given learning opportunities to increase their knowledge and understanding of sensory awareness and sensory wellbeing.	🟠🟡🟢	Sensory awareness and sensory wellbeing are integrated across the curriculum for all students. A wide variety of teaching and learning strategies are used to learn about sensory awareness and sensory wellbeing.	🟠🟡🟢

(continued)

Area of Focus	Core Success Criteria		Quality Success Criteria		Notes/Evidence
School Day	Sensory awareness is also considered outside of lessons at one other key time of the school day at least; for example, lunchtimes.	🔴🟡🟢	Sensory awareness and wellbeing are considered throughout the whole school day including break times, lunchtimes, assemblies and student movement across school.	🔴🟡🟢	
Uniform	There are optional adaptations to support individual sensory needs with uniform where appropriate.	🔴🟡🟢	The school has designed the school uniform with students' sensory needs in mind. There are a variety of options available to meet individual needs.	🔴🟡🟢	
Staff Role and Responsibilities	Sensory informed practice. Most teaching staff (including teaching assistants) feel knowledgeable and confident around sensory awareness and understand their role and responsibilities for, and the benefits of, adopting sensory aware approaches.	🔴🟡🟢	Sensory informed practice. The majority of all staff (including lunchtime and site staff) feel knowledgeable and confident around sensory awareness and sensory wellbeing and understand their role and responsibilities for, and the benefits of, adopting sensory-friendly approaches through a common sensory approach.	🔴🟡🟢	
Supporting Staff and Student Sensory Needs	Staff and students are supported to develop understanding of their own sensory needs. The sensory experiences of students, such as those with identified special educational needs and disabilities, are acknowledged and supported. Students feel comfortable to adopt their chosen sensory strategies in lessons without feeling embarrassed or different.	🔴🟡🟢	All staff and students understand their sensory needs and know their personal specific sensory strategies for (a) engaging/focusing, (b) soothing/calming. They support their own sensory wellbeing through sensory wellbeing. Students feel able to experiment, change and be flexible with sensory strategies over time. Students are able to use their chosen sensory strategies responsibly and appropriately so as not to distract other students or teachers.	🔴🟡🟢	
Offering Reasonable Adjustments	Teaching staff and school leaders understand the importance of implementing reasonable adjustments (both in class and across the school day) for the individual child, considering the impact on the whole class.	🔴🟡🟢	All teaching staff (including teaching assistants) are able to adopt 'best fit' approaches, for the greatest number in the class, across the school day, taking into account both individual sensory needs and the needs of the whole class. These adjustments are supported by senior leaders.	🔴🟡🟢	

Category	Description	RAG	Description	RAG
Behavioural Approaches	Staff are mindful of the possibility of sensory reasons or triggers for observed behaviours.	🔴🟡🟢	Where behaviour incidents are recorded, there are opportunities to record any possible sensory reasons or triggers for the episode, to establish any patterns and develop pre-emptive sensory strategies.	🔴🟡🟢
Staff Training and Development	Teaching staff (including teaching assistants) with an interest in sensory awareness and needs are identified and supported to develop their skills. Professional development opportunities are regularly provided.	🔴🟡🟢	The school ensures that all staff (including support and site staff) receive appropriate professional development, training and ongoing support on sensory awareness and sensory wellbeing. Staff feel able to experiment and be flexible with sensory strategies for the students in their care.	🔴🟡🟢
Supporting Staff Sensory Needs	Staff are supported to understand their own sensory needs and make reasonable adjustments to support themselves.	🔴🟡🟢	Staff identify their own sensory needs and are able to make adjustments for their own sensory wellbeing through sensory welldoing. All staff feel supported to find a balance between their own sensory needs, and those of their students.	🔴🟡🟢
Student Voice	Students with specified sensory needs have a voice in feeding back on the sensory aware approaches that are developed for them.	🔴🟡🟢	Student voice (of a wide range of students across the school) is included in developing, implementing and evaluating sensory aware approaches for sensory wellbeing across the school.	🔴🟡🟢
Parents and Carers	The school works in partnership with parents and carers. Opportunities are provided for parents of named children with identified sensory needs to share with the school what they know of their child's sensory needs.	🔴🟡🟢	Parents are seen as vital for the success of meeting sensory needs at home and at school. The school has a strong home/school partnership with all parents and carers around sensory needs. Opportunities are provided for all parents to share with the school what they know of their child's sensory needs, and the school endeavours to act on these with reasonable adjustments.	🔴🟡🟢
Wider Partnerships	The school is aware of the wider local support services, such as occupational therapy, for additional support for students and training for staff.	🔴🟡🟢	The school works in partnership with wider local support services such as occupational therapy, to access further training, support and evidence-based best practice. Supportive networks are established to share good practice on sensory wellbeing.	🔴🟡🟢

Further relevant audit tools are found in Chapter 7. School space sensory audit (page 210), classroom sensory audit (page 213), action feasibility assessment (Page 232) and in Chapter 9 the action plan (page 271).

Copyright material from Alice Hoyle and Tessa Hyde (2025), *Becoming a Sensory Aware School*, Routledge

Recognising your Sensory Aware School status

A Sensory Aware School would score in the audit a minimum of 15 green ticks with no more than 5 amber ticks, with no red ticks in either the Core or the Quality Standards. This would mean that enough of the required standards have been achieved to call yourself either a Sensory Aware School: Core Standard or a Sensory Aware School: Quality Standard. You could provide versions of the following text below on your school website to champion what this means to your whole school community.

Sensory Aware School: Core Standard summary

As a Sensory Aware Core Standard School, we have embedded the fundamentals of sensory awareness into our ethos, values and future development plans. Our leadership advocates for this awareness, weaving it into critical policies to create a supportive learning environment. We conduct sensory audits to identify and address areas for improvement, and integrate sensory strategies into our curriculum. Our commitment extends to providing professional development for staff and responding to student voice, ensuring that everyone in our community contributes to and benefits from an inclusive sensory-aware environment.

Sensory Aware School: Quality Standard summary

As a Sensory Aware Quality Standard School, we have deeply embedded sensory awareness into our school's ethos, values and future development plans, guided by a dynamic Assess Plan Do Review Cycle. Designated sensory champions and collaborative policy development reflect our advanced commitment. Regular comprehensive sensory audits inform our action plans, and we integrate sensory awareness throughout the curriculum and school day. Advanced training, dedicated resources and extensive community engagement, including partnerships with external services, underscore our sophisticated approach to creating an inclusive, supportive sensory environment for the wellbeing of all.

Towards sensory wellbeing

The journey for becoming a Sensory Aware School should be as follows:

- Sensory awareness – understanding our eight senses and individual sensory needs and how the sensory ecosystem impacts on them.
- Sensory inclusion – ensuring sensory needs are fully understood and met.
- Sensory wellbeing – developing whole school sensory approaches that enhance the wellbeing of students and staff.

To do this, schools will need to develop a sensory informed workforce. We hope this book is a tool to do just that.

Reflection questions for Chapter 2

1. How would you define a Sensory Aware School?
2. Reflect on your own school's sensory ecosystem; what does it look like?
3. What does sensory informed practice mean to you?
4. Where do you want to get to as a Sensory Aware School (what is your vision for change)?
5. Have the Standards for Sensory Aware Schools Self Assessment Tool helped you consider where you are as a school for sensory awareness?
6. Where are you currently in a sensory Assess Plan Do Review Cycle?

Chapter three

UNDERSTANDING OUR SENSORY WORLD

Understanding our sensory world

Throughout this book we are considering the school sensory environment and the whole community who work/study within it. We are all sensory beings with individual sensory profiles and therefore the environment is likely to have a range of different impacts on each of us depending on our unique sensory thresholds. The level of impact can also vary depending on the time of day, the things we have already experienced during the day, what else is going on at the time and how we are feeling. The information we gather from our body and our environment, what we hear, see, smell, taste and feel is known as sensory processing; this happens constantly, enabling us to function in everyday life. Our brains note, sift and filter the information coming in from all the senses to enable us to respond appropriately (or sometimes inappropriately) in any given situation. These interpretations and responses are individual to each of us. We are likely to respond differently to something if we are feeling safe and calm, rather than being about to take an exam or having just had an accident.

Our subconscious constantly processes information from all our senses, allowing us to comprehend ourselves and our surroundings, and respond adaptively or not. The process involves several steps:

- **Registration:** Initially, we register sensory input, such as noise.
- **Orientation:** We then focus on the input, orientating ourselves towards it, assessing its impact. For example, is the noise a fire bell? Do we need to evacuate?
- **Interpretation:** Next, we interpret the information using past knowledge, memory and experience.
- **Organisation:** We organise ourselves based on this interpretation, deciding whether to respond or ignore.
- **Response:** Finally, we respond – either by taking action (such as evacuating in response to a fire bell) or by continuing with our activities (if the noise is just the air conditioning).

DOI: 10.4324/9781003409106-3

Many of us effortlessly process this information automatically and easily throughout the day, without conscious awareness. However, some of us also register every tiny piece of information, evaluating whether it poses a threat. This heightened awareness can lead to a freeze, fight or flight response, influenced by past experiences and individual thresholds for registering sensory information.

My sensory systems

The image on the next page summarises our eight sensory systems. You are already likely to be familiar with five of them but less aware of the vestibular, proprioceptive and interoceptive systems. Therefore, pay particular attention to these three. We have identified some of the common behaviours that you might see for under-responsive and over-responsive reactions; however, it is important to note that you can sometimes be both under-responsive and over-responsive in the same sensory system. For example, you might like bright colours but have a strong preference for wearing sunglasses in sunshine or you might not like the sound of whistling but enjoy loud bass music.

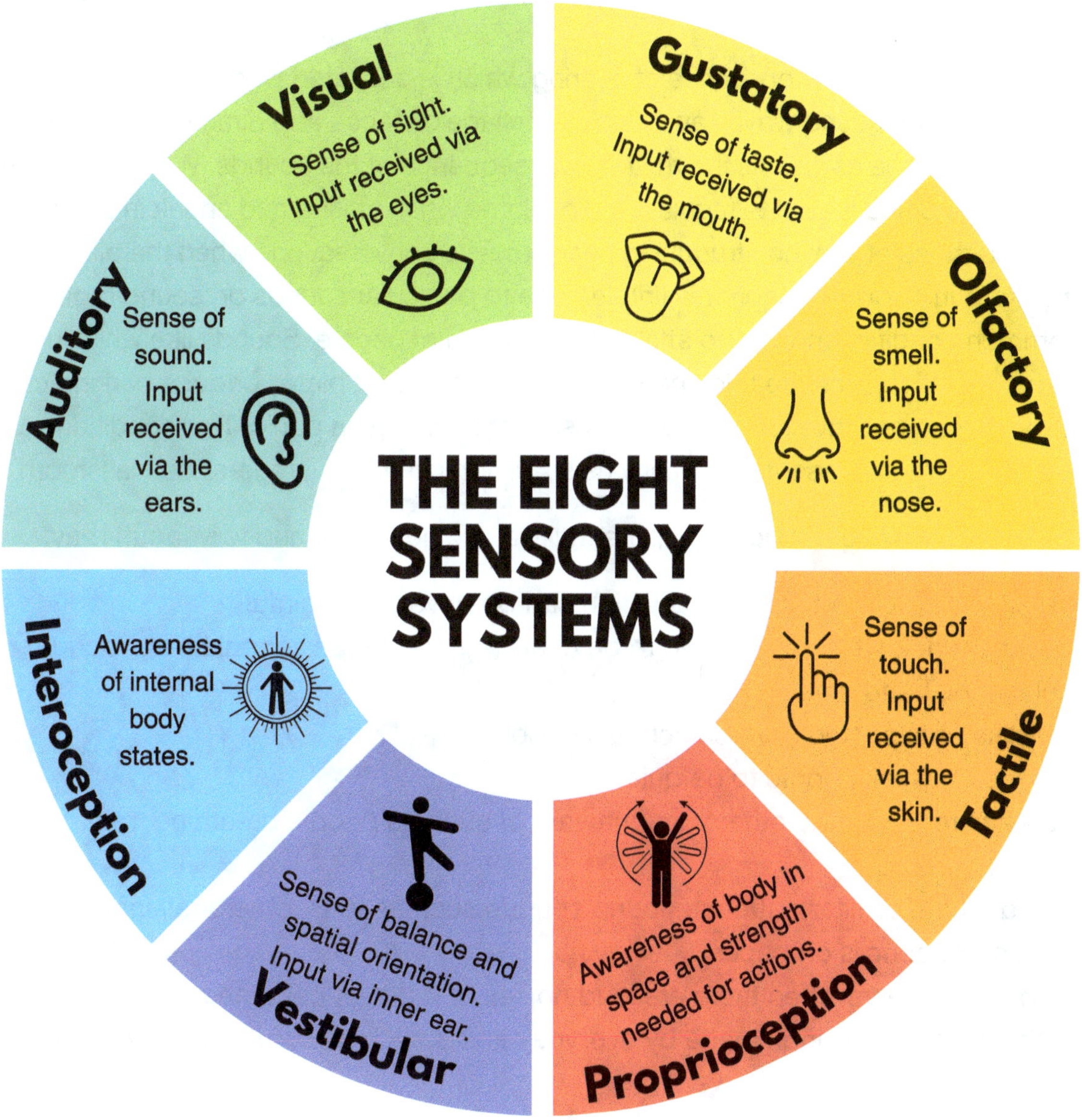

THE EIGHT SENSORY SYSTEMS

Visual — Sense of sight. Input received via the eyes.

Gustatory — Sense of taste. Input received via the mouth.

Olfactory — Sense of smell. Input received via the nose.

Tactile — Sense of touch. Input received via the skin.

Proprioception — Awareness of body in space and strength needed for actions.

Vestibular — Sense of balance and spatial orientation. Input via inner ear.

Interoception — Awareness of internal body states.

Auditory — Sense of sound. Input received via the ears.

Copyright material from Alice Hoyle and Tessa Hyde (2025), *Becoming a Sensory Aware School*, Routledge

The auditory system

The **auditory system** is our sense of hearing which is activated when our inner ear is stimulated by air/sound waves and helps us tell the distance and direction of the noise, the pitch and tone as well as the rhythm and sequence of the sounds. We are all aware of people who find it hard to regulate their volume when talking and speak in a loud voice and those of us who struggle to hear/process conversations when there is a lot of background noise. Misophonia (intolerance to particular sounds or 'sound rage') is a common condition thought to affect almost a fifth of people. Sounds like whistling, sniffing, throat clearing, people chewing, forks scraping on plates or dogs barking can cause a strong negative reaction of distress, anger and even panic. This condition could therefore be present in as many as six children in the average-sized classroom.

People who are over-responsive (potentially avoiding lots of auditory input) may:

- Dislike loud or certain sounds which can be physically painful
- Fear sounds which are known to be challenging such as school bells, vacuum cleaners, hand dryers
- Dislike unexpected noises such as fire bells
- Frequently ask people to be quiet
- Be aware of sounds others are unaware of such as people breathing, radiators, lights buzzing
- Find it hard to filter out background sounds such as fans, others talking, the sound of pencils on paper
- Cover their ears when there are loud noises or if things become overwhelming
- Dislike certain sounds made by everyday items such as some fabrics/clothing, clicking on pens, hand dryers
- Dislike working in noisy environments or be unable to work with background noise
- Avoid crunchy foods or eating with others (who may make a noise while eating).

In school this could be seen with children being unable to work in a busy classroom with others talking; developing behaviours which enable them to avoid certain noises, such as going out of the class when the bell is going to be rung or not using the toilets due to the sound of the hand dryer or refusing to wear certain clothes or to use certain regular equipment due to the noise it makes (sounds of 'squeaking clothing' as you move).

People who are under-responsive (potentially seeking lots of auditory input) may:

- Not respond to their name or voices
- Appear not to hear what is being said or miss part of conversations

- Seem to be oblivious of what is going on around them
- Need instructions to be repeated as they did not hear the first time
- Talk loudly
- Love loud noises or working with background music/noise to help with focus
- Make noises, hum or sing to self when working
- Seem to 'zone out'.

In school this could present with pupils appearing to look at the teacher during instructions and then saying, 'I didn't hear any of that' or 'I don't know what I have to do' or chatting to their neighbours or singing/humming during quiet focused work times. Under-responsive staff may have music on in the classroom while everyone is working or could prefer to do their own planning/marking while listening to music or with the radio on in the background.

The visual system

The **visual system** is our sense of sight and is the information we receive from the eyes which enables us to see colour and contrast, shape and movement. It helps us to define boundaries as we move through space and helps us pay attention and direct our actions and movements. Our proprioceptive and vestibular systems (see pages 36 and 38) work closely with our vision to assimilate our senses and enable us to function effectively. Vision is a much more familiar sense and more easily understood by us, but it is not just about visual acuity and perception and how well we can see things. We are all aware that some people love bright lights and colours and others prefer more subdued environments with more neutral colour schemes; these can affect both mood and ability to focus and concentrate or relax at home. People who are over-responsive (potentially avoiding lots of visual input) may:

- Prefer to work in dim lighting conditions or with natural light
- Frequently rub their eyes
- Become easily distracted by things around them such as others working, things on the table/board/walls
- Dislike fluorescent lighting or bright sunshine
- Be unable to find what they are looking for, particularly in 'busy' environments
- Like to work on a clear, organised desk without distractions
- Prefer neutral colour schemes and minimalist environments
- Have difficulty copying from the board.

In school this could present with some students finding it hard to find things on the wall if there is a lot of visual 'clutter', or disliking the particular light from the overhead projector or the flickering of a fluorescent light; some students or staff will put sunglasses on when they go into the playground at break times regardless of the time of the year as sunlight can be too dazzling or bright.

People who are under-responsive (potentially seeking lots of visual input) may:

- Love bright lights and sunshine
- Enjoy busy displays and environments with lots of things displayed on the walls and things hanging from the ceiling
- Enjoy wearing bright clothing and accessories
- Prefer bright colours with lots of variety and visual interest (which could be seen by others as cluttered)
- Lose their place when reading
- Become easily fatigued with school work
- Enjoy working in different visual environments
- Become distracted in class, while looking around and taking everything in.

In school this could present with children being easily distracted by what other children are doing or things going on around them, or flitting from one thing to another without being easily able to settle to their own work; their desk may be cluttered or busy with paper and books on top of each other leading to further distractions. Under-responsive staff may enjoy the classroom being very visually stimulating with a lot of information available on the walls and many different displays.

The gustatory system

The **gustatory system** gives us our sense of taste, it is obtained from the mouth and chemical receptors on the tongue and inner mouth which identify five different tastes: sweet, salty, sour, bitter and umami (savoury); this is closely linked with our tactile sense for texture and our sense of smell. Taste is very individual and we all like/dislike different foods.

People who are over-responsive (potentially avoiding lots of gustatory input) may:

- Have an extremely restricted diet/be a picky eater
- Be reluctant to try new foods
- Gag at the thought of certain foods
- Have difficulty sucking, chewing, swallowing
- Be reluctant or refuse to lick stamps or stickers
- Avoid certain textures of food

- Prefer bland tastes
- Hate, or be very sensitive to, teeth cleaning.

In school this could be seen with pupils who eat the same food daily, refuse to eat during the day or will only eat packed lunches rather than having school meals.

People who are under-responsive (potentially seeking gustatory input) may:

- Prefer strong flavours such as sour or spicy
- Over-fill their mouth when eating
- Love using electric toothbrushes
- Mouth non-food items and chew pencils, clothing, nails, etc.
- Show excessive drooling
- Enjoy a variety of tastes and textures of food
- Like trying new/different foods
- Enjoy chewing gum or eating sweets such as peppermints while working.

In school this could be seen with pupils choosing spicy or sour snacks at break times and constantly chewing pencil tops/cuffs on clothing, etc. Under-responsive staff may like to graze on snacks throughout the day, with increased textures through crunchy or chewy items such as gummy or chewy sweets, crisps, carrots/apples, dried fruits or chewing gum.

The olfactory system

The **olfactory system** gives us our sense of smell and is gained from chemical receptors in the nose which help us smell if something is musty, acrid, rotten, foul, appetising, sweet, fresh, appealing, etc. Our sense of smell is closely linked with our sense of taste and with memories (as it is processed in the same part of the brain that attaches emotion to memory); we are all aware of smells which take us back to a certain time and place in extremely vivid ways such as the smell of a certain soap reminding us of a time spent with grandparents or the smell of a cleaning fluid reminding us of time spent in hospital.

Smells can also be a major challenge for students in lessons, with many at secondary school, in particular, finding smells in specific lessons overwhelming, making it extremely hard or impossible to work within them. One student we know was unable to cope with the smell of the English classroom. The school got a diffuser with some lavender oil which helped enormously. Another student was unable to go into the science lab, but managed to do so by putting some of his dad's aftershave on his tie (which he found comforting); he was then able to attend the lessons and engage.

People who are over-responsive (potentially avoiding lots of olfactory input) may:

- Notice smells that others don't
- Be acutely aware of the different smells in school such as changing rooms, science labs, dining room, etc.
- Dislike going to certain places, such as swimming pools, grocers, dining hall, due to the smell
- Be able to identify people or places by their smell
- Refuse to eat certain foods due to the smell, which can lead to restricted diets
- Refuse to go to certain houses or see certain people due to the smells
- Gag or be physically sick at certain smells
- Find it hard to engage with some activities which have strong smells such as gardening, painting nails, washing using toiletries with strong or artificial smells.

This can be seen in school with children who struggle to engage in practical activities such as cooking or science experiments; avoid certain areas of the school; identify their own and other children's clothes by smell; shy away from teachers they perceive to have a distinct smell or who wear strong perfumes/aftershave.

People who are under-responsive (potentially seeking olfactory input) may:

- Not notice odours/smells that other people are commenting on
- Not be aware of noxious smells such as burning, gas or chemicals, so can be unaware of danger
- Excessively sniff at people or objects
- Crave strong smells and spices
- Enjoy wearing perfume/fragrance
- Burn candles while working
- Use smell as a way of helping to feel regulated such as using reed diffusers in all rooms
- Enjoy activities with varied and strong smells associated with them.

This could be seen in school with pupils who are completely unaware of the fact that the drains are blocked or are always smelling staff and pupils or items they are given; they may choose to use scented colouring pens. Under-responsive staff may prefer to wear strong perfumes/fragrances or to have specific oils or essences in the classroom such as peppermint or citrus to help with focus and concentration. Staff need to be aware of the potential impact their scent choices can have in the classroom.

The tactile system

The **tactile system** or our sense of touch relates to the information gained through the skin which enables us to tell the difference between light and deep pressure, hard/soft textures, temperatures and vibrations and if something is sharp or not. We all respond differently, and some people love the feel of soft fabrics such as velvet and others cringe at the thought. People who are over-responsive (potentially avoiding lots of tactile input) may:

- Flinch away from touch or certain textures
- Be fearful or anxious at light or unexpected touch
- Hate messy hands/face; for example, glue, paint, food
- Have difficulty standing in line between others which may lead to pushing others away
- Hate tight clothing
- Find hair washing and nail cutting traumatic and distressing
- Restrict diet depending on textures of food
- Over-react to minor cuts and grazes.

In school this could mean that the school uniform is hard to wear due to the feel of the fabric or the cut of the garment; paint/glue and messy activities are avoided or hands are washed immediately the task is finished; the feel of the paper may make it hard to write, sleeves may be pulled down to cover the hand and reduce contact with the paper or an unusual pencil grasp may develop as a way of minimising the contact of hand on paper. Over-responsive staff may choose not to wear velvet or wool clothing, buy several of the same items to make sure they are comfortable and cut out labels from clothing. Please see the section on page 244 of Chapter 8 for more information on school uniform.

People who are under-responsive (potentially seeking tactile input) may:

- Like tight clothing and often prefer to wear clothing which is too small
- Enjoy the feel of certain fabrics
- Be very 'tactile/touchy feely' with others when talking with them or sitting next to them; for example, putting a hand on their arm
- Twirl or stroke hair, fiddle with items

- Be unaware of personal space
- Be unaware of cuts and grazes until they are pointed out to them
- Enjoy walking barefoot at any opportunity
- Seek out and love messy play or become covered in paint/glue when engaging in art activities
- Not notice crumpled clothing
- Be unaware of food on their face or hands.

In school this might manifest as a student finding shoes annoying and frequently removing them whenever possible. Students might unintentionally hurt others during playtime by seeking physical contact excessively. Under-responsive staff may prefer to take shoes off in lessons, twirl their hair or fiddle with items unconsciously while teaching.

> **Personal space and body proximity and awareness combine both proprioceptive and tactile senses**
>
> In a busy school environment, the close proximity to others can be a sensory challenge for some students. Moving through crowded hallways, sitting in packed classrooms, queuing up outside classrooms or to collect lunch, or simply the nearness of others at school can feel overwhelming. This invasion of personal space may heighten anxiety and discomfort in some students, triggering a stress response that affects the student's ability to focus and engage effectively throughout the school day. Whereas other students struggle to read others' bodily cues and constantly invade others' personal space without realising, which can cause difficulties for the other person. Teachers need to think carefully about how they can support students who struggle with proximity (either can't cope with the proximity of others, or inadvertently invade the personal space of others) as part of their classroom management.

The proprioceptive system

The **proprioceptive system** gives us our sense of body awareness and is received from muscles and joints; it is activated by muscle contraction/movement which gives us our awareness of the precise position of our body in space, how our body is moving at any time, grading of movements (appropriate force/pressure of the action – not too little or too much) and is important for our motor planning. This sense enables us to remain sitting on a chair or standing without thinking about it and to accurately grade the movement of picking up a cup and drinking without slamming it on the table or pouring the liquid down our front. Proprioception is our ultimate regulation sense and is often known as the 'first aid' sense, due to the effect it has on all the senses, so students who are observed to be seeking proprioceptive input through deep pressure and resistance may in fact be trying to regulate another sense with this input.

This is the one sense to which it is generally felt that you cannot be over-responsive. People who are under-responsive and so seek this sensation (which is more frequently seen in school, as they are trying to regulate themselves in the school environment) may:

- Have low muscle tone, so prop themselves/flop against people or surfaces when sitting or standing
- Walk 'heavily' or stamp/stomp when walking
- Seek hugs and like bear hugs
- Chew on toys or pencils or grind teeth
- Miss their mouth with food and drink (misjudging distance)
- Become fatigued or tired easily
- Be 'on the go', moving in their seat, fidgeting with items
- Press hard on the page with a pencil when writing/drawing
- Use too much pressure and always break things
- Overshoot when pouring drinks or milk onto cereals so it goes everywhere
- Bump into others, furniture, doorways frequently due to poor body awareness.

In school these pupils may be always moving in their seat or fiddling, in an attempt to increase their sense of body awareness; they press very hard when writing so as to leave indentations on the page beneath (or several) and be constantly breaking pencil points and needing to sharpen them; they may at times bump into furniture or peers and can accidentally hurt others due to poor body awareness and grading of movements and 'being unaware of their own strength'. Under-responsive staff may knock things off tables, run a finger along the corridor wall when walking, or press hard on the paper when writing.

The vestibular system

The **vestibular system** gives us our sense of balance and is based in the inner ear and gained through head movements; it is closely linked with vision and proprioception and helps us to judge the speed and direction of movement, whether it is us who is moving or our surroundings, the position of our bodies in space; it also impacts our posture and muscle tone. We all respond differently to vestibular input: some people love the feel of roller coasters, running, spinning, etc., and others become easily dizzy or feel sick when travelling in cars or bending over very quickly. People who are over-responsive (potentially avoiding lots of vestibular input) may:

- Be more sedentary and avoid rapid movements
- Choose slower, calmer sports/hobbies such as yoga, walking or those which are more linear such as swimming, archery
- Move with a rigid posture or move slowly in a more stilted manner rather than exaggerating movements
- Stay away from swings, slides, playground/fairground equipment
- Prefer using stairs to lifts and escalators
- Be afraid of heights, even things which do not seem very high off the ground, such as benches during PE lessons
- Find it hard to learn to ride a bike or be fearful of bike riding
- Lose balance easily and become disorientated bending over
- Avoid games due to the movement or unpredictability.

In school this could mean that pupils move more carefully and slowly than others and walk in a stiff somewhat robotic manner, rather than moving their body a lot while walking. These children would prefer to be at the side of the classroom or playground rather than in the middle where they may become jostled and feel dizzy; they may be reluctant to join in with games or try new activities which may make them feel sick; they could find school trips stressful, with the thought of the coach journey at the start and end of the day; they may sit very still, dislike bending down to pick things up or moving quickly in dance or PE. Over-responsive staff may avoid active trips such as skiing or theme parks, may offer to be the driver rather than the passenger, get others to bend down to get things off the floor or demonstrate movements to avoid feeling dizzy.

People who are under-responsive (potentially seeking vestibular input) may:

- Love playgrounds, fairground rides and want to repeat them as much as possible
- Be seen as 'thrill seekers' with a lack of awareness of danger at times

- Appear 'On the go' at all times
- Like sudden movements or changes of direction, so are frequently active
- Have difficulty stopping or move in a frequent stop/start manner
- Love spinning/twirling and can do this a lot without appearing dizzy
- Rock in a chair when working or when standing and talking
- Balance on two legs of the chair, seeking the point of balance to increase vestibular input
- Enjoy sitting on gym balls or on rocking or spinning office chairs when reading or working.

In school these pupils could be seen as thrill seekers, choosing hobbies and lifestyles which include lots of movement and activity such as active sports. In class they will be the children who are constantly moving, changing position when working, frequently walking around the classroom, rocking on the chair, etc., and at break times they enjoy the monkey bars or trim trail or run around constantly. Under-responsive staff may spin on office chairs, mark while sitting on a gym ball and have active lifestyles.

The interoception system

The **interoception system** gives us our internal body sense and lets us know when we are hungry, thirsty, tired, in pain, makes us aware of our body temperature and when we need to go to the toilet. It also includes heart rate and breathing, as well as emotions.

People who are under-responsive or less aware of interoceptive input may:

- Not notice when they are thirsty until they have a headache
- Not feel hungry until they feel unwell or sick
- Leave it until the last minute to go to the toilet, sometimes not making it in time
- Develop constipation, sometimes with encopresis (soiling), due to reduced fluid and food intake, combined with poor timing of toilet visits
- Wear jumpers when it is hot as they are unaware of their body temperature
- Be less aware of cuts, scrapes, breaks
- Eat too little or too much at mealtimes
- Confuse internal needs with emotions, so they may feel sick when actually worried or anxious.

This can be seen in school with children who forget to eat or drink anything during the day, but become 'hangry' (hungry and angry) at home because their blood sugar is so low and they haven't noticed. Or children who do not know they need to go to the toilet until the last minute, leading to not making it in time and possibly needing to change clothing. Students or staff may be dressed inappropriately, wearing many layers and looking hot in the height of summer or having bare legs in the middle of winter as they don't notice their body temperature.

People who are sensitive (have over-responsive interoception) may:

- Feel overwhelmed by internal information/feelings; for example, butterflies in stomach, heart racing
- Find it hard to focus on external information as internal feelings are so strong
- Have difficulty concentrating if physical needs are not met
- Pick up on internal cues quickly
- Notice every small scratch or knock as a huge concern
- Notice their temperature to the extent of complaining of being hot or cold frequently
- Go to the toilet frequently throughout the day
- Show poor tolerance of being hungry and need to 'graze' throughout the day.

This can be seen in school when students and staff have an emotional response to being hungry, such as becoming 'hangry' very easily if they don't get regular snacks. They may need to go to the toilet or have a drink frequently. The slightest internal changes and sensations can be very painful and can be distracting.

Motor skills and co-ordination

Many students who experience sensory processing needs (particularly those with challenges with discrimination) will also have difficulties with motor co-ordination. It is really important for students to feel safe and in control of their own body, to be able to engage in everyday skills such as getting dressed, writing, riding a bike, swimming . When students are unsure how much strength to use for a task, if they cannot pick up an item easily, or successfully connect with a ball when kicking, they are faced with constant reminders that they are finding things harder and their efforts are less successful than those of their peers. Therefore, ongoing weak motor co-ordination skills may cause a reluctance to participate, with a resultant impact on their social skills as students become increasingly aware of the differences in their own success compared to others. Ensuring that students' motor co-ordination is assessed, understood and fully supported is essential in giving them the skills to be able to successfully participate fully in everyday life alongside their peers.

Sensory thresholds

Sensory thresholds play a crucial role in how individuals interact with and interpret their environment. We all have unique thresholds/levels for registering information. Sensory thresholds refer to the point at which an individual perceives and responds to sensory stimuli, whereby some people effectively have a fine sieve to filter information (so notice everything) and others have a wide-meshed sieve with large holes, which lets a lot of information through before they are consciously aware of it. This means that many people will notice the seam in their socks as they put them on in the morning in order to adjust them comfortably; they then filter this out for the rest of the day. However, some students will notice the seam in their socks at this level for the whole day, as if it was a potential threat, and will be unable to filter this out, meaning that this will be occupying their awareness rather than the teacher talking to the class about the lesson. Some will be unaware of information until it is pointed out to them, such as a fire bell ringing or a broken bone after a fall, as they have a much higher threshold for registering sensory input.

Our sensory thresholds can also vary based on factors such as age, genetics, past experiences and individual sensitivities. Some individuals may have lower thresholds, making them more sensitive to stimuli and prone to sensory overload, while others may have higher thresholds, requiring more intense stimuli for them to register. Often people will have different thresholds for different senses, and these are not necessarily fixed but can fluctuate. Remember that environmental conditions also vary daily, weekly or seasonally; this can also change the way we

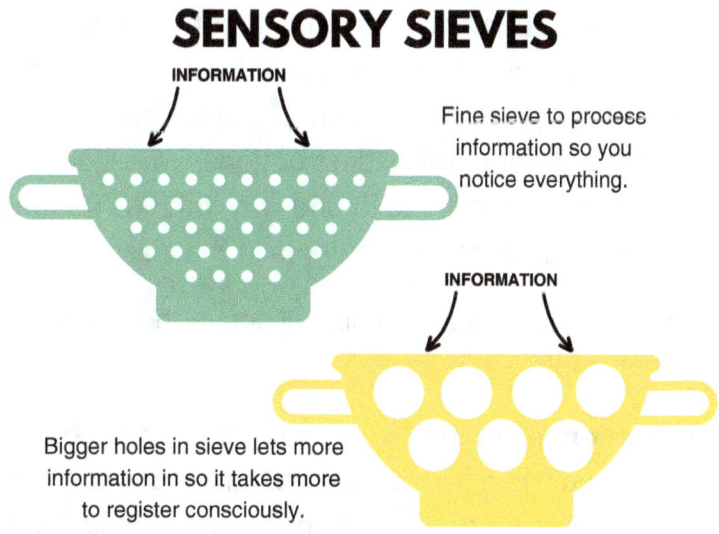

respond to things at different times. These thresholds can also vary throughout life; for example, due to puberty, ageing or certain medical conditions.

Anxiety and stress significantly impact sensory processing, often lowering our thresholds and heightening awareness of the sensory environment. This heightened awareness can lead to difficulty filtering out irrelevant stimuli and may contribute to increased anxiety. Distinguishing outward behaviours driven by sensory or emotional factors can be challenging. At times of increased anxiety, we become more distracted and unable to cope with situations which we can usually navigate with ease. For example, the sound of the coffee machine, clinking cups and other people talking in a café may lead to us being unable to engage in a conversation with a friend (which we would normally do with pleasure), which leaves us taking avoidance behaviours, such as actively removing ourselves from the situation. During times of heightened anxiety, sensory strategies can be beneficial in alleviating unease caused by too much sensory input. However, it's essential to recognise that while sensory strategies may help us manage situations triggered by sensory issues, they may not address the root cause if it is primarily driven by underlying anxiety. In such cases, a more comprehensive approach, including addressing the emotional aspects of anxiety, is likely to be necessary for effective resolution.

Sensory discrimination

Sensory discrimination is the ability to distinguish the quality and properties of sensory inputs. This includes recognising subtle differences in textures, sounds, tastes and other sensory information. In a classroom setting, a student with sensory discrimination issues might struggle to differentiate between the sound of their name being called and other background noise, or they might have trouble writing because they cannot feel the pen properly in their hand. Such difficulties can impact learning, attention and the ability to follow instructions. We all need to be aware that just because we perceive something in one way, this will not necessarily be the same for the person next to us or all the students in the class.

The most common discrimination issues you will see in the classroom are auditory, visual and tactile. For example:

- **Auditory discrimination** refers to the ability to differentiate between different sounds or auditory stimuli. It involves both recognising and understanding subtle differences in pitch, tone, rhythm and volume, as well as distinguishing between

similar or overlapping sounds. It is a very important part of auditory processing, and many students and staff find this extremely challenging which can make daily interactions exhausting, so many people will be unable to sustain focus and will tune out/opt out, as a coping mechanism. Auditory discrimination skills are crucial for various tasks throughout the day, including language development, speech perception and sound localisation.
- **Visual discrimination** refers to the ability to distinguish between similar but different images/visual input such as similar letters, like 'b' and 'd' or numbers like '6' and '9'. Students may appear confused or struggle to locate their own belongings among others, such as finding their workbook in a pile or their coat on a row of hooks. Additionally, they may have difficulty with tasks that require sorting or organising based on visual characteristics, like colour-coding materials or grouping objects by shape.
- **Tactile discrimination** refers to the ability to differentiate between different textures/tactile input and the information we are gaining through our skin. A child with tactile discrimination problems may appear clumsy, have difficulty with fine motor tasks like handwriting or be slow to get dressed and do up fastenings, as they cannot easily interpret the information they receive from holding/touching things. Most of the time, the reason some students seek a lot of tactile input or try to regulate through deep pressure is linked to poor discrimination rather than an under-responsive tactile system.

Sensory modulation and regulation

Sensory modulation and regulation are essential processes that involve receiving and organising sensory information effectively from all of our senses throughout the day. It involves managing the intensity, duration and nature of sensory input to maintain an optimal level of focus and attention. This ability allows us to adapt to our environment and respond effectively within it. We may actively seek certain sensory inputs such as chewing gum or listening to music to help us stay engaged and regulated, while avoiding other inputs which dysregulate us, such as sitting on an office chair or wearing 'scratchy' fabrics. This can mean that students who appear disruptive or are withdrawn could in fact be trying to regulate their sensory input. For example, they may cover their ears during assembly to block out loud sounds or avoid science activities which involve touching messy things. These reactions can affect our ability to engage in learning and social interactions. Preferences for sensory experiences, whether seeking or avoiding, vary amongst all of us and can change depending on a variety of factors, as already discussed.

Sensory input throughout the school day: The bottle of pop analogy

You will all know of the parents who complain of their children being 'total nightmares' at home, but at school they are never a problem. Many children save up their meltdowns for when they can finally feel safe enough to 'unmask' and let out all those big feelings.

The 'bottle of pop analogy' is often used to help people understand the experience of sensory overload. Picture a bottle of pop that's been shaken up throughout the day, and then eventually the pressure becomes too much and when opened the bottle explodes, causing a mess. This explosion is akin to a meltdown, which is a reaction to the accumulated sensory triggers and stress experienced by the individual. The image below shows an example of the kinds of triggers that might shake up the bottle.

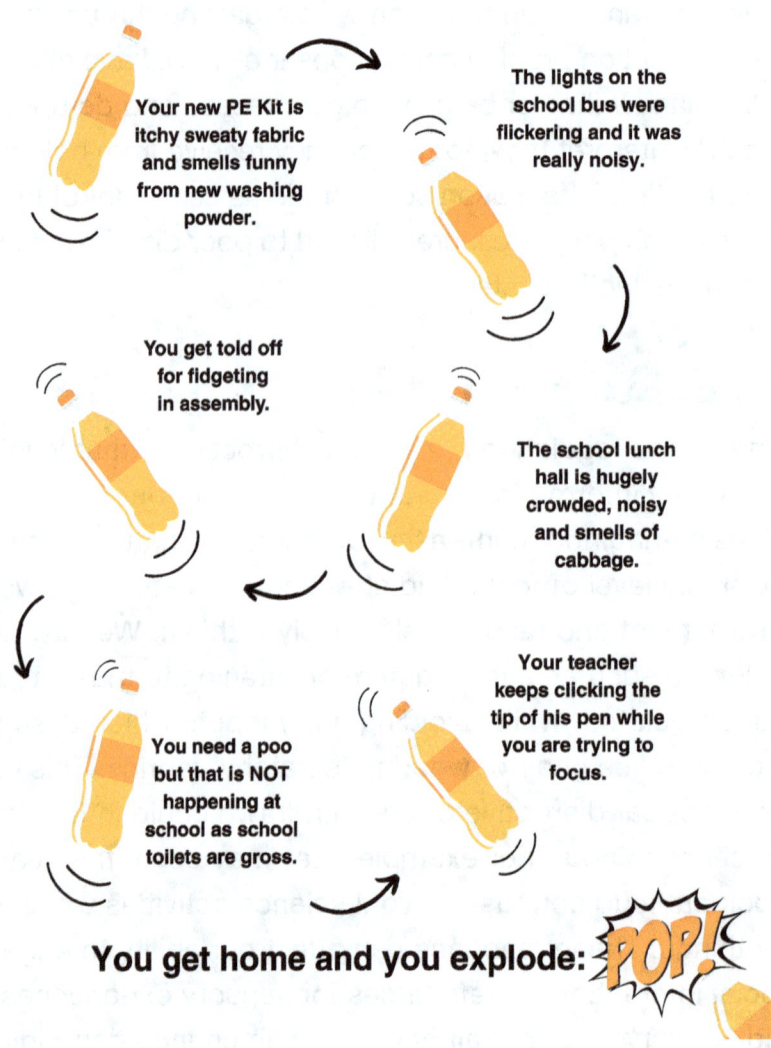

By the end of the day, the accumulated sensory triggers can become too much to handle, causing the individual to experience a meltdown – like the explosion of the shaken pop bottle. To avoid meltdowns, it's essential for individuals who are autistic or have ADHD, their families and their support network to be aware of these triggers and work together to minimise them when possible. Implementing sensory strategies consistently across the day can help reduce the effect of the sensory triggers and lead to sensory regulation/modulation to reduce the likelihood of meltdowns at the end of the day. For further information, see the infographic 'Sensory strategies make things better' in Chapter 5, page 96.

Responding to dysregulation: Think about Dan Siegel's Hand Model – flipping the lid

To better understand why it's challenging to reason or communicate with a dysregulated child, Dan Siegel, Clinical Professor of Psychiatry, developed the Hand Model of the brain (lots of videos available on YouTube) which describes the concept of 'flipping the lid', a helpful analogy. Imagine the brain as a closed fist, where the fingers wrapped down over the thumb represent the rational thinking part of the brain, and the thumb itself symbolises the emotional centre that influences physiological functions like heart rate.

In a regulated state, the thumb is held in the palm of the hand, and the fingers are down, depicting a closed fist with well-connected pathways between different brain areas. This state enables clear thinking and responsive behaviour. However, when a child becomes dysregulated, the thumb becomes active, pushing the fingers up – metaphorically flipping the lid. In this flipped lid state, the child is primarily operating from the reptilian fight or flight part of the brain, and the rational thinking part (the fingers) are less effective in acting as a brake on emotions.

Attempting to communicate reasonably with a child in this dysregulated state is not possible. The child is no longer thinking and acting clearly, as the rational part of the brain is less engaged. It's important to wait until the child's 'lid' is back down, and the brain is in a more regulated state before attempting communication. During these moments, the different parts of the brain are better connected, and the child is more receptive and capable of making better decisions. Utilising strategies to help the child regulate, such as offering comfort or a safe environment, co-regulating with the child, becomes essential before expecting them to respond effectively to reasoning or to do the task originally asked of them. Chapter 5 expands on this in the section on 'Managing behaviour through co-regulation' (page 105).

DAN SIEGEL'S HAND MODEL OF THE BRAIN

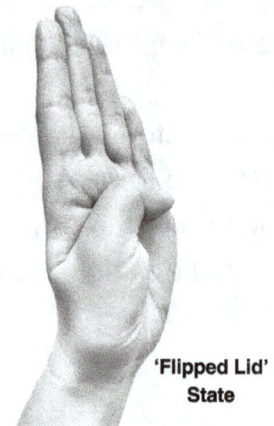

Regulated State

'Flipped Lid' State

Reflection questions

- When was the last time you felt stressed, overloaded, dysregulated and like your lid had flipped?
- What was the result of feeling like this? Was there a 'last straw' moment that caused you to 'explode' or 'collapse'?
- Can you think of all the contributory factors that led to you feeling and responding like this?
- Do you think if you had added in some sensory supports the outcome may have been different?
- Did you know the point at which things were starting to feel like 'too much'? Would you be able to identify this point in future and make changes?

These questions could also be helpful to use with students to unpack behavioural incidents.

Other available models for understanding Our Sensory States

There are a wide variety of models used to describe and explain sensory and emotional regulation. In the table on the next page, we detail some of the most common.

Understanding our sensory world

Models for Understanding Our Sensory States

MODEL	Zones of Regulation	The Arousal Curve/ Speedometer	The Arousal Graph/Bell Curve	The Sensory Quadrant
	 **ZONES OF REGULATION** — Blue Zone (REST): I feel… slow, sad, sluggish, sick so I need to… REST. Green Zone (GO): I feel… ready to go, happy, focused, calm so I can… GO. Yellow Zone (SLOW): I feel… frustrated, anxious, worried, excited, silly so I need to… SLOW. Red Zone (STOP): I feel… angry, out of control, overloaded, ready to explode so I need to… STOP.	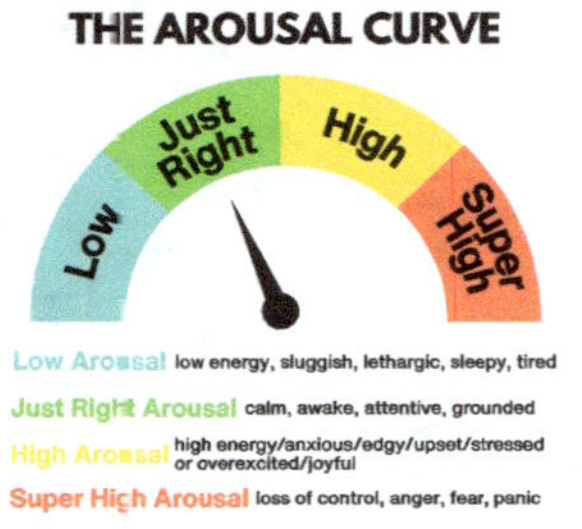 **THE AROUSAL CURVE** — speedometer showing Low, Just Right, High, Super High. Low Arousal: low energy, sluggish, lethargic, sleepy, tired. Just Right Arousal: calm, awake, attentive, grounded. High Arousal: high energy, anxious/edgy/upset/stressed or overexcited/joyful. Super High Arousal: loss of control, anger, fear, panic.	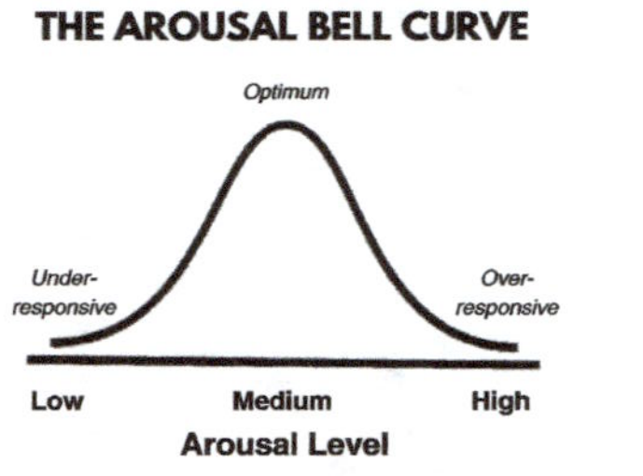 **THE AROUSAL BELL CURVE** — bell curve with Under-responsive (Low), Optimum (Medium), Over-responsive (High) Arousal Level.	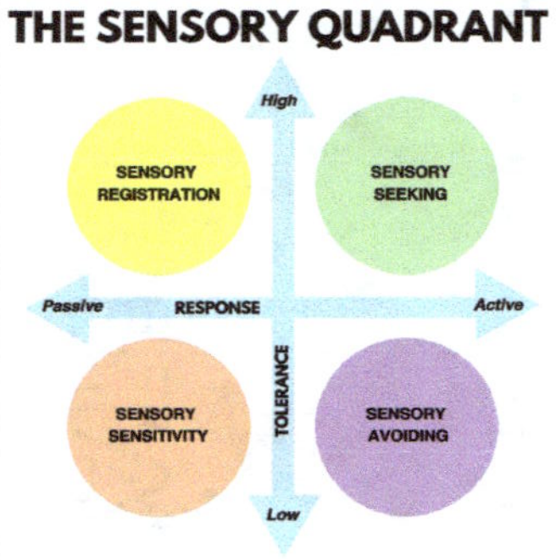 **THE SENSORY QUADRANT** — Active/Passive axis and High/Low Tolerance (Response) axis, with four quadrants: Sensory Seeking, Sensory Avoiding, Sensory Registration, Sensory Sensitivity.
Origin	Based on Leah M. Kuypers, *The Zones of Regulation* (Social Thinking Publishing, 2011)	Based on Mary Sue Williams and Sherry Shellenberger, *The Alert Program* (1995, 2 audio CDs)	Based on the Yerkes-Dodson Law of Arousal and Performance (R. M. Yerkes and J. D. Dodson, *Optimal Arousal Theory*, 1908).	Based on Winnie Dunn's Sensory Profile (*Living Sensationally*, Jessica Kingsley, 2007).
Use	Four coloured zones to describe how a child is feeling – blue, green, yellow and red.	A 'speedometer' description to describe arousal levels.	A bell curve to explain underarousal, optimum functioning and overarousal.	A way of explaining sensory processing/regulation and how a person is functioning.
Pros	• Visual • Widely used in schools • Students are able to identify zones throughout the day	• Clear movement along the speedometer indicating change throughout the day • Visually appealing and adaptable • Easy analogy to understand	• Simple visual graph • Widely used in different settings • Can easily be drawn out and explained with a young person	• Quadrant clearly sets out these four key states • More precise representation of a sensory profile • Technically more accurate – based on questionnaire responses • Winnie Dunn identifies and explains Seekers, Avoiders, Bystanders and Sensors – see her book *Living Sensationally*
Cons	• May be used inconsistently across schools • Children aren't always taught the underpinning theories behind the colours and may default to 'green zone' as they think that's the zone they are supposed to be in • It may be harder to see movement through zones	• Used in therapy but not as familiar in schools • Young people and teachers report they don't like the use of the word 'arousal' as it makes them think it's something to do with sex • Less familiar language so 'just right zone' can be harder to identify	• Needs explanation, an understanding of graphical representation is needed • Implies a journey through each state, rather than fluctuating across the states • Not as intuitive for a young person to identify where they are	• Quite technical. Takes thinking about to fully understand • This model merges responses to give an overall position which may make it harder to understand individual senses and responses • Often used by therapists for explanations rather than being school based

The models in the table on the previous page all have strengths and limitations in using with young people. In our experience, these models may be used directly in specialist schools and with SEND pupils, but their use across mainstream settings and with all pupils is limited. Rather than replicate existing models, we felt this book was an opportunity to experiment with building a new way of thinking about sensory states. We chose to do this by building on the common model of Learning Zones such as 'comfort', 'learning/stretch' and 'panic' which should be familiar to teachers and some students.

SLUG	• My body feels low in energy and tired. • My sensory input needs to be increased. • I am slow and less responsive.
COMFORT	• My body feels safe and comfortable. • My sensory input is enjoyable or unnoticeable. • I am regulated and calm.
ENGAGE	• My body feels engaged and focused (and still safe). • My sensory input is interesting and stimulating. • I am regulated and ready/alert/awake.
OVERLOAD	• My body feels stressed and unsafe. • My sensory input is overwhelming and I need something to change. • I am dysregulated. • I may meltdown or shutdown to help me cope.

When trialling this model with students, they reported they found the model easy to follow and to identify what zone they were currently in, as well as providing steps they could take to move between zones. There are questions on page 66 of Chapter 4 (under 'Thinking about your sensory states') where you can explore the usefulness of this model for yourself personally as well as student versions of this activity ('Our changing sensory states') found on page 163 of Chapter 6.

The window of tolerance

Another useful model developed by Dan Siegel in *The Developing Mind* (The Guilford Press, 1999,) is the concept of the **'window of tolerance'**, describing the optimal range of arousal for effective stress management. Visual depictions to help you understand this model are widely available online. The model uses terms such as 'hyperarousal' (meaning overstimulated and dysregulated – flight/flight responses) and 'hypoarousal' (meaning understimulated and dysregulated – freeze/flop responses). Within the window of tolerance, the nervous system is regulated and in the 'just right state', enabling adaptive responses to challenges. Outside of the window, an individual is less able to manage, and is either over-responsive or under-responsive to stimuli. In this book, we choose not to use the term 'arousal': although it is a widely used term in occupational therapy, it is less familiar in schools and after consultation with teachers and young people, they said it made them giggle due to it also being a term linked to sex; therefore to avoid this, we use terms such as 'engagement' or 'alertness' instead.

WINDOW OF TOLERANCE

Bigger window = Expanded capacity to cope.

Self care such as exercise, nutrition, rest, mindfulness, hobbies and active sensory welldoing can widen your window of tolerance, so you are better able to regulate and manage your mood, behaviour, energy, focus and ability to actively engage.

Smaller window = Limited capacity to cope.

Stress, anxiety, trauma and negative sensory inputs can cause your window of tolerance to shrink so you become dysregulated more easily, with potential for volatile outbursts. You may struggle with your mood, energy and ability to concentrate and engage.

50 Copyright material from Alice Hoyle and Tessa Hyde (2025), *Becoming a Sensory Aware School*, Routledge

This model can be very helpful for individuals, particularly young people, to understand the things they need in place to enlarge their window of tolerance; for example, getting enough sleep, eating regularly, exercising, and 'sensory welldoing'. Although this model was originally written for emotional regulation, it is very adaptable for sensory regulation. An activity on page 195 in Chapter 6 enables young people to create 'my personal window of tolerance models'. Sensory welldoing therefore can be used to enlarge our window of tolerance and so enable us to cope better with challenging situations.

A note on trauma informed practice

Working in schools, you may be familiar with the concept of trauma informed practice, which understands that trauma exposure can impact an individual's neurological, biological, psychological and social development. Individuals who have experienced trauma may have increased or reduced sensitivities due to an over-reactive or under-reactive nervous system as a result of this. Therefore, embedding sensory awareness as part of your approach to trauma informed practice may support work with traumatised children. However, specialist therapeutic support will be needed. It is beyond the scope of this book to go into much detail on trauma, but it is very important that we consider the role of trauma as part of identifying sensory needs.

Some definitions of terms used in the context of sensory processing

These terms are often used in the field of sensory awareness, so we have outlined them below to help teachers understand these terms:

- **Sensory processing:**
  This is how the brain takes in, filters and puts together all the sensory information from inside and outside the body to produce a behavioural or motor response. Sensory processing is something we do all the time; we are all constantly processing, filtering and acting on the sensory information we receive from our bodies.
- **Sensory regulation:**
  Regulation is about being at the right level of alertness for the task or the environment you are in. Different tasks and different environments will require your senses to be at different levels and regulation is the ability to adjust.

- **Sensory dysregulation:**
  Dysregulation is the opposite of regulation, where you are unable to function or participate effectively in the moment, leading to difficulties in managing emotions or behaviours effectively.
- **Sensory overload:**
  Sensory overload occurs when an individual receives an excessive amount of sensory stimuli that overwhelms their ability to process and respond effectively. This can happen when the brain is bombarded with too much information from one or multiple sensory systems. When someone experiences sensory overload, they may feel overwhelmed, anxious, irritable or even experience physical discomfort. Common symptoms include difficulty concentrating, heightened sensitivity to stimuli, irritability, fatigue, and in severe cases, panic or meltdown.
- **Masking:**
  When people try to suppress their natural responses to everyday activities and environments, in an effort to try and fit in and not 'stand out', it is known as **masking**. Over time, the effort involved in maintaining this can become considerable, leading to anxiety, distress, physical illness or self harm, triggering sensory overload with potential meltdowns, shutdowns and, in time, burnout. See the bottle of pop analogy on page 44 to further understand masking, with more information in Chapter 5, page 86.
- **Meltdown:**
  A meltdown is a term sometimes used to describe an intense and often uncontrolled emotional outburst, possibly as a response to overwhelming stimuli. 'Meltdowns' may be more common in individuals who struggle with sensory processing difficulties or who have emotional regulation challenges. We urge caution when using this term to describe observed behaviours, as it can miss nuances in the behaviours because it doesn't discriminate between a mild 'strop' or 'temper tantrum' and a 'totally debilitating loss of control', the latter being more common in autistic communities.
- **Sensory shutdown:**
  When the brain feels under threat, it only has a few options to try and keep safe. The options are fight, flight or shutdown. Shutdown is the option where the brain protects itself by shutting down and shutting out information coming in. 'Shutdown' therefore refers to a defensive response, or coping mechanism, to stress, anxiety or overload, where an individual becomes overwhelmed and disengages or withdraws from external stimuli. It involves a reduction or cessation of communication, interaction or participation in activities.

- **Burnout:**
Autistic burnout results from chronic life stress alongside a mismatch of expectations and abilities without adequate supports and reasonable adjustments in place. It results in longer-term loss of function (typically 3+ months) characterised by complete exhaustion and reduced tolerance to everything.
- **Stimming:**
'Stimming' or 'stims', short for self-stimulatory behaviours, refers to repetitive movements or actions, such as flapping hands, jumping, rocking, making noises, posturing, that individuals engage in to provide sensory input and regulate their sensory experiences or emotions. Stimming behaviours are often seen in autistic individuals. This is discussed further on page 87 of Chapter 5.
- **Sensory Integration Therapy:**
Sensory integration refers to the processing, integration and organisation of sensory information from the body and the environment. Sensory Integration Therapy is a treatment approach aiming to improve how the child's brain processes sensory information, helping them regulate their emotions and behaviour and developing important skills they need for everyday life. These therapies are only available from trained Occupational Therapists. See Royal College of Occupational Therapists, STAR Institute for Sensory Processing and Sensory Integration Education for more information.
- **Sensory diet:**
A 'sensory diet' is a range of activities that provide planned sensory input to help individuals with identified sensory processing challenges stay focused and balanced throughout the day. We don't like the term 'sensory diet', but prefer 'living sensationally' (as introduced by Winnie Dunn). The word 'diet' can imply restricted intake based on aims of loss not gain, and not a rich and varied intake throughout the day. We tend to use the terms 'sensory wellbeing' and 'sensory welldoing' so that sensory strategies are embedded in daily life. Some schools use **Sensory Passports** to help document a child's sensory provision requirements throughout the school day. This can be a useful tool, but you need to be aware of all the children who are experiencing sensory processing differences (including those who are not evident at school such as those students who mask). Our stance is that everyone can benefit from sensory adjustments and sensory welldoing for sensory wellbeing.

This chapter has been full of occupational therapy-based information, but do not panic, you do not have to be an Occupational Therapist to make use of the information in this book. Many of the strategies and approaches suggested can be used for many students, but there will always be those for whom the strategies are not enough and further help and support are needed to fully identify and understand their needs. When students are not being helped by strategies or continue to experience considerable challenges with sensory processing and motor co-ordination, then referral for further assessment, advice and support from an Occupational Therapist should be sought.

Now that you have an overview of our sensory systems, Chapter 4 'You are a sensory individual' will take you through ways of identifying your own sensory needs and those of your students, followed by Chapter 5 'Identifying and meeting sensory needs'.

> ### Reflection questions for Chapter 3
> 1. What did you know already before reading this chapter?
> 2. Was there any information that surprised you in this chapter?
> 3. Was learning about proprioception, the vestibular system and interoception helpful?
> 4. Why might knowledge and understanding about the eight senses be useful to your practice as a teacher?
> 5. Has there been anything specific in this chapter that you will take away to inform your practice?

Chapter four

YOU ARE A SENSORY INDIVIDUAL

Why is understanding our senses important?

Understanding more about our senses is crucial because they are our gateway to interacting with the world around us, and form the basis for us being able to achieve sensory wellbeing. While most of us know of the five senses explored in Chapter 3 (vision, auditory, tactile, olfactory and gustatory), there is a very limited understanding of the other three (proprioception, vestibular and interoception). In an increasingly digitally driven world, many of us are guilty of not being as in tune with our senses as humans used to be. Recognising and responding to our sensory needs and preferences, as well as supporting those of others, can help us to be more comfortable and productive in our environments.

Finding our sensory wellbeing through sensory welldoing

Sensory wellbeing refers to the state of feeling comfortable and balanced in relation to one's sensory environment. It is the ability to process, regulate and respond to sensory stimuli in a way that promotes a sense of harmony and wellbeing. Sensory wellbeing is important for everyone, but may be particularly important for neurodivergent individuals and/or those who experience sensory processing challenges. As previously discussed, sensory welldoing is the process by which sensory wellbeing is achieved. The first step in sensory welldoing is completing some sensory audits to help work out our sensory identity.

Starting point: Tuning into our senses

To help you start to think more deeply about your senses, take some time to take a sensory snapshot of this moment. What does it tell you about your sensory likes and dislikes?

DOI: 10.4324/9781003409106-4

A Sensory Snapshot

Take a moment to record all of your sensory inputs in the following areas:

Sounds: (What can I hear?) _____
_____
_____
_____
_____
_____

Smell: (What can I smell?) _____
_____
_____
_____
_____
_____

Taste: (What can I taste?) _____
_____
_____
_____
_____
_____

Touch: (What can I feel on my skin?) _____
_____
_____
_____
_____
_____

Sight: (What can I see?) _____

_____

_____

_____

_____

_____

Proprioception: (Body awareness – Are you aware of your body positioning? Are you fiddling or fidgeting? Can you accurately gauge the amount of effort needed to press the pen on the paper for writing?)

_____

_____

_____

_____

_____

_____

Vestibular: (Balance and motion – Do you feel balanced? Do you feel dizzy? Are you moving; for example, rocking or swinging?) _____

_____

_____

_____

_____

_____

_____

Interoception: (What can I feel internally? Am I hungry/thirsty/need the toilet/ stressed/tired/calm/ tense/relaxed?) _____

_____

_____

_____

_____

_____

Copyright material from Alice Hoyle and Tessa Hyde (2025), *Becoming a Sensory Aware School*, Routledge

> **Reflection questions**
> - What did you learn about yourself doing this exercise?
> - Does tuning into your senses make you more 'sensitive' to things that might otherwise not bother you?
> - Was it difficult to consider some of the less common senses such as proprioception, vestibular and interoception?
> - Can having sensory mindful moments help with overall sensory wellbeing?

Assessing your own sensory identity in more detail

The table at the end of this chapter on page 72 highlights some of the main sensory questionnaires/measures available today. Some are paid for, some need to be administered by an Occupational Therapist. As an initial option we have provided you with some reflection questions on the next page to help you think more deeply about your own sensory likes and dislikes, as understanding your own sensory needs is an important aspect of empathising with and supporting others with their sensory needs.

The Sensory Me Audit

You may wish to print this in A3.

👍 **Reflection Questions for Sensations I Enjoy/ Can Cope with** *N.B.: These questions are not an exhaustive list, they are just primers to get you thinking. If you can think of additional sensory preferences you want to include, please feel free to add them.*	👎 **Reflection Questions for Sensations I Don't Enjoy/Might Try to Avoid/Ignore** *N.B.: These questions are not an exhaustive list, they are just primers to get you thinking. If you can think of additional sensory triggers you want to include, please feel free to add them.*
👍 **Auditory (sound)** What sounds do you enjoy? What sounds do you seek? What sounds bring you joy? What sounds don't you mind?	👎 **Auditory (sound)** What sounds do you avoid? What sounds distract you from your focus? What sounds are painful?
👍 **Tactile (touch)** What are your preferred fabrics for clothing? Do you like your clothes to be a snug fit or loose? Do certain body parts; for example, feet, arms, legs, head always have to remain uncovered? Do you like hugs and physical contact with people? Do you prefer baths or showers? Do you enjoy 'messy' activities; for example, kneading dough, finger painting, gardening?	👎 **Tactile (touch)** What fabrics or footwear can you absolutely not wear, or if you do wear them you will be conscious of them and feel uncomfortable? Are you aware of the properties of fabrics you need to avoid; for example, itchy, static-inducing and clingy, cold feeling, surface feel (for example, smooth, rough, scratchy)? Are you irritated by the feeling of wearing underwear or socks and shoes or accidental touch from others? Are there body self care activities that you struggle with; for example, brushing your hair, brushing your teeth? Having a shower? Shaving? Manicures? Haircuts?

Copyright material from Alice Hoyle and Tessa Hyde (2025), *Becoming a Sensory Aware School*, Routledge

👍 **Vestibular/Proprioception (movement)** Do you enjoy activities such as going on roller coasters, climbing, horse riding, racing bikes, swinging upside down? Do you like swings and roundabouts? Do you like travelling in cars/boats? Do you need movement activities as part of everyday life?	👎 **Vestibular/Proprioception (movement)** Do you get car sick? Do you avoid certain movements like swinging, spinning or being upside down, or going excessively fast? Do you dislike the feeling of heavy blankets or duvets? Do you avoid heavy or tight clothing?
👍 **Olfactory and Gustatory (smell/taste)** Do you prefer mild or spicy food, sweet, salty or sour? Are there certain tastes, textures or smells you really love/regularly seek?	👎 **Olfactory and Gustatory (smell/taste)** Are there any foods you never eat or dislike due to taste, texture or smell? Are there any smells you don't like or avoid?

👍 **Interoception (internal body feelings)** Do you tend to graze or prefer big meals to manage your hunger and energy levels? Do you have a regular bowel habit and know when you need a poo? Do you feel hunger and thirst, so remember to eat and drink regularly? If the temperature changes to a level that is uncomfortable for you (too hot or too cold), do you take steps to adjust your clothing or environment to accommodate this?	👎 **Interoception (internal body feelings)** Do you sometimes get dehydration headaches or moments of being 'hangry' (easy to anger when hungry) because you haven't felt hunger or thirst and responded to those cues. Do you feel heat or cold differently to your peers; for example, wearing shorts in winter or jumpers in summer.
👍 **Conclusion: Your sensory day** Think about your ideal sensory day – for example, would that be sleeping in satin or cotton sheets? Waking up with the light or an alarm? Wearing loose flowing clothes? Walking barefoot in grass or sand? Feeling the sun or the rain on your face?	👎 **Conclusion: Your sensory day** Think about your sensory nightmare day – what clothing, experiences, foods would be included in this day?

How sensitive am I?

It is important to identify our levels of sensitivity to different inputs to help us find sensory balance. For example, we might not register tactile input from clothing but certain smells are intolerable. Sometimes this can vary depending on our mood, energy levels or other factors (see Chapter 3 for more explanation). Use the web on the next page to consider whether your tolerance to each of the different sensory inputs is low, medium or high. So if you have a low tolerance to light you might wear sunglasses more often, whereas if you have a high tolerance to sound you might not notice the noise from crowded spaces such as coffee shops.

You could print out and colour in this diagram if you prefer.

SENSORY SPIDER WEB
How sensitive am I?

Colour in this sheet according to whether you are highly sensitive to the sensory input or not very sensitive (low) or in the middle (medium).

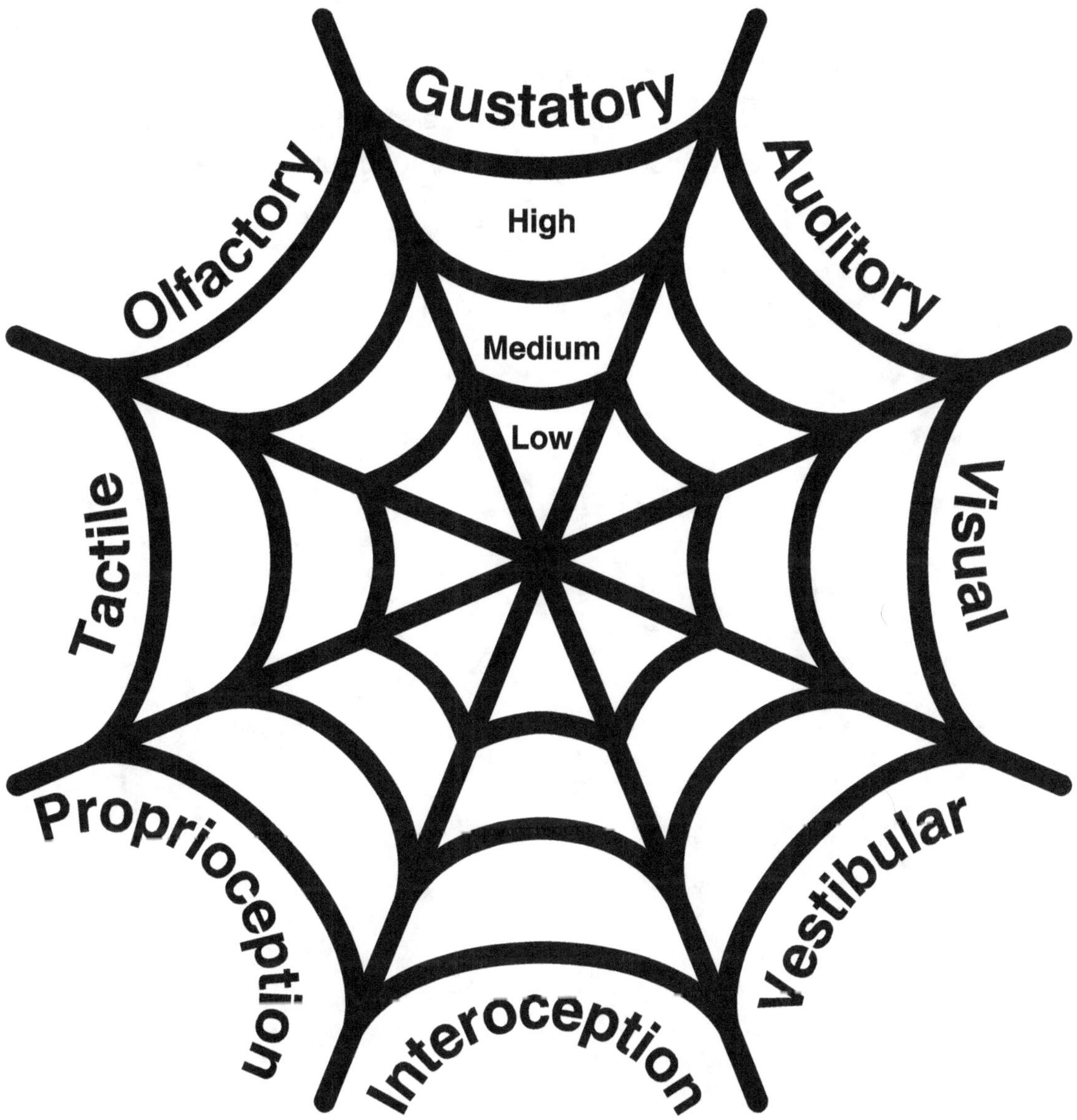

Copyright material from Alice Hoyle and Tessa Hyde (2025), *Becoming a Sensory Aware School*, Routledge

Navigating your sensory spectrum

Take a moment to revisit your sensory snapshot and consider where you would place each sensory input you noted down on the sensory spectrum on the next page. For example, the flickering light in your peripheral vision could have caused moderate discomfort, while your milky morning coffee was a sensory glimmer.

Understanding this spectrum will enable you to better navigate your sensory environments, and start to think about strategies to mitigate discomfort and enhance sensory wellbeing which are covered in more detail in Chapter 5. It can also be a useful tool for educators, parents and therapists to discuss sensory experiences with their students to help them understand themselves and is covered in Chapter 6 under 'Sensory continuums/spectrums' (page 126).

THE SENSORY SPECTRUM

Your Sensory Spectrum				
Sensory Triggers (Extreme Discomfort)	**Sensory Dislikes (Moderate Discomfort)**	**Sensory Neutral (Midpoint)**	**Sensory Likes (Moderate Comfort)**	**Sensory Glimmers (Extreme Comfort)**
Definition: Sensory inputs that cause significant distress or discomfort, making it difficult to focus or remain calm. They can lead to sensory overload or strong negative reactions.	**Definition:** Sensory inputs that are unpleasant, but not as immediately overwhelming as sensory triggers. They can cause irritation or distraction.	**Definition:** Sensory inputs that do not particularly sway one's emotional or physical state in either a positive or negative direction. They are neither stimulating nor distressing.	**Definition:** Sensory inputs that provide comfort or reduce stress but may not elicit strong positive emotions. They are often used as grounding or calming techniques.	**Definition:** Sensory experiences that spark joy, comfort and a sense of wellbeing. They are highly individual and sought after for their positive effects.
Examples: Flickering fluorescent lights, loud unexpected noises, strong perfumes	**Examples:** Background chatter in a busy café, clothing with irritating textures, mild odours	**Examples:** White noise, neutral lighting, comfortable but not particularly stimulating textures of clothing	**Examples:** Soft instrumental music, the weight of a heavy blanket, the scent of fresh linen	**Examples:** Singing in the shower, the feel of sand between the toes, the aroma of a favourite meal cooking
Impact: These provoke an immediate and often intense negative reaction, may require withdrawal or immediate intervention to manage discomfort.	**Impact:** These cause discomfort or distraction but may be tolerated for short periods with coping strategies.	**Impact:** These inputs blend into the background of one's sensory experience, neither enhancing nor detracting from wellbeing.	**Impact:** These help to soothe and calm, making environments more manageable and pleasant.	**Impact:** These elicit strong positive emotional responses, enhancing mood and overall sensory wellbeing.

Copyright material from Alice Hoyle and Tessa Hyde (2025), *Becoming a Sensory Aware School*, Routledge

OUR SENSORY STATES

Thinking about your sensory states

Using the Sensory States Model (also described in more detail on page 48 of Chapter 3), answer the following questions.

Questioning your sensory states

- What zone are you in right now?
- What zone would you like to be in?
- What sensory inputs could help you move there?
- What sensory inputs move you to 'slug'?
- What sensory inputs move you to 'comfort'?
- What sensory inputs move you to 'engage'?
- What sensory inputs move you to 'overload'?
- What sensory inputs move you from 'slug'?
- What sensory inputs move you out of 'comfort'?
- What sensory inputs move you out of 'engage'?
- What sensory inputs move you out of 'overload'?
- Is this a useful model for you to think about your sensory state?
- Can you think of a different/better analogy that works for you?

There are also student versions of this activity found on page 163 of Chapter 6. You may wish to do those as well.

Sensory triggers, sensory glimmers and sensory strategies

Use the information you have gained about yourself from this chapter to help you to identify and summarise the following:

Sensory glimmers – these are the things that you can do to spark sensory joy. They are the opposite of triggers. For example, singing in the shower.

Sensory triggers – these are the things that give you the 'sensory ick', the things that set your nerves jangling and you find it tricky to concentrate on anything else when they are present. For example, flickering fluorescent lights.

Sensory strategy – something you do to meet your sensory needs. For example, if you are feeling anxious before a test, you sniff your favourite smell (peppermint oil) on a hankie.

Use the 'My Sensory Glimmers, Triggers and Strategies Worksheet' (on the next page) to help you document this.

MY SENSORY GLIMMERS, TRIGGERS AND STRATEGIES

TRIGGERS

STRATEGIES

GLIMMERS

Thinking point: Embrace sensory joy!

We don't always tune into our sensory needs, or the tiny things we can do that make our bodies feel more positive on our sensory spectrum. What are the little things you can do to spark sensory joy? In recent years where more and more of our lives are lived digitally, we seem to have become a little disconnected with our bodies and our senses. We also now spend less time in nature; however, nature is a core source of sensory joy. For example, Tessa likes to garden barefoot to feel grounded.

For many of us, the idea of 'indulging our senses' can sometimes fill us with a sense of embarrassment or selfishness, feeling that it should only be done at special 'self care' times, rather than curating our life to be as full of sensory joy as possible, lest we become 'spoilt'. There is also an issue in that we don't like to be seen as awkward or difficult when sharing an environment with others and making demands such as 'turning the lights off' or 'opening a window'.

It is important to understand and meet your own sensory needs first, before you try to meet the needs of others. Think about it like the oxygen masks on a plane; you will be in a better position to help others with their sensory needs if you understand your own, and are working on your own sensory wellbeing through welldoing, so your window of tolerance is wide. However, make sure you do not assume that your own sensory preferences are universal experiences; you need to remain open and curious about individuals who experience the world differently to you.

Reflection questions about sensory joy

Values and attitudes

- How does the phrase 'indulge your senses' make you feel?
- Would this impact on how you do this work?
- Why do you think society is uncomfortable with the idea of indulging our senses?
- More generally, reflect on your own values and attitudes to sensory adjustments and how that might impact your practice. For example, how do you feel about students having movement breaks in your lesson?

Your sensory wellbeing

- On a daily basis, are you aware of your own sensory wellbeing?
- Current sensory wellbeing – is there anything you already do regularly that sparks sensory joy?
- Sensory welldoing – is there anything else you could experiment with doing to add more sensory joy?

Window of tolerance

- Would embracing sensory joy help to widen your window of tolerance (see page 49 in Chapter 3 for an explanation of the window of tolerance)?
- Can you write a list of strategies that you can utilise to help expand your window of tolerance?
- What things reduce your window of tolerance?

Case study: A swimming trip with added sensory joy

Imagine you are someone who enjoys swimming for the benefits of body and mind, but also wants to add a little sensory joy to the experience. You might pick a sunny day and an outdoor pool/river/lake/sea to boost your swimming experience. You decide to scoot, walk or bike there so you can enjoy the feeling of the movement on the journey there and back in the sunshine, with no stress about traffic or parking. You might ensure your swimming goggles are tinted so you can cope with the sunlight reflecting on the water and use adjustable nose clips so you don't get water up your nose. You wear a comfortable swimming costume you feel confident and happy in and it doesn't slip or ride up while you are swimming.

You choose a fabric swimming cap instead of a rubber swimming cap as you prefer the feeling on your head and you always make sure you have additional hair bands to keep your hair tied up, as you hate the feeling of wet hair flapping about. While you are swimming you might choose to listen to your favourite songs on a waterproof MP3 or just enjoy the sounds of the water or nature. You make sure you spend some time just floating about and really enjoying the sensations of being in the water. You use your favourite-smelling shower gels and hair products for a treat in a hot shower afterwards as well as a mini hair wrap towel so your head is warm and cosy as soon as you get out. You might take a warm long-sleeved towelling robe so it's soft and cosy for when you get out and much nicer than a crispy towel. You wear loose-fitting comfortable 'easy on and off' clothes so you don't have to put tights or horrible fabrics onto damp skin. You bring flip flops or sliders for the walk home to avoid the post-swim wet sock horrible feelings. Sprinkling sensory joy into small everyday experiences like this can really help you (a) enjoy life; (b) enjoy activities that sometimes we know we are supposed to do (like exercise) but avoid because they feel hard or not fun.

Reflection question

- What everyday activities could you sprinkle sensory joy into and how would you do it?

Read this:

We love Winnie Dunn's *Living Sensationally* because it's an 'easy read' book explaining how everybody has different sensory needs and how we can all make accommodations to adjust our environments for maximum sensory benefit. It is a fantastic exploration about how we can all make small and large adjustments in our lives to 'live sensationally'.

Reflection question

- What does it mean for you to 'live sensationally'?

Wider Sensory Questionnaires/Checklists Available

Type of Tool	Name of Tool	Source? Location?	Comments (availability)
Informal for adolescents/adults	Sensory patterns questionnaire (Winnie Dunn)	*Living Sensationally* (Winnie Dunn, Jessica Kingsley, 2007), pp. 45–49	This is available in one of our favourite books, it really helps individuals think about, and understand, their own sensory profile. Looking at: Seeker, Avoider, Sensor and Bystander. These are the same questions used in the *Adolescent/Adult Sensory Profile: User's Manual* (Catana E. Brown and Winnie Dunn, Pearson Assessments, 2002)
Informal for various ages – infant/toddlers through to adolescent/adult	STAR Institute for Sensory Processing: sensory checklist by age.	STAR Institute Symptoms Checklist https://sensoryhealth.org/basic/symptoms-checklist	This is available online and can help parents identify if their child has particular sensory needs and to see if additional testing should be done.
Informal for children	Sensory checklist (Lindsey Biel and Nancy Peske)	Adapted from the book *Raising a Sensory Smart Child: The Definitive Handbook for Helping Your Child with Sensory Processing Issues* (Lindsey Biel and Nancy Peske, Penguin, 2005, 2009, 2018 and beyond). Available online: www.sensorysmarts.com/sensory-checklist.pdf	This is available online. It looks at different sensory systems and identifies if a person: Avoids, Seeks, has Mixed or Neutral responses.
Informal for children or adults	Sensory preference checklist (Jamie Chaves and Ashley Taylor, 2021) (Adapted from Mary Sue Williams and Sherry Shellenberger, *How Does Your Engine Run?*.[1996])	Found in *Creating Sensory Smart Classrooms: A Practical Guide for Educators* (Jamie Chaves and Ashley Taylor, Routledge, 2021), pp. 188–191.	Available in *Creating Sensory Smart Classrooms*. Identifies behaviours which improve regulation/attention or disrupt regulation/attention for different sensory systems.
Informal for adults	NAIT Guide to Assessment of Sensory Preferences as Part of Adult Neurodevelopmental Assessment	www.thirdspace.scot/wp-content/uploads/2022/05/NAIT-Guide-to-Assessment-of-Sensory-Preferences-in-Adults-2022.pdf	Available online. Questions to help identify sensory likes/dislikes and impacts of these.
Informal for adults/children	Sensory Diet Exploration: Activity checklist	www.ot-innovations.com/wp-content/uploads/2013/09/sensory_diet_checklist_2007pdf.pdf	Activity checklist of things people may use to attain an appropriate state of alertness. Categorised into different senses.
Informal for older children, teens or young adults	The Sensory Challenge Questionnaire (Lindsey Biel)	https://sensoryprocessingchallenges.com/images/SensoryQuestionnaire.pdf *Sensory Processing Challenges: Effective Clinical Work with Kids and Teens* (Lindsey Biel, W. W. Norton & Company, 2014)	Available online and in *Sensory Processing Challenges*. Questions to help identify sensory likes/dislikes.
Informal/formal adult and youth version (7–17 years)	Multidimensional Assessment of Interoceptive Awareness (MAIA) version 2 – 2018; Youth version (MAIA-Y) – 2020	UCSF Osher Center for Integrative Health, San Francisco, CA https://osher.ucsf.edu/research/maia https://osher.ucsf.edu/sites/osher.ucsf.edu/files/inline-files/MAIA2%202018.05.27.pdf	This tool can provide interesting insight into interoception

Sensory evaluation tool for children with Autism Spectrum Disorder	Sensory Experiences Questionnaire (SEQ)	Grace T. Baranek, University of Southern California (published 2020)	Available for purchase and download
This is not an exhaustive list, there are many other sensory checklists available online or through local services. Further free toolkits on Sensory Processing can be found at The Spiral Foundation https://thespiralfoundation.org/spd-education-toolkits/			
Standardised Measure. There are five different forms, based on age from birth to 15 years (Infant, Toddler, Child) plus short form and School Companion.	Sensory Profile 2 (Winnie Dunn, 2014)	Available in the UK from Pearson Assessments: Sensory Profile 2 www.pearsonclinical.co.uk/store/ukassessments/en/sensory-profile-child/Sensory-Profile-2-/p/P100009110.html	**This needs to be administered by a trained professional.** Family of assessments provides standardised tools to help evaluate a child's sensory processing patterns in the context of home, school, and community-based activities.
Standardised Measure Age range 11 and older	Adolescent/Adult Sensory Profile (Winnie Dunn, 2002)	Available in the UK from Pearson Assessments: Adolescent/Adult Sensory Profile www.pearsonclinical.co.uk/store/ukassessments/en/Store/Professional-Assessments/Motor-Sensory/Adolescent-Adult-Sensory-Profile/p/P100009054.html	Generates an individualised profile of sensory processing across the four quadrants – Low Registration, Sensation Seeking, Sensory Sensitivity and Sensation Avoiding.
Standardised Measure. There are five age levels: Infant/Toddler, Preschool, Child, Adolescent and Adult. Covering the lifespan from 4 months to 87 years. Forms cover: Home, School Self-Report (adolescent and adult) and Driving	Sensory Processing Measure – Second edition (SPM-2), 2021 Published by Western Psychological Services (WPS)	Available in the UK from Hogrefe: Sensory Processing Measure, Second Edition (SPM-2) – Hogrefe – Online testing, psychometric test & training providers www.hogrefe.com/uk/shop/sensory-processing-measure-second-edition-95550.html And from Ann Arbor publishers: Sensory Processing Measure, Second Edition and SPM-2 Quick Tips www.annarbor.co.uk/index.php?main_page=index&cPath=250_657	**This needs to be administered by a trained professional.** The SPM-2 forms are intended to be used together as an integrated system to provide a comprehensive overview of a client's sensory integration and processing across home, school, caregiving and community settings. As such, multiple forms may be used within each age level. However, each form may also be used separately.
Standardised Measure. Age range 13–95. Forms cover: Self Report, Caregiver, Medical History and Abridged Self-Report supplement.	Adolescent/Adult Sensory History (ASH) (Teresa May-Benson and Olivia Easterbrook-Dick, Spiral Foundation, First Edition Revised, 2021)	Available online from the Spiral Foundation: Adult/Adolescent Sensory History https://thespiralfoundation.org/adult-adolescent-sensory-history-2/	**This needs to be administered by a trained professional.** A self-report assessment of sensory and motor behaviours commonly observed in individuals with difficulties processing and integrating sensory information. The assessment identifies difficulties in five key areas of functioning: Sensory Discrimination, Sensory Modulation, Postural-Ocular Skills, Praxis and Social-Emotional Functioning.

We hope that this chapter has given you insight into your own sensory needs, likes and dislikes. We want to encourage you to always think about your sensory wellbeing through active sensory welldoing.

Reminder:

> **Sensory wellbeing** – The state of feeling comfortable and balanced in relation to our sensory environment.
>
> **Sensory welldoing** – A deliberate and conscious effort to actively use personalised sensory strategies for your own wellbeing.

Remember that life is a journey, not a race, and aspiring to a sensory lifestyle is not going to be immediate, but there are plenty of little steps you can take to improve your sensory life.

W.E.L.L.D.O.I.N.G: Nine easy tips to build sensory joy in your life

Consider this handy acrostic for sensory welldoing or W.E.L.L.D.O.I.N.G with nine easy tips to build sensory joy in your life.

W – Wake Up: Think about your sensory wake-up routine – is music or light better than an alarm beep? Do you prefer to sit in bed with your coffee and wake up slowly or dive straight into a wake-up shower and get dressed so you can get motoring?

E – Eat Well: Experiment with mindful eating – how can you make mealtimes a more sensory experience?

L – Leap: Play about with body moves, stretches and massage. What makes your body feel good?

L – Look: How is your visual environment? Does it meet your sensory needs? Is there anything you could change; for example, adding more lamps/changing the colour of lightbulbs or changing the colour choices in the room, reducing visual clutter?

D – Daily Focus: Designate 5–10 minutes a day to focus on your senses. What are the positive sensory inputs around you?

O – Outfit: Organise your wardrobe based on sensory appeal; which clothes are most comfortable to you?

I – Indulge: Identify your glimmers and treat yourself to the quick wins, such as indulgent moisturiser, a luxurious bath or cosy dressing gown. What glimmers are part of your day? Is there anything you can do to further enhance them?

N – Nature: Take a 10-minute mindful walk outside, focusing on each of your senses. How do you feel before and after the walk? Or walk barefoot in the garden for 5 minutes. How do you feel during and after?

G – Goodnight: Develop a bedtime routine aiming for relaxation and better sleep, experimenting with what soothes you best. What are your top tips for sleep?

Copyright material from Alice Hoyle and Tessa Hyde (2025), *Becoming a Sensory Aware School*, Routledge

The Seagull Caveat

Where we live, seagulls are the bane of our lives. They nest on our roofs and keep us awake with their incessant squawking. During the writing of this book, we noted in some ways that our sensitivities were heightened because we were thinking constantly about our senses and sensory inputs and instantly categorised them into positive or negative inputs. Unfortunately, this had an unwelcome side effect we decided to call 'the Seagull Caveat' after Alice went for a lovely relaxing soundbath as a sensory treat which was completely ruined by the squawking of seagulls!

The Seagull Caveat is where your sensory joy is easily derailed by the slightest small thing that ordinarily you might be able to tune out or ignore, but by focusing on your senses it can make you more sensitive to everything. So with everything there has to be sensory balance – it is probably not realistic to have a life full of sensory joy all of the time. We have to live in the real world where there are seagulls and road noise and flickering lights and crowds of noisy people. So there is also something to be gained from developing strategies that help us manage our feelings about everyday situations which are beyond our control (such as squawking seagulls!), so that they can't overwhelm and derail your attempts at sensory joy.

Reflection questions for Chapter 4

1. What are the things beyond your control that you have had to learn to tolerate?
2. What strategies have you developed to manage these?
3. Are there situations you actively avoid because you absolutely cannot tolerate them?
4. Are there situations you can tolerate when you are really motivated or engaged, but not at other times?
5. Does this avoidance affect your life negatively or neutrally?
6. Are there any other strategies you could employ to become more comfortable with certain situations?

Chapter five

RECOGNISING AND RESPONDING TO SENSORY NEEDS

In the previous chapters we have looked at our sensory systems and how we all process sensory information constantly; each of us having different thresholds for registering and filtering out information (consciously or unconsciously), using a variety of behaviours and strategies in everyday life. Chapter 3 went into considerable detail about how you can recognise the specific over-responsive and under-responsive behaviours you might see for each of the eight sensory systems. So revisit that chapter if you need a reminder before going through the rest of this chapter.

This chapter focuses on how to recognise and respond to sensory needs in the classroom to embrace **sensory informed practice**. Remember that sensory informed practice involves considering the sensory needs and preferences of individuals, especially those who have barriers to education due to sensory processing needs. It involves understanding how sensory processing differences can affect a person's mood, learning, energy, focus and behaviour (Chapter 3 and Chapter 4). By incorporating the sensory-friendly strategies in this chapter, the educational approaches in Chapter 6 and the environmental adjustments and the whole school approach in Chapter 7 and Chapter 8, you will be developing your sensory aware skills and practice. Your overall aim is to reduce the potential for sensory overload or overwhelm, by creating supportive, accessible spaces and opportunities that support a range of diverse sensory needs.

When doing this work, we urge you to consider adopting a **'common sensory approach'**. You should consider what small practical changes you can make for the biggest benefits, using your common sense with your increased knowledge of sensory needs and their potential impact on learning and behaviour. Using this approach will mean you shouldn't be overwhelmed or implement unnecessary changes that don't make a difference. It is also important that your own sensory needs are met before you try and meet the needs of others, as you cannot pour from an empty cup. Look up the concept of spoon theory to help you think further about this (see also Chapter 6 on page 186 for an activity on 'Budgeting our sensory spoons'). Supporting your own sensory wellbeing will give you increased capacity to support and develop others' sensory wellbeing.

Our aim for this chapter is not to suggest every single possible sensory strategy for every single sensory need; instead we want to provide a range of universal strategies that are safe for most learners as well as comment on some targeted approaches. Some of these strategies may also be of benefit to you and colleagues as members of staff and not just for the students you work with, so keep this in mind when reading this chapter.

Why should we respond to sensory needs?

The benefits of increasing your sensory awareness throughout your teaching will lead to more regulated students and should lead to a reduction in dysregulated behaviours within the classroom and any issued consequences such as detentions. We hope this will reduce your classroom workload as well as your stress levels! Embracing sensory informed approaches may initially feel challenging and out of your comfort zone, but you will soon see, as you start to experiment with sensory informed practice and stay curious about sensory needs, that the benefits to working in this way will swiftly become evident.

How should we respond to sensory needs?

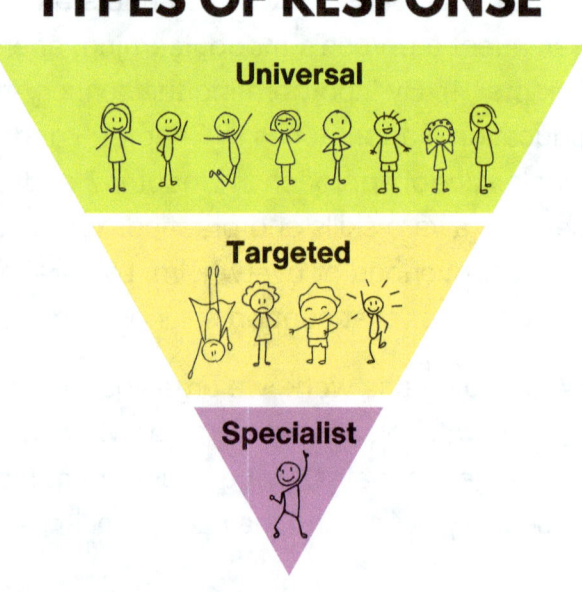

There are three different levels of response. Universal approaches for all learners in your class, targeted interventions for small groups of learners with identified needs, and then specialist individual responses which would be carried out by an Occupational Therapist or other sensory trained professional.

It is important to start small with sensory interventions, first to make it feel more manageable for you as a teacher, but also you would be surprised at how the smallest of sensory interventions, that do not require much, if any resource, can have the biggest impact and positive consequences on behaviour. Remember to use your common sense in evaluating what is possible and what works (**the common sensory approach**).

By considering and nurturing your own sensory wellbeing in doing this work, you can also become a sensory role model in your own classroom. Remember that you don't need to do this work alone. Work with teaching assistants in your classroom around implementing sensory interventions. Seek support from the Senior Leadership Team and Sensory Wellbeing Champion (see Chapter 8 for more detail on the whole school approach) to further integrate this work across the school; because if particular students are only getting their needs met in one out of five lessons in a day, they will still be dysregulated in and out of school. A whole team approach is required and will make it easier for you in your own lessons.

Recognising sensory needs

Recognising that the classroom is a sensory environment can help you to consider the impact this has on all those who work and learn within it. This will enable you to address as many sensory needs as possible, for the majority, for most of the time. The information in Chapter 3 as well as the audits in Chapter 4 and Chapter 6 will help build up this knowledge and awareness for both staff and students. As this knowledge develops, it will be important to evolve a collective recognition, through exploring and understanding, that not everyone responds to the same sensory input in the same way, so not all experiences are the same (or even fixed). Teachers will need to be aware of the potential teacher's double standard of expecting things from students we wouldn't expect from ourselves. For example, many teachers work best when moving around the classroom, but won't let their students move in the same way; or we regularly observe teachers during training sessions fiddling with their hair, rings, clothing, doodling or chewing gum/sweets to help them to focus, which they don't allow in their classroom.

Factors that can affect sensory behaviours

Sensory behaviours may change based on age (between childhood and adolescence and adulthood), and even due to hormone levels (some individuals report reduced sensory tolerances around puberty, menstruation, pregnancy and menopause). A key influence on sensory behaviours may be the presence of special educational needs. If you look at the Pyramid of Learning on page 4 of Chapter 1, you will see how fundamental sensory needs are. If you have a student who is struggling with their learning and cognition, it may be that elements of their sensory and motor development are also affected. Therefore, considering sensory/motor interventions as part of the overall package of support could also lead to gains in their behaviour, communication, social skills and their learning and cognition.

Considering the impact of gendered expectations on behaviour is also absolutely crucial in recognising and responding to sensory behaviours. There are differences between boys and girls and the way they can present their sensory needs. Girls' masking might involve mimicking peers' behaviours or suppressing sensory-related difficulties to blend in or avoid drawing attention to themselves. On the other hand, boys might display more overt sensory-seeking or avoiding behaviours, which can make their needs more visible, but also potentially misunderstood as behavioural issues rather than unmet sensory needs. This then leads to the very different diagnosis levels between boys and girls for neurodevelopmental conditions such as Autism and ADHD, and the huge gender disparities seen in specialist provision.

Many women are diagnosed later in life (including Alice), and girls who were seemingly 'fine in school' sometimes have to get to the point of crisis (self harm or suicidal ideation) for the level of need to be properly diagnosed and identified. This is a hugely common experience for neurodivergent girls who have an internalised presentation of their very real needs. Because girls are so adept at masking, this can make their struggles much less apparent to their educators in school, but they may 'meltdown' more at home in their safe space. This also reinforces the importance of clear supportive communication between home and school about needs. Overall, schools need to be aware of the impact of gender, age, hormones and additional needs on their sensory profile, and ensure that staff are tuned in enough to detect more subtle signs of sensory distress, and not just the more evident ones. This will enable them to effectively support more students, identifying and meeting their differing needs.

> **Reflection questions**
>
> - Do I see any differences in sensory behaviour between the students I teach?
> - Do gender roles and stereotypes play a role in how students behave?
> - Where behaviour represents some of the more subtle sensory-seeking or avoiding behaviours, do I still need to offer adjustments and accommodations?
> - In what ways might my own biases affect my perception of sensory behaviours in students? How can I reflect on these biases for positive change?
> - How can I support students to feel more comfortable to unmask?

What sensory behaviours can you spot? You need to be a sensory detective

Do you see students in the class who are rocking on their chair, sitting with their feet up on the seat, lolling across the table, fiddling with things, pulling their hoodie up over their head, wearing shorts in the winter or getting so hot and not thinking to take off their sweatshirt in the summer? Have you been aware that these are all sensory-seeking/avoiding behaviours? Which sensory system is over- or under-responsive? How do you know? After considering sensory systems (Chapter 3) and completing the sensory audits (Chapter 4 and Chapter 7), you will find it easier to consider possible reasons behind these overt behaviours. Using your detective skills, you may be able to reframe how you interpret the manner in which the student engages in lessons and offer strategies or adjustments to enable them to successfully engage in the lesson.

Remember it is important to think about what you want from the lesson/activity; behavioural approaches such as the SLANT approach (sit up, listen, ask and answer questions, nod your head, track the speaker) are unlikely to work for many children with sensory processing needs. Some students may be moving around the class, sitting at the back of the group, fiddling, or just looking around, and yet still be completely engaged and listening to every word that is said. This is clear when they are able to answer the question quickly when asked, but they cannot sit still, look at the teacher, make eye contact and listen all at the same time (as it uses up too much mental energy to do all of these things at the same time). You need to understand that there are many ways to sit on the chair; the right way for a child trying to regulate might look like the wrong way. Is it unsafe? Is it affecting others? Is this behaviour doing any harm?

BE A SENSORY DETECTIVE

What am I seeing, do I need to do anything about it?

Is it meeting a particular need?

Could this behaviour have a sensory element?

Are they regulated or dysregulated?

What sensory system might be involved?

Are they sensory seeking or avoiding?

Is this impacting on others?

What do I need to do, or can I do about it?

See behaviour. Consider sensory.

Guiding principle: 'See behaviour – consider sensory'

'See behaviour – consider sensory' is a guiding principle that encourages education professionals to look beyond surface behaviours and consider if there are any underlying sensory issues that might be influencing a student's actions. This perspective shifts the focus from reacting to the observed behaviours to understanding them as possible communications of sensory discomfort or overload. For instance, a student who fidgets or appears distracted or is looking around may need to do so to enable them to listen. By adopting this approach, professionals can better identify and address the sensory needs of children, thus creating a more inclusive and supportive learning environment.

Reflection questions when considering behaviour

- What am I seeing, do I need to do anything about it? *(You may not need to offer an intervention in all cases.)*
- Is it meeting a particular need? *(Thinking about behaviour as communication and meeting needs can help you shift perspective in analysing behaviour.)*
- Could this behaviour have a sensory element? *('See behaviour – consider sensory'; it is especially important to consider interoception – hangry or constipated children will display more challenging behaviours!)*
- Are they regulated or dysregulated? *(You may have a very fidgety child in front of you who is regulated and coping well; can you leave them to carry on or is their behaviour bothering others? Do they need the same level of possible intervention as a child who is dysregulated or a different level?)*
- What sensory system might be involved? *(Don't forget about proprioception, vestibular and interoception.)*
- Are they sensory seeking or avoiding? *(This will impact on any intervention you offer.)*
- Is this impacting on others? *(Does this change how you would intervene? Remember that being distracted is different to being disruptive.)*
- What do I need to do, or can I do about it? *(Not every behaviour requires a response.)*
- It may be necessary to keep a behaviour log in consultation with certain students to identify patterns:
    - What happened?
    - Where were you?
    - Who were you with?
    - Was there any lead up to this event?
    - Anything that helped or made it worse?
    - What would you do again or do differently next time?

> ### Thinking point: Spot the kids who need to chew!
>
> Take a moment to think about how many kids you see chewing on things in a school day. The illicit chewing gum, the ends of a pencil, rolled up bits of paper, etc. Did you know that chewing is a regulating activity? We have never met a school willing to allow chewing gum in school, but that doesn't stop our chewers. There is a wide range of commercially available chew jewellery (chewelry) in the form of necklaces, bracelets, lanyards, etc., which can be safely used in schools. During the writing of this book, we have increasingly used chewy and crunchy snacks to help us concentrate with great success!
>
> ### Questions about chewing
>
> - Do you teach any students who are always chewing (for example, pen lids, clothing, tops of sports bottles, bits of paper, illicit chewing gum)?
> - How do you manage that behaviour in the classroom?
> - What are your school's rules about chewing?
> - How would you feel about students using chewelry or chewable pen tops in your lessons?
> - Can you experiment with offering healthy chewy and crunchy snacks throughout the day and observe the impact on learning and behaviour?

Spotting vestibular behaviour

Case study: A batgirl at a primary school

Willow is a happy, quirky child who is 11 years old. She has been struggling academically and with concentration in Year 6 at primary school. She has meltdowns at home, but not at school. School and parents are concerned about her transition to secondary school next year. Her parents got an occupational therapy (OT) assessment as part of an application for an Education, Health and Care Plan (EHCP). The Occupational Therapist observed Willow in the playground and noted she spent the whole of break time spinning round and round on the bars. The Occupational Therapist asked the parents if they had seen Willow upside down at other times too. They realised Willow was regularly upside down: she watched TV upside down; liked to spin on chairs upside down; did a lot of inversion gymnastics practice at home; and she would often rest on her bed with her head hanging over the side, or flop upside down over things when out and about.

The OT explained that Willow needs a lot of vestibular input in order to help regulate herself. On talking to Willow about why she liked being upside down, she explained it to her mum as "all the blood rushes in and all the anxious and angry feelings whoosh out!". Now that her parents better understand her vestibular needs, they have installed a sensory swing at home (that the whole family uses and benefits from) and this can be swapped out for aerial silks, gym rings or a trapeze depending on mood. Willow also attends a 'Topsy Turvy Club' which is a gymnastics class that specialises in inversion, involving handstands, headstands and being upside down on gym rings.

Understanding Willow's need for inversion has been game changing for the family. Having daily opportunities to invert have led to a reduction in meltdowns at home. This will be particularly important, as when Willow starts secondary school, she won't find it as easy to invert as she did on the playground equipment at primary school. Although, if you have ever observed teenagers and any solo handrails around school, you will see that some will still try to invert, often to staff alarm for the health and safety implications! Through observing Willow and identifying that need, Willow now understands herself better, and the people around her are better able to support her.

Reflection questions

Can you think of any 'batkids'? How do you know?
- Are there other kids who might benefit from inversion for regulation that are not obviously hanging upside down everywhere!?
- What opportunities are there at your school for children to invert (for example, PE lessons, playground monkey bars)? Can you build in more inversion opportunities? Yoga classes?
- What opportunities are there for secondary aged children to invert?
- Can individual children be supported with inversion as part of a movement break or sensory plan?

We hope these examples have given you some insight into some sensory behavioural considerations regarding things you may see in your classroom. Use the lists in Chapter 3 to further think about the things you might see in a classroom. You also need to be aware of some common behaviours, such as masking, stimming, sensory overload, discharge behaviours and shutdowns.

How to recognise the following behaviours

Recognising different sensory states

The Sensory States Model described in Chapter 3 on page 48 is useful to think about here in terms of what a teacher will observe in the classroom.

- **Slug** – A student seems to have low energy and be tired, they may be slow and less responsive. Their sensory input needs to be increased.
- **Comfort** – A student appears calm and relaxed and comfortable, but may not be fully engaged in the lesson. Their sensory input can stay the same or be increased.
- **Engage** – The student appears engaged and focused on the activity whilst also seeming regulated. Their sensory input is interesting and stimulating, you may need to work to maintain this without overloading them.
- **Overload** – The student looks stressed and overwhelmed. They are not engaged with the task. They are likely to be dysregulated. They may meltdown or shutdown to help them cope and exhibit discharge behaviours. Their sensory input needs to become calming and soothing.

It may be difficult to always tell the difference between these stages as some students may mask internal feelings and these states are subjective.

Recognising masking

It can be extremely difficult to see signs of masking (see Chapter 3, page 52 for explanation) in school, due to the fact that many children mask their feelings/sense of overload exceptionally well and it is only evident when they meltdown either as soon as they leave school or at home. It is therefore not always easy to identify what is happening for the student due to this masking, which by its very nature started as a coping strategy (either consciously or unconsciously). By the time it is noticed in school, there will often have been a steady escalation of challenging behaviour at home. Open and honest communication between teachers and parents is essential in helping to reduce stressors in school to support the child fully and this in turn reduces the need for students to mask. See the section on working with parents on page 97 in this chapter and Chapter 8, page 257 for more strategies and support for working with parents around students' sensory needs.

Case study: Tara

Tara is an autistic girl who was 'high masking'; the only evidence observed by OT and school was a tiny amount of fidgeting with a paperclip which would not be unusual for any child. However, Tara was having significant increasingly violent meltdowns at home every day after school, and was becoming more and more reluctant to go to school, needing increasing input from parents and the school to support her to go in in the mornings. She went onto a reduced timetable which did not help. She soon became unable to go to school or even leave the house, sometimes remaining in bed in her bedroom. She experienced burnout which 2 years later she slowly recovered from, but she is still out of school.

Reflection questions

Would it have been possible to identify how stressful school was for Tara before the meltdowns started at home?
- How could school and home work in partnership to support Tara's needs and reduce the home meltdowns?
- Have you ever taught a child like Tara? How did you support them?

Recognising stimming

Stimming or stims were explained in Chapter 3, page 53. It can be difficult to tell the difference between stimming, fidgeting and regulating behaviours. Think about the things you do to help you regulate. What behaviours do you see in your classroom? Would you consider them stimming or fidgeting? See also the section on 'Legitimate fiddling' on page 109 in this chapter.

Stimming is part of the diagnostic criteria for Autism (stereotyped or repetitive motor movements, use of objects or speech) and stimming behaviours in autistic individuals may be more obvious. More overt sensory stimming examples, such as rocking, twirling, jumping, hand flapping, flicking fingers and vocalisations are harmless and can serve as coping mechanisms for individuals to regulate their sensory experiences. As a society we need to become much more accepting of these harmless public stimming behaviours, because suppression can cause mental health distress and potentially self harming replacement behaviours. How can you ensure that your students feel safe and comfortable to stim in your classroom? How can you balance stimming needs without disrupting others in classroom groups?

It is important to note that when stimming behaviours interfere with daily functioning, are socially inappropriate (for example, touching oneself or others intimately in public) or compromise safety, it may be necessary to introduce alternative coping strategies or provide support to manage the behaviours effectively.

A safeguarding note on stimming

If stimming causes harm:

Some stims can cause harm to self or others; for example, biting. When trying to change a harmful behaviour and offer alternatives, then this will need to be discussed and considered with parents and the child, because the student will need an alternative of similar intensity to meet this need. For example, trying to change self soothing behaviours (such as biting oneself) can have unanticipated consequences, with trying to stop the biting causing the child to bang their head against the wall instead to get the same level of sensory input. So harm minimisation needs to be key and schools will need to seek advice from sensory or behaviour specialists with all interventions being risk-assessed appropriately.

If stimming involves touching other people:

Students need to be taught about bodily autonomy and consent and may need redirection at school into more appropriate forms of touch, and seeking permission before a touch. It is also important to think about the life course of a particular behaviour; for example, a 5-year-old boy with special needs who regularly strokes the hair and chests of others to self soothe may not yet be recognised as a cause for concern; but when that child is a tall and strong 17-year-old, that behaviour is going to be much more complex to deal with, with potential safeguarding concerns for their safety and the safety of others.

If stimming involves the genitals:

Some SEND students who are very sensory seeking may try to self soothe through intimate self touch of the genitals (masturbation) while at school (this behaviour would be more likely to occur in a specialist setting rather than a mainstream setting). This behaviour should never be dismissed as "just stimming" as it includes a sexual as well as a sensory response which is never appropriate or acceptable in a school. Despite this note of caution, it is also important to balance that with also not shaming individuals for a common human behaviour, but clarifying that it needs redirecting to a private space at home, not school. Well-meaning special schools have been known to send particular students to the school toilets to do this as a way of offering a private space. However, a toilet in a school is not legally private, as it can be accessed and is used by a number of people. So as well as creating a significant safeguarding issue, it is also illegal to masturbate in there (Section 71, Sexual Offences Act 2003). Repeating this behaviour in public toilets outside of school carries even more risks, so this sends a dangerous message to the student. Schools need to be unequivocal that this cannot happen at school, and students need clear and specific instructions on the difference between public and private spaces and be given appropriate help, working with parents, on identifying safe home spaces for private masturbation. For more help, training and support with this type of situation, please contact Claire Lightley (www.bodysenseeducation.co.uk), Rachael Baker (www.rachaelbakerrse.co.uk) or Mel Gadd (www.sexeducationcompany.org/) author of *Masturbation, Autism and Learning Disabilities A Guide for Professionals* (Hachette, 2021), who all have a wealth of experience in supporting schools with these sensitive behaviours.

Recognising sensory overwhelm

Sensory overwhelm refers to a condition where a child's sensory system starts to get overloaded by the combination and intensity of various sensory inputs, such as sounds, lights, textures, smells or even social interactions. This leads to distress, anxiety and even meltdowns in children, making it essential for teachers to be aware of the signs and respond with sensitivity and support. You may be able to spot the signs of someone starting to feel overwhelmed: some cues may be personal to the child; for example, we know a child who gets glazed unfocused eyes, gritted teeth and starts exhibiting behaviours such as winding up those near them or throwing things on the floor when in sensory overwhelm. General clues you may spot include an increased sensitivity; for example, starting to show more extreme reactions to inputs such as covering their ears. They may avoid things they are normally able to cope with. They could become less focused, more distracted and are evidently struggling to participate. They may even have physical symptoms such as headaches or stomach aches or extreme tiredness. They could also show emotional responses such as increased irritability or anxiety with mood swings and volatile outbursts. These may be examples of the fight, flight or freeze responses of our nervous systems.

For some children, this may be a gradual amping up of responses, but for other children, it may be like a switch has been thrown with a sudden change in behaviour. The key is to regularly engage in dialogue with the students (and parents where possible) about their sensory needs and status and support them to recognise and self advocate to get their needs met.

Recognising discharge behaviour

Discharge behaviour is a term used from the Thrive approach; it refers to an explosive (fight, flight) response which could have occurred because individuals are overwhelmed by sensory input. These behaviours can manifest as volatile outbursts or attempts to disengage from the environment. Recognising the triggers and underlying causes of discharge behaviours is essential for effective intervention.

Case study: Riley

Riley has ADHD and is constantly moving and finds it hard to stay still. He is getting in increasing trouble at school, where he will lash out impulsively if things do not go his way, he will throw things, punch other children and run out of the class. Following a Team Around the Child (TAC) meeting trying to prevent an exclusion, it was decided that Riley would try a standing desk at the back of the class on a walking treadmill or a wobble board. The transformation in Riley's ability to concentrate and engage in the lesson was immediate. The discharge behaviours reduced hugely and Riley was at a reduced risk of exclusion, with an added benefit of increased social inclusion – because he wasn't so volatile with his peers anymore, he started tentatively to make friends. However, the following academic year, Riley's new class teacher did not want to have the standing desk in the classroom and made Riley sit at a table with other students. Riley's behaviour started to escalate again both at home and at school, and he began to run out of the classroom and would hide in dark tiny spaces causing panic when staff couldn't find him.

Reflection questions

- Have you taught a child like Riley?
- Would your school offer that level of accommodation to support a child like Riley?
- What is Riley seeking in the classroom and when he runs away?

Recognising shutdowns

Sensory shutdown, explained in Chapter 3, page 52, is the equivalent of the 'freeze' response. During a shutdown, a student might find it difficult to speak, interact or participate at all; they may appear unresponsive, withdrawn or disconnected from their environment. It's important to recognise and respect sensory shutdowns as a way for students to regulate their sensory experiences and manage overwhelming stimuli. Providing a calm and supportive environment and allowing the student time and space to self regulate can help them gradually re-engage and recover from the sensory overload. Some students may need time away from school to help them recover, particularly if repeated shutdown episodes have led to burnout.

Recognising the under-responsive student

You may teach some students who are under-responsive to sensory input. The students who "need a rocket put under them" or who are extremely passive in all your lessons. These students need a huge amount of sensory input to 'wake' them up and get them going.

Case Study: Kai

Kai was always seemingly tired in class, last to get started with work, never finishing work or joining in classroom discussions. His entire demeanour was sluggish. After an OT assessment, his mum increased physical activity in the mornings, which helped Kai get to school with more energy. In school, he then sat on a wobble cushion in lessons which didn't help as much as hoped. However, after discussion, the class teacher tried a wobble stool which gave increased proprioceptive and vestibular input and Kai was able to join in the lessons with hugely increased engagement and vigour.

Reflection questions

- Do you have children like Kai in your classroom?
- What interventions would you put in place for a child like Kai?
- If your intervention isn't working, how could you plan to scale it up as children like Kai need massive amounts of input to get them going?

> ### Thinking point: Reflect on your language and the lens through which you view behaviour
>
> It is helpful to reflect on and think carefully about the language you use to describe students and the way you are viewing their behaviour. A useful way to do this is using the conceptual approach of Dani Donovan's 'Two Sides, Same Coin' Venn Diagram, easily found online (one of many listed at https://adhddd.com/comics/). It clearly illustrates how negative descriptors can be changed to positive when observing student behaviour. For example, the 'dreamer' replaces the 'distracted', the 'enthusiastic' transforms the 'loud', the 'fidgety' becomes the 'energetic'. This perspective shift of the lens through which you are viewing student behaviour not only encourages a more positive view of each student's unique qualities but also reminds us of the power our words hold. Thinking more broadly, you might reimagine doodling as a coping strategy rather than a distraction or fidgeting as a regulating/focusing strategy; even daydreaming becomes a self care/respite strategy, tuning out from the overwhelm of the classroom. Carefully choosing our language so that it sees the potential in every student can enable us to empower and uplift, rather than undermine or stereotype. Remember that the messages received in childhood can last a lifetime and have lifelong consequences in the way we feel about ourselves and our abilities.
>
> It's also important to be aware of the **'double empathy problem'**. This concept highlights the challenges where people with very different experiences of the world (for example, neurodivergent and neurotypical people) interact with one another, and may struggle to empathise with each other. This is likely to be made more challenging due to differences in literal and figurative language and resultant understanding. Take some time to read up more about the double empathy problem and consider how it may impact on your professional practice and how you relate to students.

Don't panic! You are doing this work already

Think about the student you:

- Send on an errand when you see they need a break
- Hand a paperclip when they are clicking a pen and annoying everyone
- Tactically ignore when they have their hood up as it helps them focus on work
- Notice but do not comment on, chewing their pencil/cuffs while working
- Give jobs to enable them to move

- Give a scrap of paper or notebook to doodle on while they are listening
- Move to a different position in class when you see they are distracted
- Allow to fiddle with small unobtrusive items or give them Blu Tack (putty-like adhesive) when they are in class
- Tactically ignore when they are safely rocking on their chair or sitting with their feet on the seat while working.

Now thinking about these in the context of sensory informed practice, you will realise you are already making sensory adjustments intuitively that work for you and your students within your classroom. Recognising what you do already is a very good place to start from.

How reasonable is a reasonable adjustment?

Reasonable adjustments are modifications or accommodations made to ensure equal access and opportunities for people with disabilities or special needs. Determining a reasonable adjustment can be subjective and may vary depending on the context.

When considering the reasonableness of an adjustment, there are several questions to take into account:

- **Benefit to the student:** Does the adjustment improve access and participation? (If it does not offer a certain level of benefit, it might not be considered reasonable.)
- **Effectiveness:** Does it enable them to participate fully and equally in a particular situation? How effectively does the adjustment meet the individual's needs?
- **Practicality:** Is the adjustment practical and feasible to implement without causing significant disruption to the activity or environment?
- **Cost and resources:** What is the financial cost of implementing the adjustment? What resources are required for the adjustment? Is the adjustment financially feasible without straining the school's budget excessively? (An adjustment might be considered unreasonable if the cost is disproportionately high compared to the benefit it offers.)
- **Health and safety:** Have you carried out a risk assessment? (The adjustment should not compromise the health and safety of the individual or others involved.)
- **Impact on others:** Does the adjustment have a negative impact on the rights and interests of others? (Balancing the needs of all parties is important.)
- **Legal requirements:** Does the adjustment comply with relevant laws and regulations, such as the UK's Equality Act (2010)?
- **Sustainability:** Is the adjustment a sustainable solution that can be maintained over time, not just a temporary fix?

The answers to these questions can help establish whether an accommodation is reasonable or not, but we note that it often comes down to subjective individual school policies and practices rather than genuinely meeting needs through reasonable adjustments. It is important to engage in open communication and negotiation with the students and parents concerned and, if necessary, seek expert advice to determine the most appropriate and reasonable adjustments for the situation.

It is vital to understand the impact that establishing reasonable adjustments can have on supporting students' wellbeing and ability to engage. For example, please see 'Sensory strategies make things better' on the next page. As you can see, the potential for sensory overload has been vastly reduced, thanks to implementing some straightforward reasonable adjustments. Therefore the student is much more able to learn and participate.

SENSORY STRATEGIES MAKE THINGS BETTER

Various factors can impact an indvidual's ability to do a given task. The particular combination that triggers sensory overload can differ depending on a variety of factors, such as time of day, season, tiredness, hunger, stress, anxiety, transitions or something unexpected happening. Simple reasonable adjustments can have a significant impact on capacity, ability and enjoyment of required tasks.

These are the differences simple reasonable adjustments can make.

Reasonable adjustments that may be simple to implement

- The **toilet card** – to be used to leave the class for the toilet at any point, no questions asked – can also double up to get a movement break mid-lesson
- The **time out card** – to get a timed break in the lesson when needed for a movement break or sensory regulation
- **Adaptable uniform** in discussion with parents and child (see Chapter 8, page 244)
- **Ear defenders or earplugs** (see table on page 107)
- Unobtrusive **fiddle items**; for example, Blu Tack, paperclip or foam earplugs
- **Chewing**; for example, chewy bracelets or lanyards, pencil tops
- **Privacy boards or workstations** to minimise distraction
- Allowing **movement to work**; for example, allowing sitting on an office chair, sitting on a foot, wobble cushion, standing to work
- Built-in **movement breaks** – step out of the class on an errand, go around handing out books
- Consideration of **position in class** – discuss with the student what is best for them.

Thinking point: Working with parents to support students' sensory behaviours

Where possible, working with parents on their children's sensory needs can be really beneficial. How parents choose to engage with teachers/schools will be very dependent on the family. It's essential for schools to create open, non-judgmental communication channels that encourage parents to share insights without fear of misunderstanding or stigma. Offering students with SEND a key worker with whom parents can liaise to support their child can be incredibly valuable. Utilise a range of parent engagement tools such as emails, online forms to capture key information about a child's needs, regular meetings, drop-in sessions. The key is to make it as easy as possible to facilitate parent engagement, and ensure open and transparent dialogue where parents and educators can work collaboratively together for the benefit of the child. Schools might also consider offering a sensory information session that could help demystify sensory needs and help further nurture positive relationships between the school and families. Chapter 8 on page 257 covers working with parents in more detail.

Responding: Universal strategies

With an enhanced understanding of the sensory needs of all individuals in the classroom, it is important to explore what changes teachers can implement to better support their students. By using this knowledge, teachers can proactively address many of the commonly observed responses by creating sensory-friendly learning environments. Remember that anxiety can heighten sensory impacts, so adapting the sensory environment and using sensory strategies can help reduce anxious responses. You may need to modify classroom arrangements, adjust lighting and noise levels, provide sensory materials and incorporate sensory breaks into the daily routine. You may also need to reflect on your own teaching style to see how compatible it is to working in a sensory informed way. For example, Alice is a very loud teacher; over time, she has had to learn how to adjust the use of her voice to try and better support noise-sensitive students! Additionally, encouraging open communication with students and collaborating with other professionals, such as Occupational Therapists, can add further benefits.

There are many suggestions and strategies for teachers, which will help in developing a clear offer for students. Initially, universal strategies that can be 'whole class' and for almost all students will be explored, followed by targeted strategies for specific children. Wider whole school approaches such as adjusted uniform are discussed in Chapter 8. It is crucial to remember that sensory adjustments are not treated as 'rewards', but as essential accommodations to facilitate curriculum access needs. For example, many of us wear glasses and would be unable to function through the day if they were taken away. It is the same for students who need sensory adjustments, it is a need rather than a preference. It is important to consider the balance of peers; for example, the student who sings while working to help with their own regulation may distract others. Think about your classroom – there may be some students with high sensory needs; sometimes accommodating those needs could cause a cost to the majority so sometimes you may need to think about creative solutions that both support the high-needs individual and the rest of the class. It will never be possible to anticipate the needs of all the students in the class at all times, and there will always be times when responding to situations as they unfold is essential. The key to a successful approach is to stay open and curious to what students are telling us through their behaviours, and what they might need or find helpful for them.

Top tips for teachers to create sensory-friendly classrooms

- **Adopt a child-led approach** – students are supported to understand and manage their anxieties/sensory needs (but also it is important this is not at the expense of rest of the class; for example, fidget toys should be discreet and not noisy).
- **Listen to everyone's needs** – acknowledge differences and aim for common ground. You won't be able to meet all the needs at all times, but students know what works for them. The class sensory audit (Chapter 7) and individual sensory audits found in Chapter 4 will help you with this.
- **Use clear, concise SEND-friendly communication** – this can help everyone. This involves concrete language, short/chunked pieces of information with time given to process this. Information also given in a visual format will enable everyone to go back and check what has been asked rather than just spoken language which, if missed, cannot be revisited.
- **Consider seating plans** – where are students optimally seated? Where can children sit to minimise sensory overload? The front? The back? By a wall? In a corner? This is likely to be different for different students.
- **Establish a safe space** – where students feel comfortable discussing their sensory experiences. This can involve using visual aids, such as sensory stars and spiders or sensory states (see Chapter 6 for further suggestions) to help children articulate their senses.
- **Check in regularly with students** – to understand how each child is feeling and whether they require any adjustments to their environment or activities.
- **What is your objective?** – think about what you want from the situation; is it important that the student is sitting still or would you like them to be engaged in learning? Remember for many, both will not be possible.
- **Provide a Stimulating Sensory Station** – offering a 'sensory station' for time out or regulation time, with boxes of sensory activities such as fidgets/puzzles, light boxes, LEGO® and so on can benefit some students.
- **Offer a Soothing Sensory Space** – could you provide a 'sensory space' (a quiet or dark space to retreat to)? This can be through the use of dark dens, an area behind the mobile bookshelves, beanbags/cushions in the book corner, etc.

Importance of ergonomics

When considering the sensory needs of all the students in the classroom, it is also important to consider how students are seated for learning. As noted in Chapter 3, many students who have sensory processing challenges, particularly with discrimination, will also have difficulties with motor co-ordination. Ensuring that students have a physically stable base for learning is especially important for individuals with proprioceptive needs who have reduced body awareness and can become very tired in the effort of moving to seek out/gain additional input. Classrooms tend to have tables and chairs of the same size for all the children within it, but the variation in height of the children can be considerable in any year group. Ideally, students will have the option of having their feet flat on the floor, their bottom at the back of the chair and the table at the correct height. Some children will benefit from having a sloping desk/angled surface to help improve posture and ease of handwriting. If students are unable to reach the floor when sitting and are working with their legs dangling, it will require additional effort and energy to concentrate, which over time takes its toll (a foot box at the right height can easily rectify this). Some students who need some movement to help with focus and concentration like to have their legs dangling, sitting on their feet or a wobble cushion or even standing to work, to give the additional sensory feedback. It will be important to consider how students are seated to work to ensure optimal learning ability.

Utilising multisensory learning approaches

Educational trends come and go. Twenty years ago, there was an education trend for VAK (Visual, Auditory and Kinesthetic) learning where all lessons were expected to have VAK elements, attempting a move away from 'chalk and talk' and largely didactic styles of teaching. New trends such as Retrieval Practice and Concept Mapping have largely replaced these. However, these are mainly brain-based strategies and it is important not to forget about the body and the senses when thinking about what works for effective learning and memory recall. As we have seen throughout this book, students have a wide variety of responses to the sensory information they are constantly processing, which leads to learning in different ways and so students benefit from different approaches. Therefore considering and using multisensory learning remains helpful and valid for many students.

Multisensory learning is broadly learning that makes use of several senses all at once (movement, touch, taste, smell, sight, sound). Instead of just listening or watching, you also get to touch, move, and sometimes even smell or taste things related to what you are learning about. The theory is that when learning is experienced through a variety of different senses, it is more likely to aid memory and retention. In recent years, multisensory learning, particularly for SEND learners, has been increasing in popularity.

Learning visually: Almost all teachers will include visual aids such as charts, infographics and videos in their practice, and many also utilise dyslexia-friendly fonts and backgrounds as standard. It is important to be cautious with the level of additional visual learning aids in the form of posters around the room as they can prove a visual distraction from the work on the board. Permitting students to draw as well as write out responses, together with using colours and highlighters, can aid their learning and memory of the task.

Learning through listening: Teachers are often comfortable delivering much of the material and instruction of their lesson verbally, requiring students to listen in order to be able to do the work. Remember it is unhelpful to think that students can 'prove' they are listening by sitting up straight and facing forwards with eye contact, as this simply doesn't work for many students (including those who are neurodivergent). If you want to promote good listening, support students to talk about what helps them to listen: is it a doodle pad, some fidgets, a wobble seat? How can the student help the teacher know the difference between them actively listening or daydreaming? Auditory learning may also be enhanced by the use of rhythm and song to aid memory. In addition, calming music may help some groups to focus; however, this could prove distracting to some student, so how can you find that balance?

Tactile learning: Handling items can be a good way of learning. Using things like shaving foam or sandbox letters for literacy, 3D models for science and maths manipulatives like blocks or beads all help to make abstract concepts tangible which will enhance comprehension and retention. Using a variety of ways in which students record their work also helps – can they write spellings with chalk on the playground, mind map their ideas with glass pens on the windows, use dry wipe markers directly on the tables? Sometimes a shift away from pen-and- paper responses can help boost creativity and task motivation (as well as helping the students who struggle with handwriting and recording due to motor co-ordination difficulties). How can you build nature and everyday objects into the learning – for example, maths activities with sticks and leaves, or crafting with cardboard tubes? You could use modelling materials such as play dough, silver foil, tissue paper, pipe cleaners.

Learning with movement (kinesthetic experiences): In primary schools, children tend to be in the same class for most of the day, whereas in secondary school, the regular changes of classroom are a natural movement break. Movement and physical interaction with learning materials can be incredibly effective. This could be as simple as acting out historical events and scientific processes, jumping while learning times tables or spellings, sitting on a spinning office chair while revising or doing a test. Some students may benefit from sitting on a wobble cushion/ wobble stool or therapy ball or having bands on the chair legs so they can bounce their legs off. Using sign language (BSL, Makaton or creating your own signs) or body movements to learn phonics, reinforce key words or processes can also help reinforce learning.

Movement breaks: Some students who struggle with focus and concentration will really benefit from regular movement breaks (a shift to a quick movement activity to help them refocus). In the classroom, teachers can offer jobs such as "taking a message to the office" or handing out books to enable certain students to get a movement break. Teachers can also offer the whole class opportunities to stretch and move, mini-activities such as chair or wall push-ups/pull-ups, star jumps, or build movement-based activities into meeting their learning objectives. Some schools use things like GoNoodle (an online movement and learning program) or brain gym exercises to build in movement for learning. Schools may also offer corridor sensory circuits for refocusing or activity trails in the playground.

One school we work with offers whole class 'learning breaks' between every activity where all students are able to get up, go and put books away, get things out for the next activity, have a quick chat and a stretch and move. Building this in as a whole class approach means the children who really need learning breaks find learning more accessible and it is less exposing for them to get their needs met, as it's a universal not a targeted approach.

Learning with aroma and taste experiences: Whilst these inputs may not be suitable for all subjects, introducing smell and taste can be a powerful tool in subjects like geography, history and science, offering a unique perspective on cultural studies and natural phenomena. Smell is also a powerful stimulant for memory. Students could experiment with revising for a test while using a particular scent on a tissue and then using the same scent in the test to see if it aids recall. Smells that invigorate such as lemon, eucalyptus or peppermint can be particularly helpful. Care needs to be taken that the smells are discreet and not overwhelming or causing distress to anyone else.

Sensory activities and accommodations

There is a shift between primary and secondary schools from specific sensory activities to sensory accommodations, as by the time children reach secondary school, it is hoped they will be more aware of their own sensory needs and they can take more ownership over these and use the strategies that work best for them.

Our favourite sensory activities for primary school

- **Movement** – activity frames/trim trails, obstacle courses in the playground, trampettes. Whole class movement breaks with activities such as Wake and Shake or GoNoodle.
- **Tactile** – Tuff trays with shaving foam, cooked pasta, paints, fabrics, water, modelling clay, play dough, kinetic sand, maths manipulatives.
- **Visual** – light boxes or calm down jars with glitter in, bubble tubes/disco lights.
- **Auditory** – playing soothing or energising music.
- **Gustatory and olfactory** – fruit faces (making faces out of fruit and veg and mindfully sampling), different essential oils/smells for specific tasks.
- **Interoception** – 'What am I feeling?' activities, mindful body scans, heart-rate measuring activities.

Our favourite sensory accommodations for secondary school

- **Movement** – movement is built into the school day, with access to dance, drama and PE most days of the week. Specific gym sessions. Spinning office chairs in computer lessons.
- **Tactile** – permitting gloves for sensory activities in food tech, art, science. Offering different types of paper according to preference.
- **Visual** – permitting tinted/coloured glasses or sunglasses for reading or use in classrooms. Classroom position to be closer to natural rather than artificial light.
- **Auditory** – permitting earplugs or ear defenders (see table on page 107) both while working and when moving around school.
- **Olfactory** – having something you like the smell of on a hankie in a pocket or on a school tie.
- **Interoception** – toilet cards and time out cards. Regular snacks/drinks throughout the day.

Specialist provision: These are strategies for mainstream provision, as in our experience, specialist provisions have a whole sensory curriculum and sensory offering that they do very well already which naturally incorporate some of the sensory accommodations on the previous page. Many specialist provisions also offer sensory rooms (see page 226 of Chapter 7, 'Considerations for including a School Sensory Room').

Managing transitions effectively

Transitions are often extremely challenging for many students. Moving from an activity you are focused on, to another one, or to another place which may be an unknown situation is extremely stressful for many students. There is not only the change of activity and place, but this is often accompanied by increased sensory input within the transition, particularly in school with the increased noise of others moving at the same time. Managing transitions in a Sensory Aware School is about ensuring smooth and predictable shifts for students without having abrupt changes. To make transitions less daunting, teachers can provide clear, consistent cues that signal when one activity is ending and another is beginning. Preparing students beforehand with visual schedules or brief discussions about what to expect next can also help reduce anxiety. Some SEND students benefit from having transition objects. By carefully managing these transitions, teachers help maintain a calm, supportive environment that increases a student's ability to adapt.

Supporting self regulation strategies through understanding bodily sensations

Supporting students to develop their self regulation strategies as part of their PSHE is crucial. Kelly Mahler, the leading Occupational Therapist for understanding interoception said, *"Trying to teach emotions before exploring body signals is like trying to read a book in the dark. You need light to grasp the words just as you need body signals to comprehend emotions"*. What strategies do you use to support students to understand their bodily sensations? Look at Lindsay Braman's Emotion Sensation Feeling Wheel (available online). Do you agree with her assessments of how each of the emotions feel in the body with their physiological responses? This whole chapter contains lots of information on strategies that can help with self regulation and the importance of co-regulation is also explored further in this chapter on page 105. It is important to "name it, to tame it". You have to be able to describe what is going on in your body (interoception) to be better able to understand and manage those feelings. It would be important to read further around self regulation to understand these ideas further.

Responding: Targeted strategies

It may be helpful to think about responding to individuals' sensory needs in both proactive and reactive ways. Proactive strategies and support can be thought through, planned and put in place to mitigate universal needs (as discussed previously). However, there will always be times when this is not enough and it will be essential to respond to a situation with more targeted strategies (reactive) or to use more specialist strategies for specific individuals in the class.

We now focus more on the specific strategies for individual students in the classroom, some of which will be detailed in individual students' EHCPs and so will be discussed with parents and the SENDCo. Be aware that some of these suggested strategies may or may not work for an individual student; monitoring the success as they are implemented will help to refine and embed them successfully. The benefits of the changes are often evident within the classroom, but this is not always the case (particularly for those students who are masking). Therefore open communication with parents as new things are tried in school can help establish the effectiveness of these changes. For example, one outcome may be a reduction in dysregulation and meltdowns at home rather than any observable differences in school.

How targeted strategies can make a difference

- A student who is constantly on the go and seeking movement and very easily becoming dysregulated was given the role of pushing the lunchbox trolley to and from the dining hall every day. This level of proprioceptive input helped him to focus and learn after lunch.
- A student who is often flopping and propping himself against furniture and walls and almost falling off the chair started to wear compression skins under his school uniform with immediate and drastic effect, enabling him to sit up and be alert.
- A student who was chewing and crunching on pencils and pens in lessons, basically eating them, to her peers' disgust, was given a chewy bracelet, enabling her to chew something at her wrist; this enabled her to focus and join in without affecting her peers in the same way.

Managing behaviour through co-regulation

Co-regulation is an active approach used by adults in helping children to develop their own ability to regulate their emotions and sensory inputs. This involves modelling responses such as lowering the voice, offering strategies which they know will help the child and can help with reassurance and regulation. This helps the child feel understood, safe and secure, and over time, enables them to understand what works for them and to become more independent. For younger children, the adults in the classroom will need to be scaffolding their sensory strategies and regulation to ensure success. This may be the teacher recognising when the child is losing focus or becoming overwhelmed and offering a movement break or suggesting a drink or time in the quiet corner. Remember that using strategies for regulation can include things which help activating/alerting or calming for students; some strategies may be good for both and others will be specific for one. As a student gets older, they will then be able to recognise this need themselves and may choose to use strategies which work for them such as chewing gum while revising or sitting on a spinning office chair to work.

Co-regulation will be part of the behaviour management strategy in the school, aiming to pre-empt challenging behaviours occurring such as a student hurting themselves or throwing equipment/furniture. It is not always possible to identify triggers that students are experiencing, but offering support when it becomes evident that the student is starting to become dysregulated can sometimes reduce or diffuse this. At times of dysregulation, keeping language to a minimum is essential as the student will be less able to process language when in fight/flight mode. Offering co-regulation to help return the student to the just right zone is the priority, and the reflection and consequences/next steps will need to be addressed at a later date. It is important to remember that as adults we often don't solely self regulate ourselves – at times of distress we will co-regulate by debriefing with a partner or confiding in close friends, we will seek cuddles and a listening ear. Therefore, it is a double standard to expect children and young people to self regulate when their brain is still developing and we don't do this ourselves!

Sensory tools

Noise sensitivity

Noise sensitivity is one of the most common sensory issues in schools; in the table on the next page we detail some of the commonly available options including the market leaders Flare Calmer® and Loop earplugs and their pros and cons.

Noise Reduction Devices		
Device Type	**Pros**	**Cons**
Ear Defenders	• Great for reducing all types of noise • Durable • Come in a range of colours and styles	• Bulky and less portable • May be uncomfortable over long use • You need to get the right size that fits over your head and ears most comfortably • Makes you identifiably different so young people don't like wearing them
Noise Cancelling Headphones (over ear or inner ear)	• Can reduce all types of noise including low-frequency noise background noise • You can listen to music and take calls while wearing them • Stylish options and less obvious when being used for noise reduction rather than music so young people prefer to wear them	• Potentially expensive for most effective noise cancelling • Requires charging or wires which may get in the way • Could be bulky, heavy and hot to wear • Less acceptable to wear in school when schools may have rules against headphones
Loop Earplugs	• Reusable • Range of options to adjust level of sound reduction • Offers earrings/necklace accessories to reduce risk of loss • Discreet, stylish and comfortable to wear	• More varied noise reduction than other alternatives • High cost • Voice can sound distorted with some options • May irritate the inner ear for some users
Flare Calmer® Earplugs	• Reduce stress from noise by soothing peripheral sounds • Comfortable, and discreet to wear • Range of options to enhance sounds, particularly music clarity • Voice sounds usual when wearing	• Expensive • Easy to lose, especially the clear versions • May irritate the inner ear for some users (offers a soft version to mitigate this) • Can be tricky to put in correctly • Subtle effect, not for high noise reduction
Foam Earplugs	• Fair amount of noise reduction • Cheap • Easy to replace if one gets lost • Can double up as a discreet squishy fidget in a pocket	• Less durable • May be uncomfortable • Muffles sounds so wearer may not hear the teacher as well
Plastic or Silicone Tree Earplugs	• More noise blocking than foam • Reusable • Waterproof • Relatively inexpensive	• May muffle too much classroom noise • May require cleaning • Can increase ear wax buildup
Mouldable Wax or Silicone Earplugs	• Mouldable to fit perfectly in the ear • Relatively inexpensive	• Less durable; may not last longer than a few uses
Earmuffs/ Ear Warmer Headbands	• Stylish fun options • Keep ears warm • Comfortable to wear with the additional side benefit of reducing sound	• Primary function is warmth, not noise reduction • Too hot to wear in summer • Unusual to wear indoors

Some may be better to wear in school daily, others may be preferable for night-time use for sleep. Alice wears Flare Calmer® earplugs regularly in busy spaces such as classrooms, cafés and on public transport. They offer calming noise reduction without reducing the noise quality of people talking directly to her. They also do not change how her voice sounds in her head, whereas other options she tried, including Loop earplugs (which are marginally more comfortable – less itchy – to wear) did change how her voice sounded to her, so she couldn't cope with them. One of her daughters who also really benefits from noise reduction benefitted from Flare Calmer® earplugs, but unfortunately, she found they caused an inner ear itch/sensory response so she struggled to wear them comfortably. She will wear ear defenders for crowded events like festivals or fireworks, or headphones or earphones with music playing for more discreet noise reduction. So really it is a case of experimenting with the available options to find the best noise reduction sensory solution for you.

Challenge: Can students listen to music to aid focus and meet their sensory needs?

We repeatedly hear from parents who are despairing of schools refusing to allow listening to music as a reasonable adjustment; as a result, their child no longer fully accesses school, either needing a part-time timetable or being homeschooled full- time. While schools may allow ear defenders or earplugs, they often refuse earphones or headphones because of a general ban on listening to music and associated with phone bans. However, young people generally prefer to wear earphones or headphones as their noise reduction aid because it enables them to blend in rather than standing out as different when wearing ear defenders. Some studies suggest that music can have beneficial impacts on mood, focus, concentration, memory and motivation; however, this is very subjective and the type of music, the volume, whether it's solely instrumental or has lyrics will all impact on the individual preferences. This means that playing music as a whole class approach may not work for everyone in your class.

Reflection questions about music

- What are your school rules about playing music?
- Is listening to music a want or a need? What might cause it to shift from a want to a need?
- What do your students say about the school rules on playing music?

- Could you set up experiments on the impact on learning and memory when students are allowed to listen to their own choice of music?
- If phones are banned, could you experiment with going with different technology such as MP3 players or using the computer rooms for listening to music while working?
- Can groups of students agree on a type of music genre that helps them concentrate for a revision lesson or another lesson requiring focus. The students who prefer not to (for sensory reasons) could experiment with earplugs or ear defenders. At the end of the experiment, the students could do self reflection questionnaires to see if the music made a difference.

The importance of fidgets

Fidgets became quite the fad in recent years. Schools are starting to move away from the idea that to prove concentration, children need to be sitting up straight and still, eyes on the teacher, etc. Many children actually listen better with something to fiddle with. (As an adult, Alice can often only listen properly if she is knitting or crocheting – and has that as a reasonable adjustment in some of the longer meetings she needs to attend!). Some schools are now using the term 'concentrators' instead of fidgets, due to the fact that fidget toys tend to have a bad press and be misunderstood. This recognises that sensory stimulation and feedback can help learners concentrate in the classroom.

Legitimate fiddling

Remember, if you are a fiddler, then it is possible to discreetly fiddle with anything without the need for specific fidgets, such as the end of a zip, the edge of a button, the seam in trousers, the corner of a name badge, a label in clothing, the end of a pencil and so on. Reminding students of this can reduce anxiety as they are still able to fiddle even if they have forgotten a specific fidget, and it is a strategy that is available to them at any time, in any situation, without planning. A parent many years ago called it 'legitimate fiddling' and this continues to describe it well, ensuring that students take responsibility to fidget unobtrusively, actively using items to fiddle with and learning how to use them discreetly and appropriately; for example, not flicking, throwing or trying to break them. If the fidget item becomes the focus of attention in itself, then it is not helping with concentration and focus on the lesson and so is not a successful strategy.

10 of the best (quiet and discreet!) classroom fidgets

1. **Blu Tack** – it's an old favourite, but a small amount of Blu Tack goes a long way. We don't want it on the carpet, but having a tiny lidded pot of it in a pocket is great.
2. **Paperclip or pipe cleaner** – a small piece of wire to bend in interesting shapes. Care needs to be taken if it breaks and a sharp edge is created.
3. **Silver foil** – a small piece can be scrunched into interesting shapes or torn into smaller balls. The same goes with paper, although it offers a less tactile response.
4. **Foam earplugs** – these can act as small discreet squishies.
5. **Chain fidgets** – you can get ones for a finger or a hand, providing a soothing repetitive motion.
6. **Marble in mesh** – this is a single marble sewn into the same mesh as used in the childhood 'finger trap' toys. You can silently squeeze the marble up and down and change the shape of the mesh to create different-sized 'marble cages'.
7. **Anxiety rings** – there is a huge range of rings available (if rings are allowed as part of school uniform), offering a range of spinning or twisting options. We especially love the spiky sensory rings which also offer an acupressure sensation (they can't be worn as a ring long-term, as they would affect circulation, but moving the ring up and down the finger provides significant calming input).
8. **Stretch toys** – the mini stretch toys you get can be great, but be careful, as they can sometimes accidentally or deliberately get pinged across a room!
9. **Stress balls** – ideally not the ones filled with gel that can burst, but the harder foam ones can be good to squish.
10. **A piece of ribbon or thick string** – (or a stretchy worm) to twirl between fingers can be really helpful.

Don't forget the power of a pencil case

All of the above fidgets can be kept in a pencil case, and remember that the pencil case choice can also deliberately help with sensory needs – for example, reversible sequins, glitter gel, furry, multiple zips, compartments to sort, or transparent so students can see contents. These pencil cases will offer something tactile to discreetly fiddle with and aid concentration.

Sensory bumbag

Using a bumbag for individual students can work well to ensure that they have the necessary sensory support with them at all times, which they can use as needed. Parents often create these to give to the child at the end of the school day or on family outings. Initially these can be set up by a parent or teacher, but as the student becomes more aware of their own sensory needs, they can choose what goes into this. Contents often include items such as a fidget item, a chewy snack, something to smell, sunglasses, earbuds, something soothing like a lip salve or hand cream. Alongside this, many students will also have a weighted lap pad or shoulder wrap to help with further regulation; these can be offered in the car at the end of a school day.

Sensory products for movement and weight

It is always important to discuss the use of these items with students and parents before they are tried, to ensure they are happy to experiment with them and know why they are being used. These items will not work for all students and the use of them should not be enforced if the student expresses a dislike for them. In general, if students find them useful, they will remember to use them by taking them to the carpet/hall and making sure they have them in class where needed. If the items are regularly left behind, then it is possible that they are not helping in the intended manner, so you should explore with the student why this is. If it's not offering any sensory benefit to the student, stop using it. However, some students may feel embarrassed about being the only one in the group using the product, so how can they be supported to use the products if they need and benefit from them? Can you provide the same thing for other students who would also benefit, to encourage peer norming?

\multicolumn{3}{c}{**Pros and Cons of Sensory Tools**}
Sensory Tool	**Pros**	**Cons**
Movin' Sit Cushion	<ul><li>Provides additional proprioceptive and vestibular feedback/increases body awareness</li><li>Enables movement to aid concentration</li><li>Improves posture and enhances core stability</li><li>Can be used on a chair or floor (for carpet time/assemblies)</li><li>Has different textures on each side such as soft spikes or small bumps to offer a choice</li><li>Lightweight and portable</li></ul>	<ul><li>Some students do not like the feel of movement – in which case, follow students' preference.</li><li>Not helpful for students with balance issues</li><li>May cause distractions for others</li><li>More suitable for primary school use</li><li>Can deflate and then not effective</li><li>Can be uncomfortable to sit on for long periods</li></ul>

Sensory Tool	Pros	Cons
Wobble Stool	• Provides more intense proprioceptive and vestibular feedback/body awareness • Can help with focus and attention • Enables movement while working	• Many schools are not willing to use it in mainstream classes for safety reasons • Can be unstable • Can be distracting for other students if the child on the stool is moving excessively • Can lead to poor posture if incorrectly used
Therapy/Gym Ball	• Provides more intense proprioceptive and vestibular feedback/body awareness • Can help with focus and attention • Enables movement while working • Can help improve posture and core stability	• Many schools are not willing to use it in mainstream classes for safety reasons • More suitable for primary school use • Can be unstable • Risk of student rolling off if not concentrating • Can be distracting for other students if the child is moving excessively • Takes more space than a wobble cushion or stool
Peanut Ball	• Provides increased proprioceptive and vestibular feedback/body awareness • Can help with focus and attention • Enables movement while working • More stable than a gym ball • Can help improve posture and core stability	• More suitable for primary school use • Not suitable for all ages/heights of children • Can be distracting for other students if the child is moving excessively • Takes more space than a wobble cushion or stool
Spinning Chair	• Provides intense proprioceptive and vestibular feedback/body awareness • Can help with focus and attention • Enables movement while working • More stable than a ball • Can help improve posture	• Can be distracting for other students if the child is moving excessively. • Needs clear safety guidelines. • **Do not use** for children who are over-responsive to vestibular input as it can cause dizziness
TheraBand/Resistance Bands of Various Strengths (around Chair Legs)	• Can help with focus and attention • Enables discreet movement/fidgeting of legs while working • Gives proprioceptive feedback/increased sense of body awareness • Reduces need to stand up and move around • Inexpensive and easy to install	• Can be distracting for other students. • Can snap if over-stretched/used • Can make a noise • Potential for misuse
Commercially Available Foot Fidgets	• Can help with focus and attention • Enables discreet movement/fidgeting of legs while working • Gives proprioceptive feedback/increased sense of body awareness • More durable than TheraBands • Reduces need to stand up and move around	• Can be distracting for other students • More suitable for primary school use • Can make a noise • Some can roll away under the table causing additional distraction • Potential for misuse

Sensory Tool	Pros	Cons
Fidget/Fiddle Toys (see page 109 for further information)	• Gives proprioceptive and tactile feedback • Can help with focus and concentration • Wide variety available • Students can fiddle with everyday items such as buttons, end of zip	• Can be distracting for other students • Can become a distraction for the students themselves • Can make a noise • Commercially produced fidgets can break • Student can become reliant on a specific fiddle toy • Can have safety concerns
Weighted Shoulder Wraps or Lap Pads	• Can help with focus and regulation • Provides calming deep pressure • Gives proprioceptive feedback/ increased sense of body awareness • Easy and portable to use around school • Student can remove when not needed	• Need to ensure correct weight for student • Not suitable for all students • May make student feel hot • In extreme circumstances, it can be thrown and therefore cause safety risk • Shoulder wraps maybe embarrassing to wear (lap pads are a bit more discreet) • Less available at secondary school as heavy to carry around (a heavy backpack does the same thing)
Weighted and/or Compression Vests	• Can help with focus and regulation • Provides calming deep pressure • Gives proprioceptive feedback/ increased sense of body awareness • Easy and portable to use around school • Some enable students to adjust pressure themselves as required • Student can remove when not needed	• Need to ensure correct weight/size for student to be effective • Not all students like the feeling, so it is not always helpful • Students can find them hot to wear especially in hot weather • Students can find it embarrassing to wear
Weighted Blankets	• Provides calming deep pressure • Gives proprioceptive feedback/ increased sense of body awareness • Can be used at specific times for regulation/calming; for example, when student is overwhelmed • Can be available in the sensory room/dark den for regulation throughout the day **N.B.:** See guidelines published by Royal College of Occupational Therapists	• Essential to ensure correct weight for student to be safe • Not all students like the feeling, so respect this and **do not enforce it** • Not suitable for general use in the classroom, but in specific places in school/classroom • Students can find them hot to use especially in hot weather • Heavy to move • Need to consider hygiene as not easily washable
Sensory Swing	• Provides vestibular input • Can have a calming effect on some students • Variety of types	• Generally used in therapy or sensory rooms • Needs to be installed correctly to ensure it is structurally safe • Need to consider sufficient space to swing safely • Needs to be used by trained staff • Unless staff are specifically trained, **do not use** it for children who are over-responsive to vestibular input as it can cause dizziness.

General classroom strategies for all students

10 strategies for alerting/activating (raising a child or young person from under-responsive to engaged)

1. Small in-class movement; for example, chair push-ups, wrapping legs around the chair
2. Larger movements: press-ups against wall or star jumps/ trampette/ trampoline
3. Movement break: take a message to the office, do a job in class
4. Breathing exercise such as bunny breath: take three quick sniffs through the nose and one long exhale through the nose
5. Change of scene: new location in school or classroom
6. Change of position: for example, standing desk or sitting on an exercise ball, link fingers and stretch arms away from body, roll shoulders
7. Drinking: through a sports bottle or straw
8. Sitting: wobble cushions and Therabands on the chairs
9. Teach strategies: like hand pressure massage, pulling/massaging earlobes, pushing hands on top of head
10. Sensory circuits: a corridor/hall filled with specific activities.

10 strategies for soothing/calming (lowering a child or young person from over-responsive to engaged)

1. Weighted equipment: for example, lap pad, shoulder wrap, jacket, weighted blanket
2. Movement: for example, Theraband on a chair, wall/chair push-ups
3. Weight bearing and resistance: carrying a heavy tray or backpack
4. Breathing activity: for example, belly breathing – place your hands on your stomach, close your eyes, breathe in through your nose for 4 seconds, expand and hold for 7 seconds and breathe out through your mouth and feel your belly deflate for 8 seconds, repeat
5. Chewing or drinking through straws and sports bottles
6. Dark den: moving to a darker space

7. Use of privacy boards: to cut out extra visuals
8. Ear defenders: to reduce extra noise
9. A designated classroom job: provides positive alternative activities to help calm the student, such as wiping the white board, moving chairs, sharpening pencils, hole punching papers, handing out or collecting materials
10. Doodling: for example mindful colouring books or a doodle pad alongside work.

Top tip: Get creative with ideas and think outside the box!

One sensory child we worked with couldn't cope with the feeling of bare skin rubbing on a table as she was trying to write. She also couldn't cope with her sleeves bunching up and getting in the way of her work. A long fingerless glove in a comfortable snug- fitting fabric for her writing arm has solved this issue for her. For another child, just the change of paper (from scratchy to smooth) made it possible for him to write with his arm and hand resting on the paper, leading to increased comfort as well as fluency of writing. Another child we know loved using squishies, but would get very stressed at the thought of a teacher telling her off for 'playing' with them (even though she had an EHCP that allowed fidgets as a reasonable adjustment) or losing them at school. It turned out that simple foam earplugs did the trick for her just as well – discreet in her pocket and easy to replace and not at all 'toy like'. A third child would chew any pens, but a 3 cm long bit of aquarium tubing over the end of any pen gave enough of a 'bite' sensory response for the pens to be protected and served as a cheap and easily replaceable (once worn or dirty) pen cap.

Exam concessions

Remember sensory needs and strategies when students are taking exams or assessments, so they are fully supported to be able to concentrate on the exam rather than wasting energy trying to focus. For example, a quiet plain room can reduce visual and auditory distractions, plus sitting on an office chair and building in rest breaks to allow movement. Ensure a silent digital clock to reduce anxiety about being unable to read an analogue clock, without getting distracted by the ticking. Be aware of avoidable distractions such as noisy shoes, squeaking/clicking, the rattle of keys, clicking pens on/off, computer servers. Discuss with students what works best for them well before exam concessions are arranged to ensure that the arrangements meet their needs, rather than offering 'one size fits all' solutions. We know of a teenage boy who failed a GCSE because in the exam the invigilator sat on a seat in front of him wearing a flowery dress which he found massively distracting. He put his hand up and tried to explain that her dress was distracting him. But she laughed at him as she thought he was being silly and didn't move position. For that exam, he only managed to write his name and returned home totally broken and devastated. We also know of another teenage girl who was supposed to do exams on her own; however, she couldn't cope with the smell of the solo tiny office she was offered and actually preferred to be in a room with others working hard, as it helped her to concentrate, as long as she could sit at the back to get outside for her rest break without disturbing others.

> ### Reflection points
>
> - How do you meet individual student needs in exams?
> - Are students asked in more detail about their specific needs before tests and exams, or are arrangements just based on provision available in school such as extra time or rooms/invigilators available?
> - Are students able to articulate their needs for tests and exams and is this listened to and responded to?
> - How do the SENDCO and the exams officer work well together (in conjunction with recommendations from Educational Psychologists and OTs) to meet needs effectively?

Specialist strategies

The aim of the strategies and approaches suggested in this chapter is that they can be implemented in schools either for whole class use or for individual students. There will always be students for whom the strategies are not enough and further help and support are needed to fully identify, understand and support their needs. When students are not being helped by sensory strategies or continue to experience considerable challenges with sensory processing and motor co-ordination, then referral for further assessment, advice and support from an Occupational Therapist should be sought. Some students will already have been seen by an Occupational Therapist and may have outcomes and provisions written into their EHCP. This could include the adoption of a sensory diet or specific sensory integration therapy (see explanation in Chapter 3, page 53). In these instances, it will be important to liaise with the Occupational Therapist, regarding the strategies and supports that are recommended for the specific student to ensure the best outcomes whilst they are in school. In primary school, the person who does this liaison would be the class teacher and/or SENDCO, and at secondary level, this is likely to be the SENDCO and/or named SEND Keyworker who may be a teaching assistant. All the key information should be recorded on their Individual Education Profile (IEP) which all their teachers should have access to.

Final considerations

- Before moving on from strategies, just one note of caution. It is important when working with students to **think about age-appropriate strategies and the possible longer-term unintended consequences** of these becoming embedded behaviours. For example, think about long-term implications of sensory seeking behaviours in adulthood – stroking an adult or preferring to go without some clothing may be acceptable when in primary school, but this behaviour will not be appropriate or acceptable in the wider community as an adult. When discussing with parents and the student how to support behaviours (which may become embedded as behaviour rather than just meeting a sensory need), considering the long-term implications is essential. You could use **Recognise Replace Reduce Reflect** as an aid for thinking through interventions for potentially problematic behaviours. To find out more, listen to the podcast on 4Rs for Addressing Challenging Behaviour by Dr Pooky Knightsmith.
- **Think about your own school day.** Working in large busy classrooms can cause sensory overwhelm. Work out the times of the day when you need quiet and calm, and make sure you plan some 'sensory joy' into your morning and evening routines as these are particularly crucial to ensure your day starts and ends well. Think about 'living sensationally' and punctuating the day with sensory activities to sustain/meet your sensory needs and widen your window of tolerance.
- Develop awareness of **your sensory impact on others**. Meeting our own sensory needs can have an impact on others around us – in both positive and negative ways, so be aware of the effect of the noise of heels on the floor, the smell of perfume or aftershave, bright clothing or large jewellery/dangly earrings, clicking pen tops or scrunching paper, tapping feet or excessive movement around the classroom. You need to also support your students to do this for each other, as meeting their own sensory needs may have sensory implications for others and the key is balance and fairness.

- Be aware of the **risk of becoming hypersensitive** to certain stimuli that were previously manageable as you become more aware of your own sensory needs. Consider coping strategies, including mindfulness and distraction techniques, to manage sensory inputs effectively.
- **Developing tolerance** of some sensory inputs needs to be considered rather than always avoiding them. As adults we live in a sensory world and it is not possible to eliminate or reduce all sensory input, however challenging it seems at times. Teaching students the strategies which help them to tune in and tune out can help them develop life skills. See the Seagull Caveat on page 76 of Chapter 4 for some questions that may help them reflect on this.
- Be vigilant to the **changing reactions to sensory triggers** depending on the level of anxiety or the build-up of difficulties, leading to this trigger being the last straw. For example, the extractor fan may be tolerated when calm and regulated, but be impossible to manage at the end of a bad day. See 'Sensory strategies make things better' on page 96 for more information.
- **Good enough is good enough** – it is not possible to be perfect all the time. We can't get it right for everyone all of the time, but just trying helps.
- Consider a **common sensory approach**. Is it feasible? Is it realistic? Is there a cost? Does it have long-term implications for adult life? Use common sense to pick your battles rather than feeling you need to address everything.
- Reflect on the **scale of responses** you feel you have the capacity to offer. You can't do it all, there is a minimum, medium, maximum. The bare minimum is listening to the individual student and acknowledging what they need.
- **Community support** – joining or creating groups (for staff or students in person or remotely via Facebook or WhatsApp groups) for communities or practice or peer support can help build supportive networks, provide opportunities to share successful strategies and build nurturing friendships.
- Our ultimate goal with this work is to develop the **child or young person's sensory autonomy** so that they can recognise and manage their own sensory needs. All sensory strategies need to be implemented consensually in dialogue with the student. For any intervention, you need to start with the child in mind and tailor it to their needs, collaborating with them for the best outcomes. Remember that in adulthood, they may well be able to choose to live a sensory lifestyle that is vastly different to the one they were forced into as a child or young person. For example, Alice wore tights to school every day until she was 16 and basically hasn't worn them since, and the thought of wearing them now makes her shudder! There are lots of activities in Chapter 6 that will develop

students' own sensory awareness through a wide variety of session ideas aimed at improving their own understanding of their sensory identity, sensory needs and thinking about their sensory wellbeing through sensory welldoing.

> **Reflection questions for Chapter 5**
> 1. How can your students tell you their sensory needs?
> 2. Can you recognise when behaviours may have a sensory basis?
> 3. What sensory interventions do you use already in the classroom?
> 4. Which new sensory interventions have you learned in this chapter that you may want to try?
> 5. How will you assess the impact of any sensory interventions?
> 6. What is the bare minimum you could offer in terms of sensory strategies?
> 7. What would a medium offer of sensory strategies look like?
> 8. What would a comprehensive 'maximum' offer of sensory strategies look like?
> 9. What other resources (time, sensory tools, support) do you need to effectively implement sensory strategies?
> 10. How can you collaborate with wider staff, SEND specialists and Occupational Therapists, to develop and refine sensory strategies in your classroom?

Chapter six

DEVELOPING YOUR SENSORY CURRICULUM

It is absolutely vital that we teach all young people about their senses and their sensory needs.

Modern society and a life lived online has meant that young people can be disconnected from their bodies and bodily sensations. We believe it is a fundamental life skill to be able to recognise, articulate and make adjustments for sensory needs. The activities in this chapter aim to get students thinking about their senses, what their individual needs and preferences are and how to articulate them. It also aims to think about collective needs and preferences and how these can be managed where there is a conflict.

The official inclusion of sensory education in the curriculum varies across the world. In most places, it is limited to learning about the five senses as part of the science curriculum. However, there is a growing recognition of the importance of addressing diverse learning styles and sensory needs in education, particularly in early years education and special educational needs programmes. This tends to be in the format of 'multisensory learning' activities that engage children and enhance the learning experience, rather than educating children directly about their senses (for more information on multisensory learning, see page 100 of Chapter 5).

While educating children about their five main senses may be common, particularly in the early and primary years, across the world, it would be unusual for schools to include detail on the other three sensory systems (proprioception, vestibular and interoception). Some of the activities from part 1 (page 138) can help explain proprioception and the vestibular system, while activities from page 141 can help explain more about interoception. While sensory education is often limited to science lessons, we would like to point out that wellbeing (with a focus on mental and physical health) would also be another core curriculum strand into which sensory education logically fits. We would argue that sensory wellbeing contributes significantly to both mental and physical health.

This chapter initially sets out what we feel the key learning objectives should be for your sensory curriculum, and how to establish a safe learning environment to do this work. The chapter is then divided in four parts with activities exploring each theme in more detail;

- **Part 1: Learning more about our sensory selves (pages 126–162):** This part starts to explore in more detail what the main different senses are, including the three that might be less familiar – interoception, vestibular and proprioception. It includes information about sensory likes (glimmers) and dislikes (triggers) and enables us to consider this on a spectrum.
- **Part 2: Understanding our sensory regulation (pages 163–177):** This part aims to help students understand how our sensory states can change and the difference between feeling regulated and calm, and dysregulated and potentially angry/upset/frustrated, potentially leading to meltdowns or shutdowns.
- **Part 3: Recognising, responding and respecting sensory differences (pages 178–188):** This part starts to build understanding of how we can recognise, respond and respect our unique sensory identities and support others.
- **Part 4: Embracing sensory wellbeing for ourselves and our community (pages 191–201):** The final part considers how sensory wellbeing can be embraced for all and includes how to consider student voice in school as a key way of developing sensory wellbeing across the school.

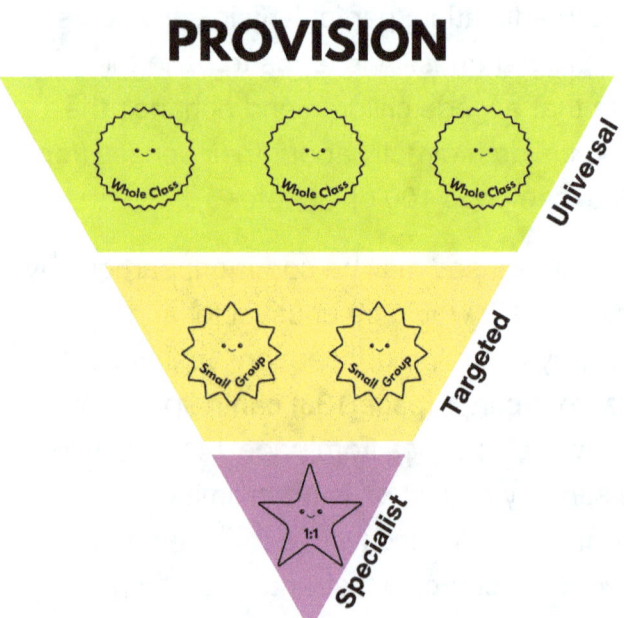

Each activity includes a brief summary of the activity, a guide to the recommended age of participants, the estimated time the activity will take and the resources the activity will require, as well as whether this activity is suitable for mainstream or specialist education, and whether it can be taught to the whole class, small groups or 1:1. Therefore this chapter can offer universal whole class approaches, opportunities for small group interventions and even offers activities for more 1:1 sessions from an educational or occupational therapy professional.

There are more than 50 different activities to try in this chapter. The aim is NOT to do every single activity with all students (this is likely to be impossible!), but rather to use this chapter as a 'pick and mix' to choose the best activities most suitable for your learners to develop your school's sensory curriculum. We would recommend you select the activities you feel will work best for your students with their needs, level and ability in mind, and the time and resources you have available.

The eight key learning objectives for sensory awareness, sensory inclusion and sensory wellbeing

Below we have identified the eight key learning objectives for a sensory curriculum. The activities in this chapter will each cover one or more of the learning objectives. Select and adapt the most important learning objectives you want to cover with your learners.

1. List what our eight senses are and explain what sensory wellbeing and welldoing are.
2. Recognise and articulate our sensory likes (including sensory glimmers) and dislikes (including sensory triggers) on a sensory spectrum.
3. Describe sensory strategies we can use to (a) soothe and calm; (b) activate, excite and energise our nervous systems.
4. Experiment with relevant sensory strategies (welldoing) and note any changes or improvement to our sensory wellbeing as a result.
5. Consider what makes each of our individual thresholds for sensory reactions change (window of tolerance) and think about what support we might need from others.
6. Think about how we can recognise when our nervous systems are in overload and what steps we can take to help us regulate.
7. Think about how we can recognise when other people are starting to be overloaded and what steps we can take to help others regulate.
8. Discuss how individual sensory needs can impact on others with different sensory needs. Also explore how fair balances can be negotiated using the principles for sensory welldoing which are 'Taking Care of Me', 'Taking Care of You', 'Having an Equal Say', 'Learning as We Go'.

Principles for sensory welldoing

Taking Care of Me – It is important that I actively look after and take care of my own sensory needs and wellbeing through sensory 'welldoing'.

Taking Care of You – I will try to also support your sensory wellbeing where reasonable* to do so.

Having an Equal Say – My right to sensory wellbeing is no more or less important than your right to sensory wellbeing – where there is a conflict of needs*, let's talk about it and find a solution that works for all of us!

Learning as We Go – It is important to stay curious about our sensory worlds and what we are learning about ourselves as a result. Our needs may change in time and space and that's okay; noticing, learning and reflecting is a key part of sensory welldoing.

These principles are adapted from an original ditty by Jenny Walsh which aims to teach ethical interactions, developed from research by Moira Carmody. A version of this ditty is also published in Alice Hoyle and Ester McGeeney's book Great Relationships and Sex Education: 200+ Activities for Educators Working with Young People (Routledge, 2019) and used to structure their chapter on relationships.

*In some cases, individuals may have diagnosed additional needs that require reasonable adjustments and supports – for more on this, see page 94 on 'How reasonable is a reasonable adjustment?' in Chapter 5.

Before doing any work on the senses and getting students talking about their senses and feelings in ways that might feel quite personal to them, it is important to have a standard PSHE-style group agreement in place. The principles of sensory welldoing above have also been adapted into a group agreement on the next page to further help with practising these principles. Students should feel free to add in anything else they feel would help support them to participate in the sessions.

A sample group agreement for sensory sessions

Taking Care of Me – Be kind to yourself. Don't put yourself down. Be open to learning, sharing and discussing, but make sure you are comfortable with what you share. If any of the material in a session upsets you for any reason, take a breather. You have a right to pass on anything in these sessions. Seek further help and advice if needed.

Taking Care of You – Don't put others down and be kind and respectful to each other. Listen well to each other's contributions. Don't make assumptions about anyone else's feelings or behaviours. Don't be judgmental.

If your teacher hears something that might require more support, we might need to pass it on and work with you to get you some help (educators can't promise confidentiality).

Having an Equal Say – Everyone has an equal right to talk and be heard, so take it in turns to speak and listen to each other. You might not always agree, but it is important to challenge the statement, not the person, and respect that we are all different with different life experiences and needs. Let's use words we all understand – if in doubt, check.

Learning as We Go – We are all learning together, these may be new ideas for many of us, feel free to ask any questions, there is no such thing as a silly question and it's okay to make mistakes. Stay curious!

Part 1: Learning more about our sensory selves

❝❝We didn't realise how helpful and important it was to think about our senses and sensory processing as a type of learning experience, like a maths or science lesson. Everyone should learn this stuff! When can we do more!?❞❞
Year 4 and Year 6 students from the School Council in a primary school

Sensory continuums/spectrums

 A quickfire movement-based activity which opens up the conversation about sensory preferences and how we all have different experiences and preferences.

 Mainstream and specialist, whole class and small groups (works best if six or more in the group).

 All ages.

 10–20 minutes.

 Labels – Love this, Neutral about this, Hate this.

Pin three signs across the classroom – 'Love this', 'Neutral about this', 'Hate this'. Read out the following list of sensory inputs and ask students to move to the label they feel fits best for that sensory input. If movement is an issue for some students, you could do the same with 'thumbs up thumbs down' for each input or smiles or frowns or other ways your students signal likes and dislikes, depending on the levels of ability within your groups.

- Smell of fresh-cut grass
- Whistling
- Swinging upside down
- Swimming
- Scratching nails down a blackboard

- Eating with a wooden fork
- Drinking fizzy drinks
- Listening to loud music at a crowded concert
- Sitting in silence
- Spinning on a roundabout
- Being outside in the rain
- Wearing a shiny nylon shirt
- Having a long hot bath
- Having a cold shower
- Filing your nails
- Listening to someone else file their nails
- Wearing velvet
- Climbing to a height
- Wearing wool
- Going on a roller coaster
- Wearing shiny fabrics
- Brushing your teeth
- Being up high and looking down
- Getting a tight hug
- Being in a big crowd
- Being in your swimming costume on a hot day on a sandy beach
- Playing in the snow
- Travelling in boats and cars
- Walking barefoot outside
- Playing with mud
- Crunching ice
- Having a massage
- Getting a haircut.

For each statement you read out, ask students in the group to move to the corresponding label of how they feel about the input. Ensure that you have a group agreement in place and do not let students make fun of people who have different preferences from them. Take feedback from the groups by asking the following questions: What is it that you love/hate about it? If you don't have particularly strong feelings about this one, is there anything that would make this change (for example, whistling might be okay if you are whistling, but being surrounded by a group of people with penny whistles might move you to a different position)?

Reflection questions for students

- Where were most of my own sensory preferences in the love, neutral or hate zone?
- What did I learn about my own sensory preferences doing this activity?
- Are there any sensory inputs that are more universally hated/liked?
- What did I learn about other people's sensory preferences doing this activity?

Extension activity: Sensory spectrums

Use the list on the previous pages to further differentiate each sensory input according to where it falls on the sensory spectrum for them. Encourage students to expand their list with wider examples so they start to build up a picture of their own sensory triggers, dislikes, neutrals, likes and glimmers.

THE SENSORY SPECTRUM

Sensory Triggers (Extreme Discomfort)	Sensory Dislikes (Moderate Discomfort)	Sensory Neutral (Midpoint)	Sensory Likes (Moderate Comfort)	Sensory Glimmers (Extreme Comfort)
Definition: Sensory inputs that cause significant distress or discomfort, making it difficult to focus or remain calm. They can lead to sensory overload or strong negative reactions.	Definition: Sensory inputs that are unpleasant but not as immediately overwhelming as sensory triggers. They can cause irritation or distraction.	Definition: Sensory inputs that do not particularly sway one's emotional or physical state in either a positive or negative direction. They are neither stimulating nor distressing.	Definition: Sensory inputs that provide comfort or reduce stress but may not elicit strong positive emotions. They are often used as grounding or calming techniques.	Definition: Sensory experiences that spark joy, comfort and a sense of wellbeing. They are highly individual and sought after for their positive effects.

Sensory dice

> **"**Young people reported having the dice makes having to think more fun.**"**
> Monica Parry, Deputy SENDCO in a large secondary school

 A quick dice game to help small groups of students or individuals start to talk about their senses with either their peers or a professional working with them.

 Mainstream and specialist, whole class, small group and 1:1.

 All ages – for younger years, keep it simple with one dice and solely focusing on glimmers or triggers.

 10–20 minutes dependent on student focus levels.

 One or two labelled dice – one six-sided dice labelled for the senses 1 = smell, 2 = sound, 3 = taste, 4 = touch, 5 = sight, 6 = movement); an optional second dice with "Sensory Glimmers", "Triggers" or "Strategies" each marked on two sides of the dice.

A simple version of this game would be to ask the group (of up to eight students) to take it in turns to roll the dice. They can play it in rounds of *"Sensory Glimmers"*, *"Triggers"* or *"Strategies"* and for that round, they roll the senses dice and give one answer for that sense. For example, if the round is *"Glimmers"* and a student rolls a *"sound"*, they might say "bird song". Or if the round is *"Strategies"* and they roll *"sight"*, they might say "wear sunglasses outside". Students have a right to pass if they get stuck and there isn't a winner or loser, students are just using the dice to help prompt them to talk about their sensory preferences and needs.

If you want to increase the complexity of the game, instead of playing in rounds, you can add in the second dice labelled with what the focus is (*Glimmers, Triggers* or *Strategies*) so students have to come up with a corresponding answer to whatever combination they have rolled, and all students have to give an answer before the dice is moved on. This way students hear the similarities and differences in the preferences and needs of their group.

Alternatively, if you really want to challenge them and make this more of a game, the second dice can just be a six-sided numerical dice and students need to give the number of answers as specified by the numerical dice. For example, if the round is *"triggers"* and the student rolls a *"touch"* and a *4* they would need to say things like "slime, velvet, itchy labels, cold baked beans". You can add in a 10- or 20- second timer as a time pressure, but in keeping with a mutually supportive ethos; if they struggle, then others in the group can help them. The aim of the game is to gain confidence in thinking about and listing sensory likes, dislikes and options that can help them. So there do not need to be winners or losers.

Extension task

Ask students to design their own dice game that gets people thinking and talking about their own sensory preferences and needs. For example, using dice of different sizes with different numbers of sides.

Quickfire sensory education activity ideas

These activities work well for mainstream and specialist, whole class as well as targeted smaller groups with a recommended group size of more than four to encourage discussion.

> *"These activities were brilliant for our students – all students enjoyed them. The main learning was that afterwards, the pupils understood that everyone experiences the world differently so might react differently."*
> Kate Truscott, Eclipse Education (an alternative provision setting)

5,4,3,2,1 – Sensory grounding technique (Age: All ages) – ask the group to take some deep breaths. While they are focusing on the breath, they should focus on five things they can see (for example, sunlight, book, desk, my hands, the board), then four things they can feel (for example, feet on the floor, snug clothes, the smooth desk, hair), three things they can hear (for example, clock ticking, rain, chatting in corridors), two things they can smell (washing powder, school dinners) and one thing they can taste (chocolate milk).

Sensory raisins (Age: All ages) – having checked the group for allergies, offer each student a single raisin. In pairs they should describe to each other what it looks like, what it smells like, what it feels like, what its taste and texture is, what it sounds like when being eaten. Encourage a real focus on the sensory experience of eating a raisin. Ask the group how they found that experience and their visceral responses. Some people find eating (particularly crunchy or chewy snacks) to be regulating, and can discuss what foods they find regulating. Explain that this was an example of eating mindfully, whereas sometimes eating for regulation involves eating quickly without conscious thought, discussing how they found mindful eating.

Gloved sweets (Age: All ages) – task a student with opening a wrapped sweet with gardening gloves on while they are having a conversation with you. Normally, opening a sweet is a tactile activity where you can talk and do it through touch alone. The gardening gloves force this activity to become visually led, as you can't use your tactile sense, which then makes it much harder to continue the conversation and you need to concentrate more. Explain that when one sense is impaired, we have to rely on our other senses which can sometimes bring its own challenges, such as using more energy and becoming tired at the end of the day or having less focus on what is happening around you (lesson/teacher talking). Ask the group what reasonable adjustments would be fair to help the person in gardening gloves access the sweet (answers might include: not having wrapped sweets, having someone help open the wrapper for them, having a machine that dispenses unwrapped sweets, having easy- unwrap sweets). Explain that this could be what it feels like for children who have difficulties with tactile discrimination and motor co-ordination when tackling everyday tasks. It's important we think about accessibility and how we can make things more accessible for everyone.

That dress – differences in perception (Age: All ages) – use the image of the viral blue and black/white and gold dress (photo available online) where people couldn't agree which colour it was. See how your group perceives the dress. Then listen to the piece of viral online audio that says "green needle or brainstorm" and ask which words students heard. These examples highlight how different our experiences can be of the same input. Use some of the online filters that show how dogs, cats or birds perceive the world. Explain that we will all have slightly different levels of different sensory receptors which accounts for this difference.

Squeak peak ears – How old are my ears? (Age: All ages) – listen to a hearing test video online which shows the hearing test frequencies and at what age you stop being able to hear them. This is a noise that becomes increasingly higher pitched (squeak) and can be a little unpleasant to listen to. Offer noise-sensitive students the option to use earplugs or ear defenders or opt out of taking part by moving out of the room for the task. Have everyone in the group raise their hands, dropping them when they stop being able to hear the frequency. There will be some variation across the class because we all tune in slightly differently to noises, and may have more or less sensitive hearing. Reassure students that this is not a medical hearing test, but if they have any concerns about their hearing as a result of this activity, they should speak to their GP.

Focus distraction – Who saw the balloon? (Age: All ages) – to help students empathise with people who have ADHD or difficulties with attention, a fun activity is to be doing a planned lesson on senses, but at some point in the lesson, have a stooge walk past the window or side of the classroom holding a balloon in the air. Make no comment about this, but later on in the lesson, ask the class to recall what colour the balloon was. Some students will remember because it distracted them from the task they were doing (and they then found it difficult to return to the task); others will not have noticed the balloon because they were focused on the task. As a group, discuss what makes you distracted and what makes you focused, and notice the differences. Some people need to listen to music, doodle or to spin or wriggle in their chair to help them focus, others need total stillness and no visual distractions.

Distraction concentration – Can we remember if distracted? (Age: All ages) – ask students to remember a short sequence of numbers (for example, 4662) whilst also copying a short paragraph from the board. While they are doing this you should play a piece of music and steadily increase the volume. Watch how long it takes the children to get distracted and look around the room. Take feedback from the group about how easy it was to remember the number while writing and having their auditory input overloaded. Explain that we all have different focus levels and some people get easily distracted while some can manage with multiple inputs; this can be task-dependent as, if the task is fun/interesting, it can be easier to block out wider distractions. Ask the class how we can support everyone in the class to concentrate when they need to.

Fidgety folk (Age: 11+) – during a session on the senses, ensure you scatter around paperclips and short pipe cleaners on some of the desks and chairs before the lesson but don't make any comment on it. At some point during the lesson ask who is playing with a paperclip/pipe cleaner and see how many children are. Point out that for some people, fidgeting with something helps them concentrate and focus on what is being said and can help relieve anxiety. Lead a discussion into whether they think fidget toys are just a gimmick or really work. Ask them about the challenges of having fidgets in the classroom and whether they can be distracting for others. Talk about 'legitimate fiddling' and how if someone needs to fiddle to concentrate, a fidget toy is not the only option, but something small and unobtrusive such as a button on a shirt, a zip end, the edge of a lanyard, etc., can give the same sensory support without distracting others. Share the challenges as a teacher of having fidgety folk in the classroom and ask the class to think about a Fair Fidget Use Charter and how students can show the teacher they are still listening and retaining the information.

A sensory body scan

This activity is adapted from one found within *Great Relationships and Sex Education: 200+ Activities for Educators Working with Young People* by Alice Hoyle and Ester McGeeney (Routledge, 2019).

 This activity provides the opportunity for participants to pay attention to their bodies, their senses and their breathing. Through this activity, young people can learn techniques that can be repeated in their everyday lives to help with relaxation, bodily awareness and self care.

 Mainstream and specialist, whole class, small group. This activity may feel too intimate to do lying down in a 1:1 so you could trial a seated version or share an online version to do on their own in their own time.

 All ages.

 20 minutes.

 A sensory body scan video or script (a huge range is available online).

If possible, ask a local yoga teacher to come in and facilitate a session with your group as a way of teaching students the techniques for tuning into their senses, relaxation and bodily awareness. Where this is not possible, guide students through a simple body scan. Please note: not all students will feel able/comfortable to be in a room with others and close their eyes, so check in with the group first and offer an alternative activity in a different room for those who do not want to participate.

Ask participants to sit or lie somewhere comfortable depending on the space available. Read out the body scan script slowly, making sure you take your time, or play a body scan video.

Once the body scan has finished, ask the students to reflect on the activity.

Discussion questions for students

- How do you feel after taking part in that activity?
- What did you enjoy?
- Was there any part of your body you paid attention to, in particular, whilst doing this? Did any part of your body feel particularly stiff, sore or relaxed?
- Were you able to notice the sensations in the different parts of your body during the scan?
- When doing the activity how did you feel about the sensations you experienced in that moment compared to how you feel generally in other situations and environments?
- What might be the benefits of doing this activity every day/regularly?
- What might be the challenges of doing this activity every day/ regularly?

Ask students if they are interested in trying to do this activity regularly to see if it affects how they feel about their sensory wellbeing. Where there is interest, ask them to agree how often they will try the activity and for how long, and whether this will be individually or as a group. Agree to discuss again as a group after the agreed time period to see if they have observed any differences or improvements.

Extension task: Personalised body scan

Students can try and write their own personalised body scan that helps them focus on their preferred sensations or areas in need of focus for relaxation.

Our nervous and sensory systems: Research and presentation

 This activity asks students to research aspects of our nervous and sensory systems that particularly interest them and share their findings with the whole group.

 This activity may be best suited to a mainstream whole class; however, you may wish to explore a single research area from the list below with a small group if appropriate.

 13+.

 Minimum 1 hour. Can be spread over different lessons.

 Range of links to online resources such as YouTube videos and BBC Bitesize; books about the nervous system and senses.

Depending on the group, you could focus on one research area or allow them to pick from the following research areas, or come up with your own (the list below is not exhaustive!):

- Explain how sensory inputs are processed and responded to by the body? (Ensure you think about conscious/active and unconscious/reflexive responses.)
- Choose a sensory system (auditory, visual, olfactory, gustatory, tactile, vestibular, proprioception or interception) and design a 5-minute activity that explains it to someone else of your age, encouraging students to focus on the lesser-known senses.
- Are our sensory inputs perceived equally by different people? What might be happening in our different bodies to cause different reactions to the same input? In pairs, compare and contrast your individual responses to different sensory inputs. What does this teach you about yourself and the other person?
- What role do the neurotransmitters oxytocin, serotonin, dopamine, cortisol and adrenaline play in the body? (Students can pick one or more.) Can we write a menu of activities that can boost certain neurotransmitters like oxytocin, serotonin or dopamine (examples available online) or reduce or calm other neurotransmitters like cortisol and adrenaline.
- Choose an animal – compare and contrast their sensory system with that of a human. For example, birds can perceive ultraviolet light and dogs have a very heightened sense of smell, etc.

- Can you explain 'flight, fight or freeze', using Dan Siegel's Hand Model (see page 45) to explain what is going on in the brain and body?
- Look at Lindsay Braman's Emotion Sensation Feeling Wheel (available online). Do you agree with her assessments of how each of the emotions feel in the body with their physiological responses? Can you redraw your own version for how certain emotions feel in your body?
- Kelly Mahler, an Occupational Therapist, said "Trying to teach emotions before exploring body signals is like trying to read a book in the dark. You need light to grasp the words just as you need body signals to comprehend emotions". Do you agree/disagree with this statement? Why?
- How is Virtual Reality (VR) being used to treat sensory processing issues or other neurological conditions?
- How is online life changing the way our brains work and particularly our sensory systems and our attention?

Students can choose to make posters, PowerPoint presentations, short video animations or clips, junk models, etc., to aid their explanations.

Sensation stations

 This activity enables students to experience a variety of different sensory stimuli and think about their personal preferences. This activity organises the sensory inputs so students can focus on one sensory input at a time, and if needed, can focus on one input per session.

 Mainstream and specialist, whole class, small group and 1:1.

 All ages – this activity works particularly well for the upper primary and lower secondary age ranges.

 20 minutes.

 Range of sensory items from lists on the next page (N.B.: You will need to check allergies in your group before you do this activity).

Set up different sensory stations around the room with various materials. Each station should represent a different type of sensory experience. For example:

Station 1: Textured materials (fabrics, sandpaper, various materials such as glass, tile, wood, etc.)

Station 2: Scented items (essential oils, scented candles, a lemon and peeler, herbs and spice pots)

Station 3: Visual stimulation (colouring books, kaleidoscopes, stunning photos, sand flowing through an egg timer, etc.)

Station 4: Auditory experiences (soft music, white noise, percussion instruments)

Station 5: Taste experiences – a range of sweet and savoury tastes and textures, with small amounts to explore (raisins, blueberries, dried mango, carrot sticks, cereal, lemon slices, peppers, jelly, etc.)

Station 6: Proprioceptive input (stress balls, resistance bands, push-ups against the wall or chair push-ups)

Ask small groups of students to rotate through each of the stations, spending a few minutes at each one. Encourage them to pay attention to each item at the station and which of their senses are being stimulated by it. For example, kaleidoscopes may also be noisy, tastes include textures and smells, etc. Can they put the items at each station in an order from best to worst? Do others in the group agree? There are no right or wrong answers in this task, it is just designed to get the students talking, thinking and feeling about their individual senses.

> *We loved making sensory boxes and exploring them.*
> Kate Truscott, Eclipse Education (an alternative provision setting)

Advanced extension activity for older teenagers: Sensation stations – Tube maps

Depending on their ability, students could use online Tube map generators, or just design their own, to think about how they could create a sensory map of themselves. Each line of the Tube map should correspond to a different sense. The lines can intersect at points where both senses are stimulated. For example, 'Lemon station' might interact with the smell and taste lines. Students could choose if they would do one for the things they enjoy or one for things they really dislike. Or they could do one end of the line for their favourite sensory inputs, the middle of the line for neutral sensory inputs and the other end of the line for negative sensory inputs. Their maps may get complicated, but this is okay as our sensory systems are complicated and this is a creative and playful way of trying to illustrate some of that.

Activities to help explain our proprioception and vestibular senses

Flamingo legs – Can we balance with our eyes closed? (Age: All ages) – ask students to stand on one leg and see how well they can balance. Ask students to then close their eyes and watch what happens to their balance. Explain that balance is not just visual, but works alongside our proprioceptive and vestibular senses. Closing our eyes makes our body rely just on our proprioceptive and vestibular input which may make balancing harder.

Turning in tune – Can we process directions quickly and correctly? (Age: 7+) – ask the group to stand up quickly without thinking about it. They need to do a half turn left followed by a quarter turn to the right without giving any further explanation or demonstration. Look where people have ended up (many of the class will be in different positions and it helps if the teacher gets it wrong too). It's very important not to let anyone in the group shame anyone else for "getting it wrong" or "not knowing left from right", but to use this example to explain that we all have very different processing speeds and for some of us, the time needed to translate a quick movement instruction into making our bodies move is really hard. Other people may have over-responsive vestibular systems and this movement may make them feel dizzy which makes them choose to move more slowly. Ask the group to think of things that could help us (for example, more processing time, a sign on the wall showing left from right, modelling the moves, practising the moves).

Herd of elephants (Age: All ages) – ask the group if they have heard the expression "you sound like a herd of elephants"; ask them why people might say that about other people. Point out that the force we use to walk, go up and down stairs, etc., is different depending on the individual. Some might be considered 'heavy footed' while others are more 'light footed'. There is nothing wrong with either, it's just different ways of moving. Ask the class to experiment with walking about the space like "a herd of elephants" or like some tiny mice. Ask them to reflect on how they move generally. Processing proprioceptive information varies for all of us and it is really common to have differences in how we grade our movements, so some people might regularly slam doors and cupboard doors shut and they might not have meant to, but they process the force needed to close the door differently to the actual amount the door needs to actually close.

Pour you (Age: All ages – particularly good for primary age range) – you may want to do this activity outside as it can get messy! Have a range of jugs and tea pots and containers of different sizes and opening sizes (for example, wide bowls or tall narrow jars). Ask students to experiment with their pouring skills with one smooth attempt at filling the small container to the brim. Older students can make this much harder by only having narrow-aperture containers. Discuss what makes pouring easy or hard, ask how they judge how far to tilt their jug and how they know when to stop; is it easy or hard to get the pour just right? If you misjudged your pour, was it too much or too little? Explain that proprioception involves us using our eyes and hands to work together to predict when the container is nearly full and then slowing our pour so it stops at the right time. This can be hard for lots of people to get right!

Rub a dub (Age: All ages – particularly good for primary age range) – offer students a range of brass or leaf rubbings where they need to capture the details of leaves or brass plaques by placing a paper over them and rubbing a crayon or pencil on the paper's surface. Experiment with applying different levels of pressure while rubbing. This gives students a hands-on way to understand how the force we apply through our hands affects what we feel and the outcome of our work. Some rubbings will appear faint and delicate with light pressure, while others will be bold and detailed with stronger pressure. This activity utilises our proprioceptive sense, which helps us gauge the amount of force needed for tasks, and our tactile sense, as we feel the texture through the paper. A simpler version of this task is for them to experiment with pressing hard and pressing lightly with their handwriting and watch what happens to the quality of their letter formation and speed of handwriting and notice how their hand feels afterwards.

What's my name again? (Age: All ages) – students can further understand proprioception by simply writing their names. First, they write their names with their eyes open, then close their eyes to try once more; this taps into muscle memory and helps show that handwriting is not inherently a visual task once it has become automatic. It highlights the critical role of proprioception in movements without direct visual direction. Discuss how tiring this must be for students who have poor proprioceptive processing, so they need to look at the task while they are doing it rather than it being automatic. This activity can also be tried with doing up buttons with eyes open and closed.

You spin me right round (Age: All ages – particularly good for primary age range) – offer a variety of 'movement stations' set up around the room (for example, a spinning chair, a small, safe rockable item like a rocking toy, a balance beam or line on the floor to walk along, a small slide or ramp). Explain that everyone has different preferences for how they like to move. Allow the students to visit each 'movement station' in turn. They can spin in the chair, rock on the horse, balance on the beam and gently slide down the slide. Ensure supervision for safety and encourage students to try each activity at least once, but it is important to respect their choice (because if students are highly sensitive to vestibular input, it is possible to make them feel physically sick very quickly – which can then take a long time to recover from). After visiting all stations, ask the students how they felt about each type of movement. Did they enjoy the feeling of spinning, rocking, balancing or sliding the most? Or did they prefer to be still? Talk about how some people love the feeling of moving fast or spinning, while others might not enjoy it as much and prefer being still or moving slowly. Highlight how these preferences relate to the vestibular system and its role in our lives. Explain the vestibular system, emphasising how it helps us balance and understand our body's movement in space.

Push me, pull you (Age: All ages – particularly good for primary age range) – start by asking students to do a simple fine motor task such as writing their name, doing up a button or threading beads. Then ask students to experiment with activities like lifting various weights, doing push-ups and crab walking to activate their proprioceptive sense, which helps them become more aware of where their body parts are without looking. After these movements which increase their body awareness, ask them to repeat the fine motor task. This allows them to see if the proprioceptive activities like lifting or pushing make the fine motor task feel harder or easier. Some students might find tasks easier after 'waking up' their muscles, while others might not notice a change, showcasing our unique sensory experiences.

Developing your sensory curriculum

Activities to explain interoception
Scale it: My interoception dashboard

 A fun activity that enables students to create a personalised scale and moving dashboard that can help them work out their relative internal states on various scales.

 Mainstream and specialist, whole class, small group, 1:1.

 11+.

 30 minutes.

 Examples of various hunger, tiredness, pain scales found online depicted in different ways, with pens, colouring pencils, card, scissors, split pins.

It is common for young people to struggle to read their internal cues. Sometimes plotting how you feel on a scale can help. We used ChatGPT to help us write the following sample scales.

Hunger Scale

- **Starving:** Intense hunger, weakness, dizziness and inability to concentrate. Immediate nourishment is crucial.
- **Famished:** Strong hunger sensations, stomach growling and increased irritability. Eating soon is important.
- **Hungry:** Noticeable hunger, feeling the need to eat soon. Some stomach discomfort may be present.
- **Neutral/satiated:** Neither hungry nor full. Comfortable and satisfied. This is the optimal state of balance.
- **Full:** Slightly uncomfortable feeling of fullness. Content but not overly so.

- **Stuffed and feeling sick:** Uncomfortably full; overeating has led to discomfort, nausea and regret. It may be necessary to rest and allow the body to digest.

Pain Scale

- **No Pain:** Absence of pain, feeling completely comfortable and at ease.
- **Mild pain:** Slight discomfort or twinges, easily tolerable. Pain is noticeable but not bothersome.
- **Moderate pain:** Noticeable pain that may be distracting, but does not significantly interfere with daily activities.
- **Moderately severe pain:** Intense pain that interferes with daily activities and may require some attention. It's difficult to ignore.
- **Severe pain:** Very intense pain that limits daily activities. It may be challenging to concentrate on anything other than the pain.
- **Excruciating pain:** Overwhelming and unbearable pain, possibly causing emotional distress. Immediate attention and intervention are needed.

Energy Level Scale

- **Energetic:** Feeling vibrant and enthusiastic and on it!
- **Engaged:** Feeling fully awake, alert and ready for activity.
- **Neutral:** Neither tired nor energised. Feeling balanced and comfortable.
- **Mild fatigue:** Noticeable tiredness that may impact concentration and performance. Rest is desired.
- **Severe fatigue:** Overwhelming tiredness, making it difficult to focus and perform tasks. Immediate rest is necessary.

Toilet Need Scale

- **No Urgency:** No sensation of needing to use the toilet; feeling comfortable and not rushed.
- **Low to moderate urgency:** A mild to moderate awareness of the need to use the toilet, but it's manageable for a short time.
- **High urgency:** An uncomfortable and urgent need to use the toilet. Finding a toilet promptly is advisable.
- **Emergency:** The most urgent level, indicating an imminent need to use the toilet. Immediate action is necessary.

Stress Scale

- **Very relaxed:** Description: Calm, at ease and completely relaxed. Indicators: A sense of tranquillity, low heart rate and a clear mind.
- **Relaxed:** Description: Feeling comfortable and relatively stress-free. Indicators: Minor concerns, manageable workload and a moderate level of mental and physical ease.
- **Neutral/moderate:** Description: A balanced state, neither relaxed or stressed. Indicators: A moderate level of alertness, dealing with typical challenges and a baseline level of stress that is not overwhelming.
- **Stressed:** Description: Experiencing noticeable stress and tension. Indicators: Increased heart rate, heightened awareness of challenges and a sense of pressure or urgency.
- **Very stressed:** Description: Overwhelmed, high levels of stress and struggling to cope. Indicators: Extreme tension, difficulty focusing and a feeling of being unable to handle the current situation.

Ask students to select a sensory state; for example, hunger, tiredness, energy levels, breathing, bladder, bowel, pain, discomfort, anger, social battery.

Get them first to consider what the extreme ends of each scale would be for them and what the midpoint is. Then they can choose how many intervening points there might be. Some might do a 3-point scale, some a 10-point scale. It doesn't matter, whatever works for them, but the key is there is a clear graduation between the points on the scale. Students should write out the language used to describe each point of the scale and what imagery they might use to depict each point. Emojis are often a popular way to do this, but people have also used speedometers, different dog or cat breeds, footballers or cartoon characters, etc., to depict the different points on the scales. Have a look at a range of examples online to get some ideas.

When they have their scale design, text and imagery decided, they can draw and write the scale/s neatly on a card. A small slit should be cut along the length of each scale with a small arrow cut out of card and attached using a paper fastener/split pin to enable them to move the arrow up and down the scale depending on where they are in the present moment.

Depending on the abilities of the group, you can either get everyone to work on the same sensory state at the same time, or whichever one they feel a preference for thinking about more. If time allows, do two or three different sensory states. You can do this on one sheet and make it look like a sound mixing board – clips from the Pixar movie *Inside Out* (2015) might help to make this point, but with senses rather than emotions. Encourage students to check in regularly with their sensory states using their new sensory scales and dashboards.

HALT for interoception awareness!

This activity is adapted from an activity within *Great Relationships and Sex Education: 200+ Activities for Educators Working with Young People* by Alice Hoyle and Ester McGeeney (Routledge, 2019). Shared with permission.

 An activity that introduces a mnemonic for students to use when they are feeling out of sorts, with some suggested remedies for the situation.

 Mainstream and specialist, whole class, small group and 1:1.

 10+.

 10–15 minutes.

 The HALT infographic.

Introduce the HALT (Hungry, Angry, Lonely, Tired) mnemonic. The idea is that when we notice we aren't feeling good, we stop (Halt!) and think: Am I Hungry? Angry? Lonely? Tired? This can help us decide what to do next to look after ourselves, as sometimes the solution can be more straightforward than we think (get something to eat, get some sleep, find someone to hang out with). Task students with creating a card containing information about the strategy that can be kept in a wallet or pocket to remind them of the strategy when they need it. Share with them the example on the next page or examples found online.

WHEN NOT FEELING GREAT, THINK, AM I...
H.A.L.T?

Hungry?
Grab a healthy snack to boost your blood sugar. Don't let yourself become hangry.

Angry?
Take some deep breaths, punch a pillow, do a brain dump of rage on paper.

Lonely?
Reach out and connect with others, phone a friend, speak to the people you live with.

Tired?
Take a break, have a nap!

Extension activity: Interoception mnemonics

Students can explore alternative strategies that they think would be helpful to use to assist people to think about their interoception needs and come up with new mnemonics to help explain them.

Sensory stars

> *Pupils did enjoy this and engage; however, I found they were more likely to talk about what they didn't like instead of identifying positives/glimmers. However, pupils really appreciated the term 'glimmers' as they hadn't heard this before, and in conversations were able to identify far more 'glimmers' than when I have tried to engage in conversations about this previously.*
>
> Monica Parry, Deputy SENDCO, a large secondary school

This activity is adapted from the Jo Adams RU Ready pack (not available online) and shared with permission.

 An exploratory and experiential activity that uses object-based learning as a stimulus for discussions around how sensory inputs can make us feel.

 Mainstream and specialist, whole class, small group and 1:1.

 All ages (if literacy is an issue, you can skip the worksheet and just focus on the experiences of different sensory items).

 20–30 minutes.

 Handout for each participant with a blank Sensory Star, a wide range of objects designed to stimulate the senses, a blanket.

Sit in a circle and set out on a blanket in the centre a wide range of objects that can be used to stimulate the main senses: touch, taste, sight, sound and smell. Objects can include perfumes, oils, scented candles or orange peel for smell; pictures and colourful objects for sight; sound bowl and musical instruments for sound; chocolate, vegetables and fruits for taste; smooth- and rough- textured objects such as soft scarves, smooth stones, lentils, fidget toys such as spiky acupressure rings for touch (and movement in a limited way). It's important to check for allergies before any tasting begins.

Ask participants to spend some time exploring the objects and experiencing the ways in which they stimulate different senses. Ask them to think about how stimulating each of the five senses can make you feel. Answers may include relaxed, calm, hungry, sleepy, excited.

Students should consider if there is any difference between the sensory glimmers, the sensory inputs that spark sensory joy, the sensory engagers, the sensory inputs that stimulate and energise us, and the sensory soothers, the sensory inputs that soothe, calm and relax us.

Give each participant a Sensory Star handout or ask them to draw their own star on a blank piece of paper.

The task is for participants to draw or write their favourite sensory glimmers, engagers and soothers (some of these may be the same thing) for each sense against the corresponding point on the triangle. It can either be one of the sensory inputs provided or something else (for example, the smell of freshly cut grass).

Depending on the ability level of the group, you could ask them to use the Sensory Star sheet to solely record their sensory glimmers, or they could also add in their sensory soothers and engagers, either in different colours with a colour code, or with a heart (glimmers) an up arrow (engagers) or down arrow (soothers) next to each input to clarify its impact.

Students can keep their Sensory Star handout to remind them of the sensory experiences they most enjoy. Have a discussion about things participants could do in their everyday lives to stimulate their senses and how this might help to soothe and relax them if they feel stressed or anxious, or energise them if they feel tired and lethargic.

Discussion questions

- Did we find anything new about ourselves doing this activity?
- In our group were there any universal glimmers or engagers?
- Why is it important to use some sensory inputs to help engage us?
- Why is it important to try and find sensory joy from different sensory inputs?
- Can you ever have too much of a good thing?

MY SENSORY STARS

These are all my favourite sensory inputs that I like to experience which help spark sensory joy and/or help engage me.

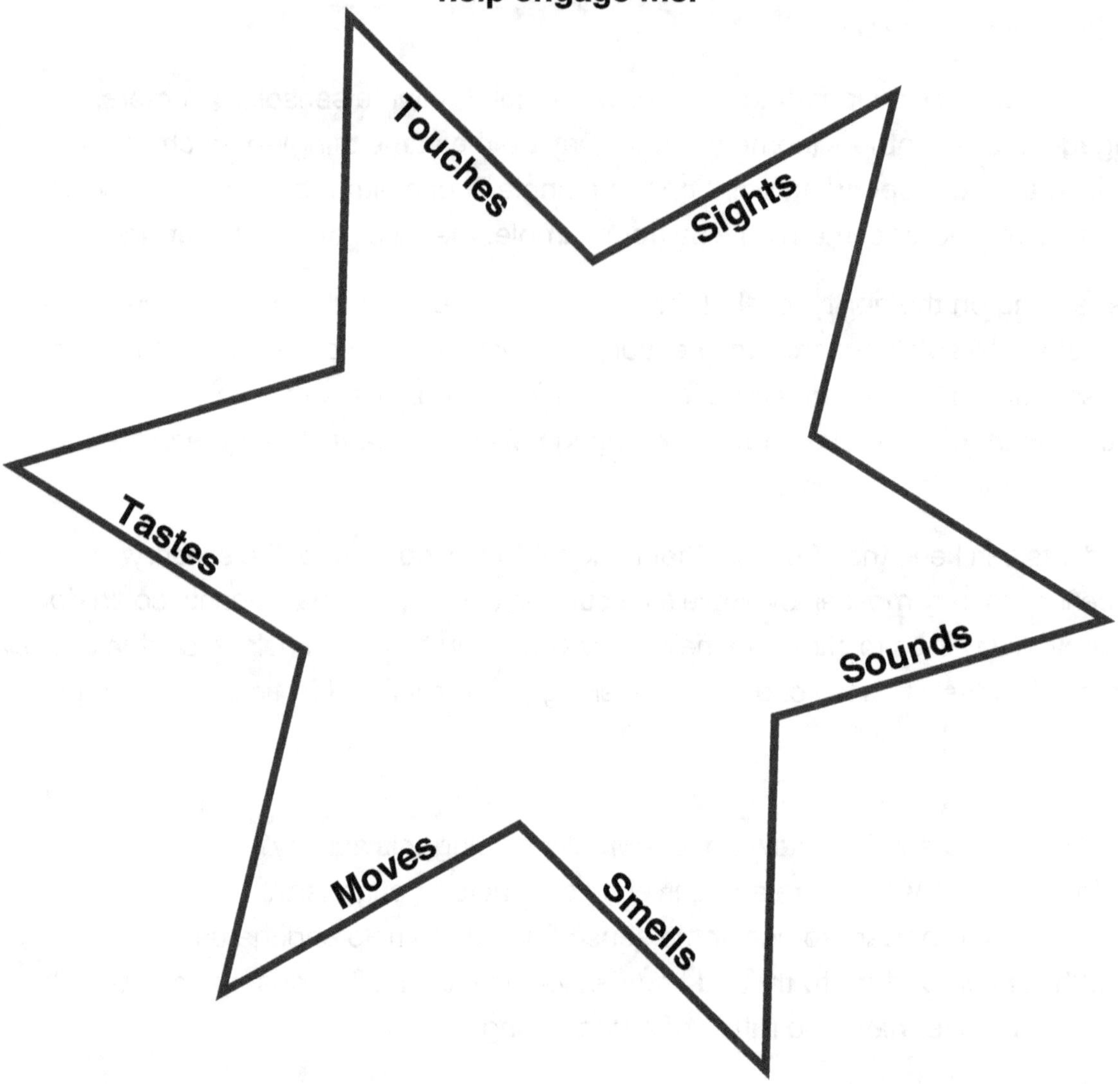

Touches

Sights

Tastes

Sounds

Moves

Smells

Draw and write around the inside and outside of this sensory star.
Be as colourful and creative as you like! Keep this to refer back to.
Do things change?

Cat food: Experiencing and explaining sensory triggers

 A lighthearted and memorable activity that opens up the group conversation around sensory triggers and helps students understand about different sensory thresholds. It involves the teacher eating a spoonful of 'cat food' (chopped-up Mars Bars in orange jelly in an empty tin) as a way of causing a collective visceral sensory response of disgust, then using this feeling to think about individual sensory responses to various stimuli.

 This activity is best suited to mainstream whole class provision.

 This activity is more suitable for 11–13-year-olds.

 20 minutes.

 Pre-prepared 'cat food' in a tin.

Warning: Do not attempt this activity if this type of activity does not fit in with your teaching approach and style, it's important you feel comfortable professionally to do this style of activity. This activity is also possibly not suitable for students who are already sensitive. Potentially if there were any students who you would be concerned about having an adverse reaction, you could give them the role of 'observer', telling them what is really in the can in secret and asking them to record people's reactions; that way they're still included, but you're preventing a potential panic.

Before the lesson prepare the following:

Use a thoroughly cleaned empty tin of baked beans or other human-grade food with a cat food tin label stuck around it. Prepare some orange jelly in a bowl and leave to set. Chop up a Mars Bar into small cubes. Just before the lesson begins, mix the chopped Mars Bar into the orange jelly so it resembles cat food and put in the tin. (Warning: don't do this too far in advance of the lesson as the ingredients will dissolve into each other, creating a chocolate sludge). Place a plastic 'tin lid' (for example, a Pringles lid) over it for hygiene. Take a spoon and the tin into the lesson.

At the start of the lesson, remind students of the group agreement including their right to pass. Warn students you are going to do something unexpected in the lesson that many students will find disgusting, explaining that the purpose is to think more deeply about our sensory responses and reactions. Remember in advance to establish a role of observer for particularly sensitive students or give them an alternative task to do in another space.

During the lesson, ask students to come up with a list of words that describe how they feel about looking at cat food, then add to the list with words that describe how they might feel about smelling cat food, then add to the list words that describe how they might feel about touching cat food. The responses are likely to increase in disgust levels. Finally ask students to ask for a list of words that describe how they might feel about eating cat food. As you do this, take a spoon of 'cat food' and eat it! The class will erupt in disgust, some children have been known to say things like "Urgh, I can smell it!", etc. (they obviously can't because it's not cat food), but comments such as this show how powerful our senses can be, including tricking us sometimes.

Explore the list of words on the board, which may include things like disgust, feeling sick, icky, unsettled, smelly, etc. Make sure you record a range of internally brain-interpreted feelings as well as more physical nervous system responses such as shuddering, feeling cold and clammy or hot and sweaty, etc. Ask students to think about whether there are any sensory inputs that cause a similar reaction as 'eating cat food' did for them just now. List them on the board. For example, nails on a blackboard, eating with wooden forks, the taste and texture of cold baked beans, someone whistling, going for a cold-water swim. Add tally marks for the numbers in the class who feel the same way about that sensory input. Point out that while eating cat food generally causes a fairly universal disgust response, those disgust responses will all be on more individual levels from mild to extreme disgust because we all have different tolerance levels. We will also have different mental and physical reactions to the eating of cat food (as with any sensory input), some being on the more immediate 'visceral gut reaction'-type level, and some being on the more cognitive level of naming feelings and emotions.

Discussion questions

- Did we all experience the same level of disgust to eating 'cat food'?
- Even when we realised it wasn't actually cat food, would we want to eat the Mars Bar in an orange jelly mixture because it looks so much like cat food?

- What three words describe my personal response to seeing someone eat 'cat food'?
- Are there other things that also cause me to feel a similar level of response?
- How does it feel when others feel the same as I do about certain sensory inputs?
- How does it feel when I am the only one who feels like that about a certain sensory input?
- If we know someone has an aversion to a certain sensory input, how can we support them?
- Is it ever okay to deliberately cause a sensory response in someone else?
- What strategies can we have in place for when something causes such responses?

N.B.: Especially for the more literal members of the class, it is very important that the teacher reveals that the cat food is pretend cat food, made from Mars Bars and orange jelly before the end of the lesson and reinforces it several times!

Sensory spiders: A traffic light tool to explain sensory triggers

"We used sensory stars and spiders as part of our pupil support plans. They helped staff more fully understand the child so they could recognise triggers and offer strategies to support."

Kate Truscott, Eclipse Education (an alternative provision setting)

 A worksheet activity that helps students to think about and record their sensory triggers and rate them on a traffic light scale of Red (cannot tolerate), Amber (can tolerate in some situations), Green (don't like, but can cope with).

 Mainstream and specialist, whole class, small group and 1:1.

 All ages but most suitable for 8–13 age range.

 20–30 minutes.

 My Sensory Spiders Worksheet, red, orange/yellow, green pens and other colours.

This activity is adapted from a widespread sensory recording activity used by Occupational Therapists. We love these creative examples found in Sensory Ladders https://sensoryladders.org/sensory-spiders/, where that particular activity records enjoyable sensory inputs rather than sensory triggers.

Explain to the group that we know that some people love spiders, but sometimes spiders can make people go EEK! or trigger a negative reaction. We sometimes call these 'sensory triggers' or the things that give you the 'sensory ick', the things that set your nerves jangling and you find it tricky to concentrate on anything else when they are present; for example, flickering fluorescent lights.

Ask the group to discuss "What sensory inputs do you dislike?", giving them examples such as "itchy clothes" or "black olives" or "spinning on a roundabout". Ask students to each fill in their Sensory Spiders Worksheet for their own triggers and ask them to think about as many examples for each sensory input as they can. When the group has done this, ask them to colour code them Red, Amber, Green – Red (cannot tolerate), Amber (can tolerate in some situations), Green (don't like, but can cope with.)

MY SENSORY SPIDERS

(or things that make me go EEK!)

We love spiders really, but we know sometimes they can make people go EEK! Or trigger a negative reaction. What sensory things make you go EEK! and you actively avoid them? We sometimes call these sensory triggers. When you have noted these down, can you colour-code them Red, Amber, Green where Red = 'Cannot tolerate.', Amber = 'Can tolerate in some situations.', Green = 'Don't like, but can cope with.'

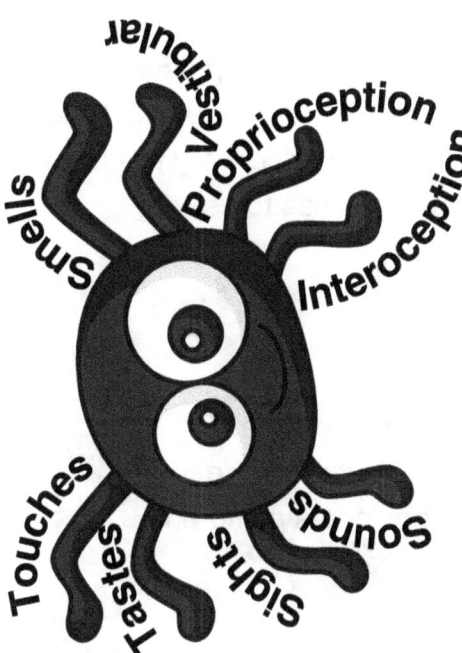

For example, our Reds might be things like wearing wool (touch) and eating fish (taste) as we cannot do them AT ALL, our Ambers might be things like disco lights (sights) and concert music (sounds), but we can do it in small doses, and our Greens are feeling hangry (interoception) or running (proprioception) where we aren't keen, but it's okay really. Think of as many examples for each leg as you can and there is no right or wrong answer as this worksheet is personal to you.

Copyright material from Alice Hoyle and Tessa Hyde (2025), *Becoming a Sensory Aware School*, Routledge

For example, their Reds might be things like wearing wool (touch) and eating fish (taste) as they feel they cannot do them AT ALL; their Ambers might be things like disco lights (sights) and concert music (sounds), but we can do it in small doses; and their Greens are feeling hangry (interoception) or running (proprioception), where we aren't keen, but it's okay really. Encourage them to think of as many examples for each spider leg as they can, and there is no right or wrong answer as their worksheet is personal to them.

Discussion questions

- What did we learn about ourselves and our sensory triggers doing this activity?
- Can we always avoid our sensory triggers?
- What strategies can help us cope with things that trigger us?
- Whose responsibility is it to protect us from the Red triggers we cannot cope with? Ours? Our parents? Our friends? Our teachers?
- What can we do if one of our sensory triggers is something that sparks sensory joy in someone close to us?

My sensory body

 Completing a body outline that helps students think about the full range of sensory inputs going on for them.

 Mainstream and specialist, whole class, small group and 1:1.

 All ages.

 30 minutes.

 My Sensory Body Worksheet, pens, colouring pencils.

Show the students the 'Sensory inputs and their impact' diagram (full sized image is also available on Page 3 of Chapter 1 and online materials). Ask students to get creative, making their own versions using the My Sensory Body Worksheet' (on the next page). Ensure they consider interoception, proprioception and vestibular inputs as well as the main five sensory inputs. Ask them to reflect on how the sensory inputs affect them and how they could display this on their worksheets. If appropriate to the students you are working with, you could ask students to share their sheets with each other and discuss the similarities and differences.

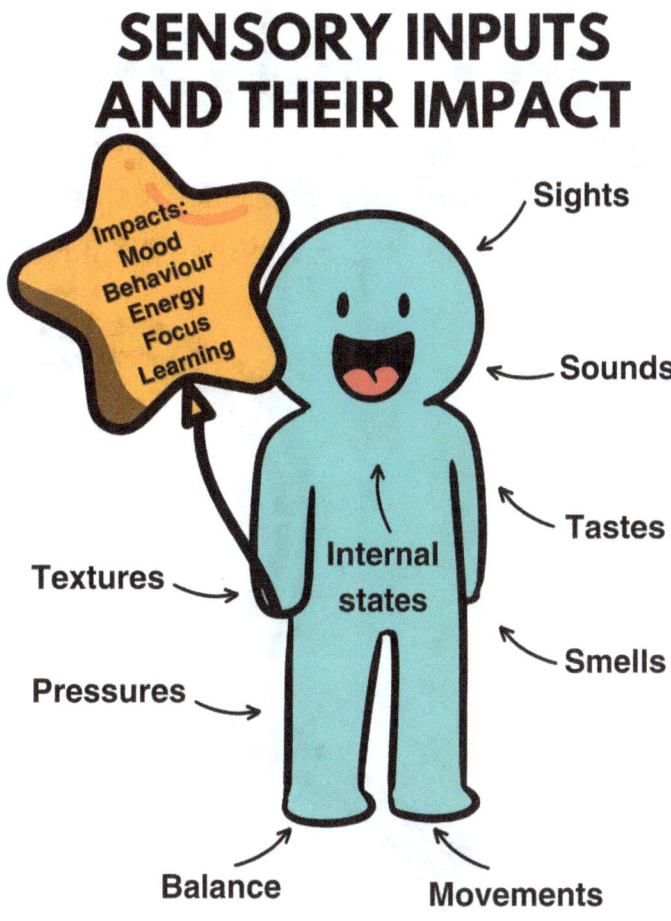

Discussion questions for students

- Did you learn anything new about yourself doing this activity?
- Which sensory input affects you the most? What about the least?
- How can your senses impact your mood?
- Can you remember a time where a sensory input significantly impacted your behaviour or focus?
- Can you think of an instance where a sensory input had a different impact on someone else than it did on you? Why might that happen?
- How can your senses impact your behaviour?
- Do your sensory inputs impact your energy levels?
- Do your sensory inputs impact your ability to focus?
- How do your sensory inputs in the classroom influence your ability to learn?
- What strategies could you use to manage sensory inputs that are overwhelming or distracting?

MY SENSORY BODY

What sensory inputs are you experiencing? How do they affect you? Draw and write your responses inside and outside of the body diagram. Get creative and colourful.

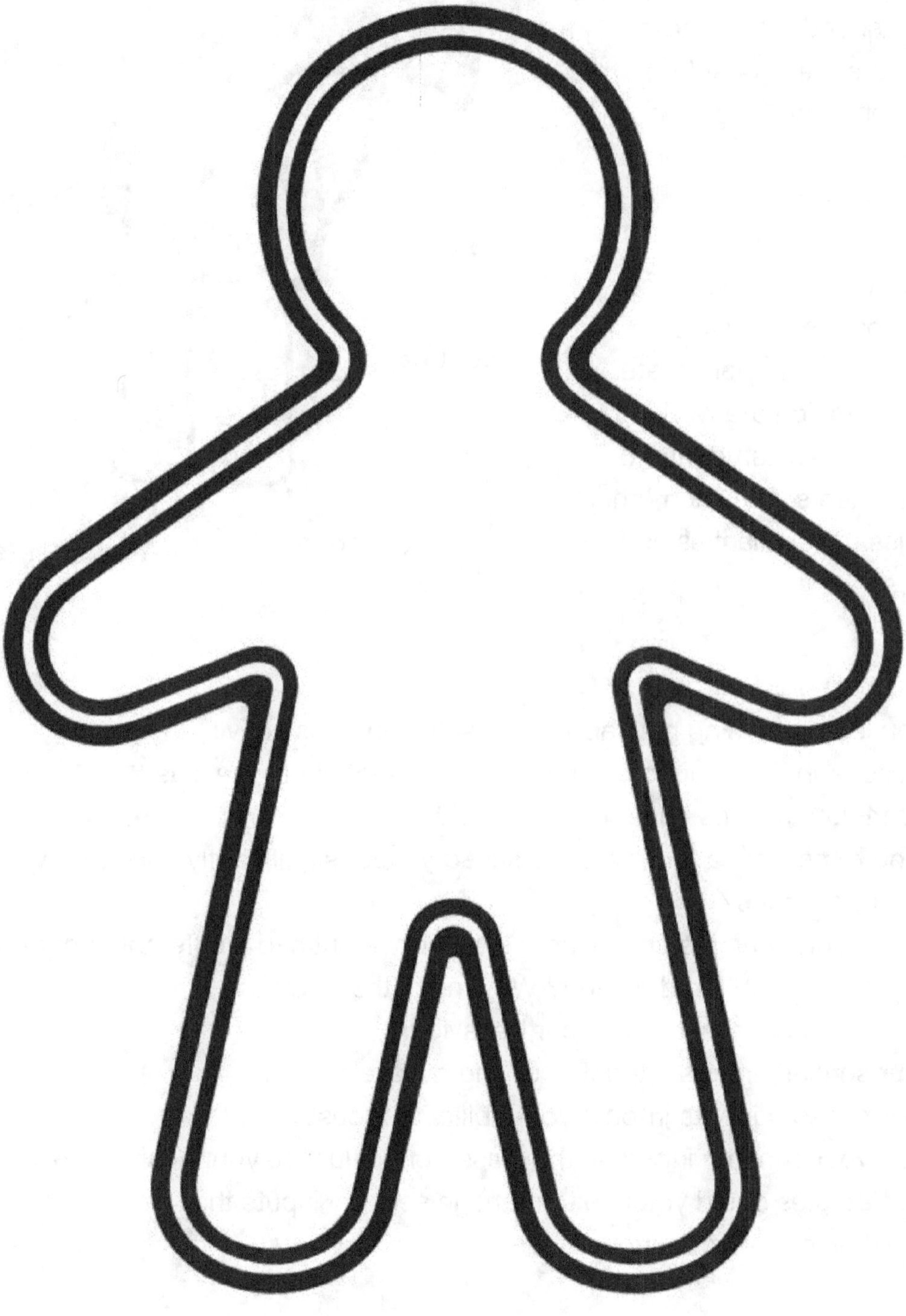

Sensory me

 Completing a worksheet that helps students reflect on their understanding of their sensory preferences and sensory dislikes (triggers).

 Mainstream and specialist, whole class, small group and 1:1.

 All ages; younger/SEND students may need help completing their worksheets using a scribe or alternative recording. One option could be to record videos of students talking about their sensory self, inline with school policy on recording students.

 30 minutes.

 Sensory Me Worksheet, pens, colouring pencils.

In order to help students fill in this worksheet, they will need a reasonable understanding of the eight senses from the previous activities in this chapter. This is a more student-friendly version of the Sensory Me Audit in Chapter 4, page 59. You may want to also look at that to help formulate further prompt questions for your students. However, be aware that some questions (around toileting) might yield more personal responses, so ensure you don't inadvertently create an expectation that students share anything they are not comfortable with. Your group agreement will help with this.

Students can draw or write in the boxes to capture their responses on the worksheet. Let them get creative, the more colourful the better. If they like birdsong they could draw a bird, for example. Small groups can share their work with each other and compare and contrast their findings. If drawing/writing is an issue, students and staff could do this more as a shared discussion activity with staff responding. If verbal responses are not possible, then parents and professionals working with the child can contribute to help build up a sensory passport. It may be particularly helpful to do this activity with a particular student in your class (if they have known sensory processing needs), to gain new insights in how best to support them.

Sensory Me

Reflection Questions for Sensations I Enjoy/Can Cope with	Reflection Questions for Sensations I Don't Enjoy/ Might Try to Avoid/Ignore
👍 **Auditory (sound)** What sounds do you enjoy?	👎 **Auditory (sound)** What sounds do you avoid?
👍 **Visual (sight)** What do you enjoy looking at?	👎 **Visual (sight)** What don't you enjoy looking at?
👍 **Tactile (touch)** What things do you like to touch and feel (for example, fabrics or textures)?	👎 **Tactile (touch)** What things do you not like to touch and feel (for example, fabrics or textures)?

👍 **Olfactory and Gustatory (taste/smell)**	👎 **Olfactory and Gustatory (taste/smell)**
Do you prefer mild or spicy food, sweet, salty or sour? Are there certain tastes, textures or smells you really love/regularly seek?	Are there any foods you never eat or dislike due to taste, texture or smell? Are there any smells you don't like or avoid?
👍 **Vestibular/Proprioception (movement)**	👎 **Vestibular/Proprioception (movement)**
Do you enjoy activities such as going on roller coasters, climbing, horse riding, racing bikes, swinging upside down?	Do you get car sick? Do you avoid certain movements like spinning or being upside down, or going excessively fast?
👍 **Interoception (internal body feelings)**	👎 **Interoception (internal body feelings)**
Do you feel hunger and thirst, so remember to eat and drink regularly? Do you always know when you need the toilet? Does your clothing usually match the season (for example, warm coat in snow)?	Do you sometimes get 'hangry' (easy to anger when hungry) because you haven't realised you are hungry? Do you sometimes leave it until the last minute to go to the toilet because you either haven't realised you needed to go or are ignoring the sensation? Do you feel the cold?
👍 **Conclusion: Your sensory day**	👎 **Conclusion: Your sensory day**
Think about your ideal sensory day and what clothing, experiences, foods would be included in this day.	Think about your sensory nightmare day – what clothing, experiences, foods would be included in this day?

Copyright material from Alice Hoyle and Tessa Hyde (2025), *Becoming a Sensory Aware School*, Routledge

Sensory Jenga

This is adapted from an activity published in *Great Relationships and Sex Education: 200+ Activities for Educators Working with Young People* by Alice Hoyle and Ester McGeeney (Routledge, 2019). Shared with permission.

 A powerful yet fun activity that encourages participants to think, reflect and discuss their own sensory needs and those of others.

 Mainstream and specialist, whole class, small group and 1:1.

 All ages (questions can be adapted to the age of students and the activity leader can read out the sentence prompt if there are literacy needs).

 10–30 minutes.

 Jenga sets prepared with sentence starters (you will need one set per 4–8 participants – you can divide one set between three tables with much smaller towers).

Before the session, get hold of a standard Jenga set (you can buy versions online for about £4). Using a ballpoint pen (other pens will bleed into the wood), write a sentence starter or sense or sensory input on each block (see following list). If you want to do this with a large group (8+), you will need more than one Jenga set. To play the game, set up a tower of Jenga blocks per group. Four–eight participants generally work best; however, this activity can also work well in a 1:1 session. You may need to adapt the statements on the blocks to the needs of the group. Each participant then takes it in turn to draw out a block from the tower, trying not to knock down the tower in the process. Once a block has been withdrawn, the participant should read what it says and give an answer. If the student struggles, the other students in the group are allowed to help them with ideas for an answer. The ethos of the game should be mutual support. If working in groups of less than four, you can also have everyone in the group answer the same block before moving on to share experiences, but larger groups tend to get restless if it takes a while until their 'turn'.

The game continues with the tower growing (or blocks being placed into a bag) until the tower is so unstable it collapses. You may want to have the tower on a carpet or mat to reduce the sound as it collapses if you have noise-sensitive children in the group. With a mutually supportive ethos, it shouldn't matter who caused the tower to collapse – it isn't about losing; often the students simply want to play another round as they really value the opportunity to talk about their senses and their feelings in a safe space. It can be helpful to have a group agreement in place to help build this mutually supportive ethos.

Example sentence starters:

1. My favourite taste is...
2. My favourite smell is...
3. My favourite sound is...
4. My favourite things to touch are...
5. My favourite sights are...
6. My favourite movements are...
7. A sensory input that can make me feel stressed is...
8. A sensory input that can make me feel calm is...
9. A sensory input that can make me feel engaged and alert is...
10. The worst taste is...
11. The worst smell is...
12. The worst sound is...
13. The worst things to touch are...
14. The worst sights are...
15. The worst movements are...
16. Eating a crunchy snack makes me feel...
17. Taking a deep breath helps me because...
18. If I go upside down, I feel...
19. I don't like the following sensory inputs...
20. I love the following sensory inputs...
21. I am okay with the following sensory inputs...
22. I am not okay with the following sensory inputs...
23. To feel calmer, I can...
24. To wake me up, I can...
25. To help me concentrate, I can...
26. If I am feeling stressed, I can...
27. If I am feeling angry, I can...

28. If I am feeling sad, I can...
29. If I am feeling anxious, I can...
30. If I am feeling overwhelmed, I can...
31. In my body right now I am feeling...
32. This morning in my body I was feeling...
33. My sensory strategies are...
34. The best fidget for me is...
35. Tuning into my senses is important because...
36. My senses are...
37. My favourite sense is...
38. My least favourite sense is...
39. Interoception means...
40. Vestibular means...
41. Gustatory means...
42. Olfactory means...
43. Tactile means...
44. Proprioception means...
45. Visual means...
46. Auditory means...
47. My senses are amazing because...
48. My body feels good when...
49. A sensory wish for the future is...
50. A sensory dream day would be...
51. A sensory nightmare day would be...
52. My best sensory tip for calm is...
53. My best sensory tip for learning is...
54. My best sensory tip when feeling overwhelmed is....

There is value in revisiting this activity when working with a group over a period of time. In our experience, young people value the opportunity to practise sharing things about themselves and listening and learning new things about their peers. Remember to adapt the statements to the needs of your group. You don't have to use all the blocks for every game.

Part 2: Understanding sensory regulation
Our changing sensory states

 A mapping and discussion activity that explores how each of us have different sensory needs and things that move us to different states of being.

 Mainstream and specialist, whole class, small group and 1:1.

 8+.

 20–30 minutes.

 Counters for each student.

This Sensory States Model discussed further in Chapter 3, page 48 is our way of exploring different sensory states. It builds on a common model used in education called 'the Comfort, Learn/Stretch, Panic Zones'. Explain the model to the students:

This is where when your body is in each of the states, it will feel as follows:

Slug – You feel low in energy and tired. Your sensory input needs to be increased. In this zone you will be slow and less responsive.

Comfort – Your body feels safe and comfortable in this zone. Your sensory input is enjoyable or unnoticeable. You are regulated and calm.

Engage – Your body feels engaged and focused (and still safe). Your sensory input is interesting and stimulating. You are regulated and ready/alert/awake.

Overload – Your body feels stressed and unsafe. Your sensory input is overwhelming and you need something to change. You are dysregulated. You may meltdown or shutdown to help yourself cope.

OUR SENSORY STATES

SLUG	• My body feels low in energy and tired. • My sensory input needs to be increased. • I am slow and less responsive.
COMFORT	• My body feels safe and comfortable. • My sensory input is enjoyable or unnoticeable. • I am regulated and calm.
ENGAGE	• My body feels engaged and focused (and still safe). • My sensory input is interesting and stimulating. • I am regulated and ready/alert/awake.
OVERLOAD	• My body feels stressed and unsafe. • My sensory input is overwhelming and I need something to change. • I am dysregulated. • I may meltdown or shutdown to help me cope.

Divide the class into groups of six; each group should have a large Our Sensory States diagram printed in A3 and a counter each as well as an individual My Sensory States Worksheet. Initially ask the group members to describe how they think their body feels in each state, asking them to think about their heart rate, breathing, tummy or gut feelings (sensations felt in the stomach area), muscle tension, focus levels and awareness of their senses. Ask students to place a counter on the diagram for which state they feel they are in currently.

Make up your own list of sensory inputs and/or ask students to also come up with their own examples, such as:

- Drinking a fizzy drink
- Having a cuddle
- Spinning upside down
- Closing your eyes and taking a deep breath
- Using a weighted lap pad
- Stroking velvet.

If appropriate, you could also have a range of sensory inputs (fidgets, smells, fabrics, etc.) for students to test some of these things out to help think what zone they are in.

For each sensory input, students should place their counter in the zone that they think that sensory input would put them in. Each student response will be different and they should be given time to share and discuss some of their answers and how that feels for them. If appropriate, you may want to mix up the groupings partway through the activity to support wider learning about each other.

To finish, ask students to complete a blank My Sensory States Worksheet. Using a different colour, they can note down some of their key sensory inputs that can put them in each zone. For example, being in bed under a weighted blanket might help someone move into the comfort zone; bouncing on the trampoline might help get someone into the engage zone; and lots of background noise or light flickers might move someone to the overload zone. Students can colour in, then decorate their sheets as a personal *aide-mémoire* for thinking about their different states of being, and their personal strategies for changing how they are feeling.

Discussion questions for students

- What did we learn about ourselves doing this?
- What did we learn about others doing this exercise?
- How can we support our own sensory needs to help us to be calm and comfortable when we need to be? What about supporting others in our class?
- How can we support our own sensory needs to help us to be engaged and ready for learning? What about supporting others in our class?
- If we are in the overload zone, what strategies can we use to help us get out of it? If our friend is in the overload zone, how do we know? How can we tell? How can we help them?

This activity can be revisited at different points over the year as answers may change and the list of initial sensory inputs can be infinite, creating a different activity each time. This way students become familiar with the language and comfortable with the ideas and strategies they can use to help themselves and others.

MY SENSORY STATES

Use this sheet to record either things that move you into one of the states, or things that move you out of a particular state. Get creative and colourful. Keep this sheet to revisit over time in case things change for you.

OVERLOAD

ENGAGE

COMFORT

Slug

Copyright material from Alice Hoyle and Tessa Hyde (2025), *Becoming a Sensory Aware School*, Routledge

Sensory states: My own analogy

 An activity that encourages students to come up with their own sensory states.

 Mainstream and specialist, whole class, small group and 1:1.

 8+.

 20–30 minutes.

 A copy of the Our Sensory States diagram, a copy of the table in Chapter 3, page 47 (under 'Other available models for understanding our sensory states'; focus on the ones your school is familiar with or using already).

Explain that people use lots of different analogies and models to think about sensory states such as the ones found in the table 'Models for Understanding Our Sensory States'. Broadly, the three main states are: 'Lethargic', 'Just Right' and 'Energetic'.

Share with the class some other possible examples, such as relating sensory states to the three different states of water:

Block of Ice State – In this state, you are sluggish, lethargic, don't want to move, immoveable, hard to engage,
Water Flow State – In this state, you are in flow, fulfilling your potential, in a good place to learn and engage, feeling safe and comfortable.
Gas Clouds State – In this state, you are bouncing off the walls, zipping about, you have too much energy, not able to focus or concentrate.

Or they could think about a **sensory zoo** of apathetic animals to zippy ones; for example, sloth to cheetah. Students could consider which animals they would be in each state; for example:

Slow zoo – sloth, koala, tortoise, turtle
Just right zoo – pig, frog, spider
Fast zoo – kangaroo, jaguar, road runner, a crazy kitten or excitable puppy.

Task students with inventing their own creative analogy that works for them to explain their three states. They should choose their own language to describe each state (or they may prefer to use words such as Zone or Area, or another word). Encourage them to draw and write this out and make it their own.

Stand up, sit down, flop

> ❝❝*Pupils really enjoyed this one, they commented that they liked the movement options, especially 'flopping'. They engaged far more than they would have with solely verbal answers. Pupils commented that they felt more able to 'be honest when just doing movements' when compared with having to speak their answers.*❞❞
>
> Monica Parry, Deputy SENDCO, a large secondary school

 A useful activity that helps learners consider the scale of their responses to sensory inputs.

 Mainstream and specialist, whole class, small group and 1:1.

 All ages.

 10–30 minutes.

 A copy of the list of sensory inputs from the 'Sensory continuums/spectrums' activity on page 126 of this chapter.

Using the list of sensory inputs, ask students to respond as to whether this sensory input helps wake us up/make us more alert; if so, they should stand up. If it has no difference – we feel just right/okay with this input – they can remain seated; and if this input, makes them sleepy/lethargic, then they can 'flop' onto their desks. Students will have individual responses to this activity. Therefore, it's just introducing them to the idea of how different sensory inputs can change how we feel, from supporting us to feel just right, to making us more aware/alert or making us sleepy and lethargic. Students should try and come up with their own examples of things that make them more alert/engaged (move them to the engage zone) or that calm and relax them (move them towards the comfort zone) and the things that have no effect on them.

Further activities to explore sensory needs and regulation

Social Battery badges (Age: 10+) – task students with creating their own 'Social Battery' badges to wear on their school uniform (there are plenty of examples online) to help them communicate to others how they are feeling at any given moment. These badges are quite popular in neurodivergent communities.

Better than 'Stand up, sit down, flop'? (Age: 10+) – task students with creating their own version of the 'Stand up, sit down, flop' activity described on page 169. For example, they could point a finger up or down to denote energy levels, with their hands in a heart or a thumbs up for sensory glimmers; or they could create traffic sign analogy cards they could hold up like STOP or GO or PARK. Encourage students to get creative and play their versions of the activity with each other.

Sensory passports (Age: All ages) – task students with creating a one-page profile about their sensory needs to show at a glance what they need. Adults can help scribe for younger children. They should include information like Name, Age, Photo, Sensory Glimmers…, Sensory Triggers…, Sensory Engagers…, Sensory Soothers…, People Need to Know…, You Can Help Me by….

Pyramids of sensory needs (Age:12+) – share the two pyramids on page 4 in Chapter 1 (the Hierarchy of Needs and the Pyramid of Learning); both depict our sensory needs as a foundational building block for both wellbeing and for learning. Explain each model and ask the group members whether they agree with the models. Challenge students to come up with their own visual representation of where sensory needs fit within life, wellbeing and learning.

What is the window of tolerance? (Age: 11+) – provide students with a range of different Google images that describe the 'window of tolerance' as well as the version on page 50. Ask what they like and dislike about each explanatory image. Ask students to sketch a brief image that explains the window of tolerance to their peer group. See activity on page 195 in this chapter for a crafting arts-based version of this activity.

Bottle of pop analogy (Age: All ages) – take the students outside for this potentially messy activity. Have two 500 ml bottles of pop. Ask students to stand in a circle. Pass around the first bottle of pop and ask students to say one sensory stressor in their day (for example, noisy classrooms, itchy uniform). For each one they say, they can give the bottle of pop one shake (the children will want to shake it more, but stop them!). When everyone has added their stressors, ask the students to stand back while you open the bottle at arm's length and watch the explosion. Explain that this is the bottle of pop analogy where people might seem like a 'fine' bottle of pop in school, but explode at home because of the stressors of the school day. For the second bottle of pop, pass it round once adding in the stressors, but for the second round, each student needs to suggest a sensory strategy that can help with coping in school (for example, wear ear defenders, go to a quiet place at break time); for each strategy mentioned, they should twist the bottle top a tiny bit to release a small amount of pressure and quickly tighten it up again (the teacher will want to supervise this or do this part themselves). At the end of the round, take the lid off fully and the pop bottle will not explode. This explains how sensory strategies can help people to cope in school. You can also use the diagram of the pop bottle analogy in Chapter 3 on page 44.

Defining our responses (Age: 11+) – ask students to come up with class definitions of the following words (select the words most appropriate for your group): overwhelm, underwhelm, overload, overstimulated, understimulated, meltdown, shutdown, temper tantrum, emotional outburst. Ask students to ensure they use words to describe the physical feelings of being in each state, including commenting on breathing, heart rate and muscle tension and whether they are in control of their responses or not. Ask if there are different levels of responses from less to more extreme. Point out that the terms 'meltdown' and 'shutdown' specifically are commonly used in autistic communities to describe a more unavoidable response that the individual has no control over and is often caused/exacerbated by external sensory inputs. The group needs to collectively agree a range of terms that work for them to use in sessions generally to describe overload, etc. They should feel free to get creative with their terms – the 'screaming heebie jeebies', 'flip out', 'hissy fit', 'freak out', 'seeing red', 'blow a fuse', 'in a tizzy', 'go ballistic' or 'collywobbles' being other examples. It is important not to imply that any of these specific responses are wrong or bad behaviour, but to try to encourage viewing them neutrally, as reactions that have occurred because of a certain set of circumstances, and to encourage thinking about what changes to situations could lead to different outcomes.

Non-verbal communication of overwhelm (Age: 7+) – when we are in an 'overwhelm' state, it becomes very difficult for us to communicate as our 'lid has flipped' (see Chapter 3, page 45) and we will therefore struggle to process verbal instructions and find it difficult to find words to communicate what we are feeling. Ask the group to come up with a range of ways they can non-verbally communicate that they are overwhelmed. Show them the wristbands available online that are red and green, where you can turn to the green side and show 'I am okay/talk to me' or the red side 'I am not okay/leave me alone'. These can be used to non-verbally communicate current feelings. Look up videos online for the sign language/Makaton signs for overwhelmed. For example, one sign is sweeping your arms (palms facing your head) up and over your head. Another possible sign is as follows: raise your arms in front of you level with your shoulders; bend arms at the elbow to right angles in front of you with your palms facing you; move your forearms in a crossing motion across your face and repeat this motion a few times. Alternatively, you can use your hand, repeatedly lifting your fingers from a fist shape with your thumb tucked inside your fingers to show your lid has flipped (see diagram on page 45 of Chapter 3). Ask the group to come up with their own ways and signs they want to use to communicate non-verbally that they are overwhelmed. Ask them to share these signs with their close friends and family and practise using them. If appropriate, some students may want to share these signs with their teachers.

Sensory detectives (Age: 10+) – ask students to play detective with the last time they had a significant emotional response to something. What happened? How were you feeling? What happened before the event? What sensory inputs were you experiencing? Was there anything that could be done differently to change what happened?

12-sided sensory regulation dice (Age: 11+) – use a dodecahedron dice (the net for which is widely available online to print onto card). On each of the 12 sides, write a strategy for regulating that works for you. In times of dysregulation, roll the dice and do the sensory regulation strategy.

Sensory icebergs

 An activity that helps students explore and articulate the observable and hidden elements of our sensory identities, using the metaphor of an iceberg.

 Mainstream and specialist, whole class, small group and 1:1. This activity may be better in a small group and 1:1 due to the likelihood of sharing more personal information. Ensure you have ground rules set up with your group to ensure a safer space to do this activity.

 11+.

 20–30 minutes.

 Sensory Iceberg Worksheets, colouring pens.

Begin by explaining the concept of an iceberg and how most of its mass is hidden beneath the water's surface. Relate this to how people often have underlying sensory needs that aren't immediately visible. Ask students to annotate their Sensory Iceberg Worksheets, Above the waterline, students will draw or write about the sensory behaviours that are visible to others; for example, covering ears, squinting or avoiding certain textures. Below the waterline, they should write or illustrate the internal feelings and challenges they might experience, which aren't visible to others, like feeling overwhelmed by noise, discomfort from bright lights or anxiety in crowded spaces.

Allow students to share their icebergs with the class if they feel comfortable. Discuss how different each iceberg is, highlighting the unique sensory experiences of each individual. Facilitate a discussion about the importance of understanding and respecting these hidden elements just as much as the visible ones. Bring in a conversation about masking and how hard it can be to constantly hide how you feel in order to fit in. Another way of thinking about this could be visualising a graceful swan gliding across the water surface, while their legs are pedalling frantically to keep up.

Conclude with reflecting with the students whether this activity helped them understand themselves or others better. Encourage students to discuss strategies that could help manage the sensory needs they illustrated below the waterline.

A SENSORY ICEBERG

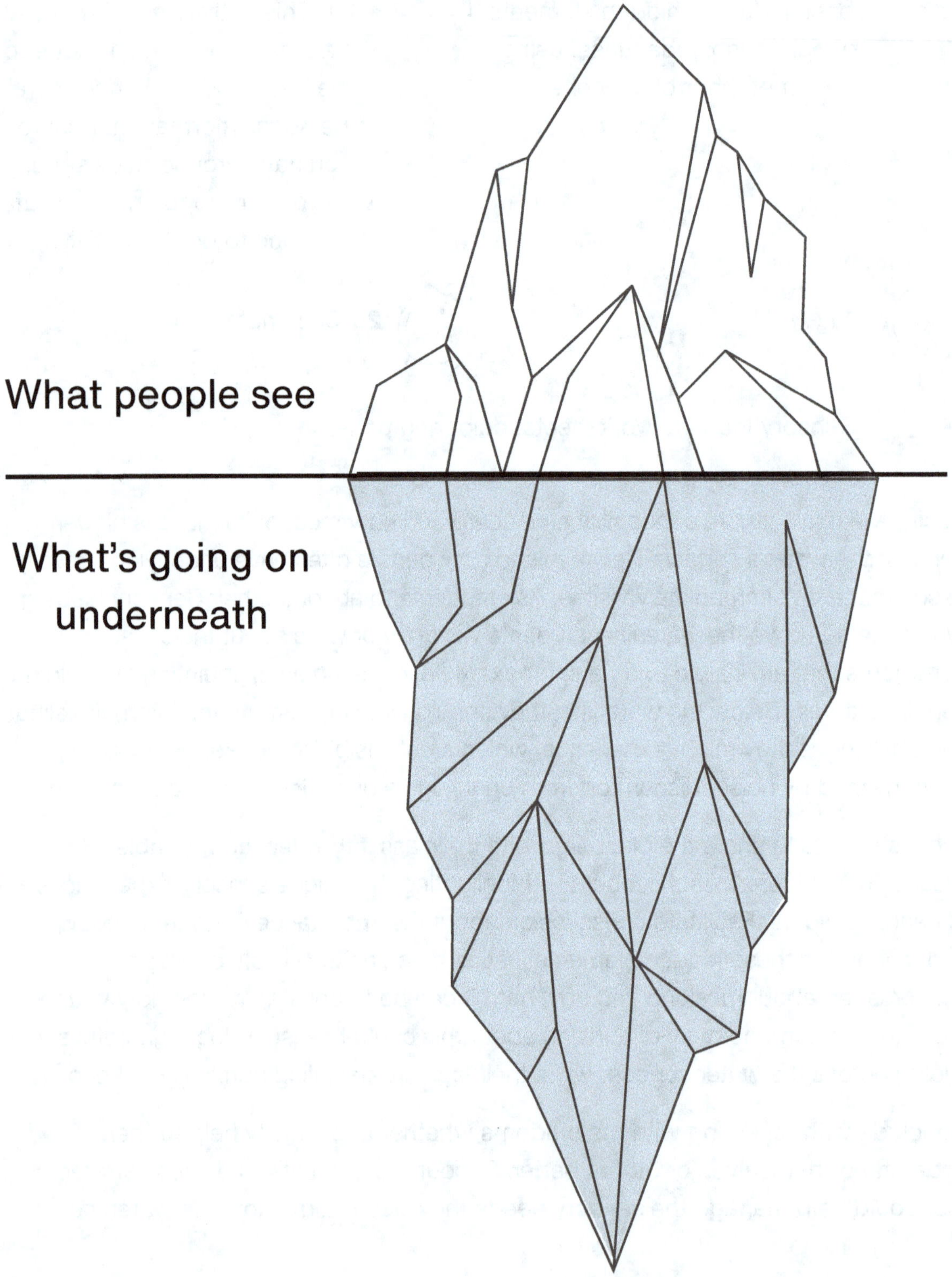

What people see

What's going on underneath

The Sensory Flower: A Situation and Solutions Analysis

This activity is adapted from 'The Mind Flower' found within *Great Relationships and Sex Education: 200+ Activities for Educators Working with Young People* by Alice Hoyle and Ester McGeeney (Routledge, 2019). Shared with permission.

 This activity adapts a common model used in cognitive behavioural therapy (CBT) for breaking down how our thoughts and feelings about situations affect how we respond to them. It tries to encourage students to think about perspectives other than their own, and to think about how possible sensory interventions could help change the situation.

 Mainstream and specialist, whole class, small group and 1:1.

 11+.

 40–50 minutes.

 Pen and paper, copy of The Sensory Flower Worksheet.

The worksheet portrays a large blank flower, with five petals around a circle. The petals are labelled as: 'What am I thinking?', 'What am I feeling emotionally?', 'What am I feeling physically?', 'What external inputs are affecting the situation?', 'What do I do/How do I respond/react?' The circle in the centre is labelled 'Situation'. The teacher also draws the flower on the board and models the activity for the participants.

THE SENSORY FLOWER
A Situation and Solutions Analysis

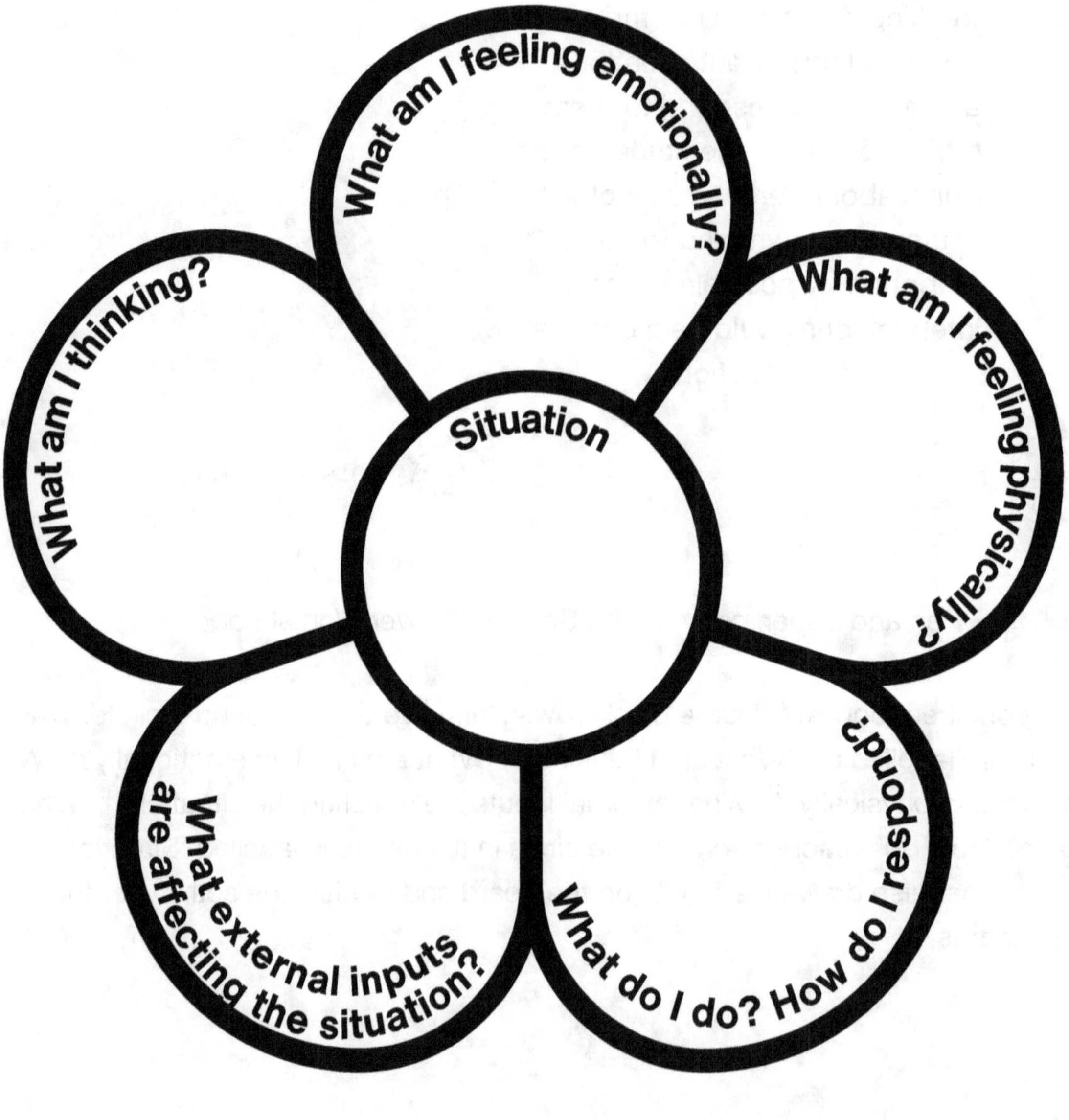

- What am I feeling emotionally?
- What am I feeling physically?
- What am I thinking?
- Situation
- What external inputs are affecting the situation?
- What do I do? How do I respond?

Ask participants to think about a common scenario that young people experience in their everyday lives that is challenging, stressful or difficult; for example, they are running late for school and not having a chance for breakfast, their parents are shouting at them, they can't find their PE kit.

Start by summarising the scenario in the middle of the flower. Next, ask participants to brainstorm how they might think, physically and emotionally feel in this scenario, and what they might do/how they might react as well as if there are any other external inputs they can think of (for example, a loud ticking clock or a strong smell from PE kit trainers).

To extend this activity, you could have some students act the person who is late, and others could do the activity as the parent who is shouting at them because they are late. Try and probe beyond the 'correct' way of responding and think about good and bad thoughts, feelings and actions. Write responses in the relevant petals. Explore the similarities and differences across the group in how people could respond to the same scenario. Use the diversity of responses to highlight that it is not the situation itself that makes us feel or act in a certain way (as shown by the diversity of responses across the group). Rather it is our perception and reactions towards the situation that lead us to feel a certain way.

Show participants the relationships between the petals and between what we think, feel and do. For example, a hangry meltdown at our parents when we are late for school could have been avoided if we had had a quick piece of toast and asked our parents nicely if they could help us look for our PE kit. Sometimes the solutions are intrinsic (I need to do something to help myself) or sometimes extrinsic (someone else can do something to help me).

Ask students to revisit the flower and to think of any sensory interventions they could make to create a different outcome to the situation. For example, taking a deep breath could help you feel calmer and lower your heart rate which then might mean you are able to talk more calmly rather than shouting. Or having a crunchy snack can help regulate the blood sugar and the crunch helps work out some of the tension from the moment and then you feel more regulated and able to look for your PE kit more methodically and logically rather than in a rushed and panicked way. Ask students to experiment with using this model for other situations in their lives to see if breaking down situations into their component parts can help provide clarity and perspective and possible interventions for better outcomes.

Reflection questions for students

- What have you learnt about yourself from doing this activity?
- Do you think you are led more by your thoughts, your emotions, your physical feelings (interoception)?
- Is it always easy to change something in the moment for a better outcome?

Part 3: Recognising, responding and respecting sensory differences

A sensory audit of a school day

 Students complete a record capturing how they feel at different points in the day, what the causes were and how things could be made better. This supports students to really think about their daily needs as a whole and how they can better help themselves.

 Mainstream and specialist, whole class, small group and 1:1.

 11+.

 All day – students should be given the sheets the day before and asked to complete them at designated points throughout the day.

 The School Day Sensory Reflection Worksheet. Pens. A clipboard may be useful.

Using the 'Our Sensory States Model' depicted on page 164, ask students to complete the following audit during a school day. They should flag whether they are in Slug, Comfort, Engage or Overload, consider what caused it and what could make things better.

When you next see the group, ask small groups to compare and contrast their findings about the different states they found themselves in across the day. Ask them to identify the common triggers that changed their states in a negative direction and common strategies that moved their state in a more positive direction.

Ask them to experiment with strategies across the week to see if their daily experiences improve as a result of the things they are trying.

The School Day Sensory Reflection Sheet			
	My Body Feels… (Or my body is in what sensory state?*)	**Why (what caused this)?**	**How Could Things Be Made Better?**
Before school			
Arriving at school			
First lessons			
Break time			
Lessons before lunch			
Lunchtime			
Afternoon lessons			
Assemblies			
Home time			

Copyright material from Alice Hoyle and Tessa Hyde (2025), *Becoming a Sensory Aware School*, Routledge

My personal space: Too close for comfort

This activity is adapted from an original activity on consent called 'My Body Boundaries: Too Close for Comfort' found within *Great Relationships and Sex Education: 200+ Activities for Educators Working with Young People* by Alice Hoyle and Ester McGeeney (Routledge, 2019). Developed originally for work Alice did with the PSHE Association. Shared with permission.

 An interactive activity in which participants use their bodies to think about their personal space needs and practise communicating them.

 Mainstream and specialist, whole class, small group.

 11+.

 10–15 minutes.

 None.

Line the group up in two lines facing each other about 3 metres apart (ensuring individuals in the rows have at least an arm span of space between each person in the row) and identify them as Row A and Row B. Ask Row A to slowly take small steps forward. The facing person in Row B should try to communicate (using words or body language) once they feel uncomfortable with the proximity of the person opposite them. Person A must stop when they have registered the other person's discomfort in that position.

You may have students in your group who struggle with proximity, standing in line, etc. It would be better for them to be in Row B with sufficient space around them and make sure they are comfortable to participate or they may prefer to opt out and observe instead.

Continue until everyone on the opposite line has reached their final position. It is likely that the Row A lines will be variable due to different levels of proximity comfort. Keep the participants in their lines for a discussion of the following questions:

- How did it feel when people were getting too close? *(Answers might include: I wanted to move away, I felt uncomfortable, I wanted to push them away.)*

- Why do you think people in Row B said "Stop!" at different distances *(Answers might include: people have different levels of comfort with personal space; depends on the relationship between person A and B; depends on how clear the communication was between person A and B.)*
- For Row Bs: How did it feel to communicate your discomfort? How easy or difficult was it? Was that listened to and respected? How would it have felt if the person opposite you had kept taking a step forward even when you had communicated your discomfort?
- For Row As: How did it feel to try and read someone else's discomfort levels? What signs did the other person give you that communicated their discomfort? Are verbal or non-verbal signals easier to understand? How did it feel seeing that other people were able to go further/less far than you?

To extend the activity, swap the rows over so that Row A gets a chance to communicate their proximity discomfort and standing still and Row B takes the steps forward.

Discussion questions for students

- What did we learn about ourselves and others doing this activity?
- How easy is it to communicate our needs verbally?
- How easy is it to communicate our needs non-verbally?
- What sorts of things can we say if trying to communicate our needs?
- How can we communicate what we need on a physical non-verbal level?
- How easy is it to respond to the needs of others when stated verbally?
- How easy is it to respond to the needs of others by picking up non-verbal cues?
- What advice would you give someone who is worried about sharing their sensory needs?
- Would living by the ditty "Taking care of me, taking care of you, having an equal say and learning as we go" help ensure all of us get our needs met? How?

Overloaded! The last sensory straw that overloaded the camel's back

> ❝Pupils had never heard of the phrase 'the straw that broke the camel's back' before, yet they found it a very useful concept to help them understand the phrase 'sensory overload' by doing the activity in this way.❞
>
> Monica Parry, Deputy SENDCO, a large secondary school

 A game to help students think about how people can get overloaded, and how sensory strategies can help reduce the chance of overload.

 Mainstream and specialist, whole class, small group and 1:1.

 10 +.

 30 minutes.

 One Sensory Camel Worksheet per player. A set of sensory straws (lolly pop sticks written on or card strips printed in a pot to draw out). You can also buy a game called 'The Last Straw' by Paul Lamond Brand which has a wooden camel and wooden sticks to do this activity.

Ask students if they have heard the phrase "this is the last straw!" and what context it is used in. People usually use it as an idiom to describe the latest in a series of difficult events that makes you feel like you cannot tolerate the situation any longer. It is from a longer old English proverb, "it is the last straw that breaks the camel's back". This session could form part of a wider conversation about idiom use which may be particularly useful for pupils on the Autism Spectrum who may find literal rather than figurative language easier to understand. There are many available illustrated books that can help explain idioms and metaphors such as *What Did You Say? What Do You Mean?* by Jude Welton and Jane Telford (Jessica Kingsley, 2004).

Give each student a picture of the camel with five spaces in for straws. Each student starts with one sensory straw already taking up a space on their camel. Each person takes it in turns to draw out a sensory straw which will either have another sensory input (which adds to the load) OR a sensory strategy/accommodation that has a value of -1 so one sensory input straw can be removed from their camel's back. The first person to get to five straws on the camel's back has lost the game as they are now OVERLOADED. Students can also come up with their own examples of sensory inputs and strategies to continue game play.

OVERLOADED!
The last sensory straw that overloaded the camel's back.

First player to five sensory straws is OVERLOADED!
Sensory strategy straws help take one load away.

Copyright material from Alice Hoyle and Tessa Hyde (2025), *Becoming a Sensory Aware School*, Routledge

Possible Sensory Inputs and Strategies/Accommodations	
Sensory Input Straws	**Sensory Strategy/Accommodation**
Clothes are too tight and itchy	Took a movement break -1 straw from the camel's back
Lights are bright and flickery	Have a snack -1 straw from the camel's back
I am hungry	Wore comfy clothes -1 straw from the camel's back
I didn't sleep well	Wore noise cancelling headphones -1 straw from the camel's back
Someone is wearing a strong scent	Wore coloured glasses for visual stress -1 straw from the camel's back
Someone is tapping their pen	Bounced on trampoline before school -1 straw from the camel's back
The classroom is too loud	Got into sensory swing after school -1 straw from the camel's back
Someone is whistling	Had some chillout time with my iPad after a period of socialising. -1 straw from the camel's back
Someone asks a question and doesn't give you thinking time	Got a good night's sleep -1 straw from the camel's back
The sun is reflecting off the board	Had a movement break in a double lesson -1 straw from the camel's back
I need a poo but won't use school toilets for that	Did some deep breathing -1 straw from the camel's back
I need a wee but feel too embarrassed to ask to go in a lesson	Allowed to leave lesson a few minutes early to miss the crowds -1 straw from the camel's back
I am thirsty	Used a bottle with a straw to keep hydrated -1 straw from the camel's back
The corridors are overcrowded.	Had a really active playtime -1 straw from the camel's back
The teacher's high heels click clack during our exam	Was allowed to eat lunch in a quiet zone of school to help recharge for the afternoon. -1 straw from the camel's back
Own example	Own example
Own example	Own example
Own example	Own example
Own example	Own example

Discussion questions for students

Adapt the following questions depending on the age and ability of the group you are playing with.

- Do sensory inputs affect everyone in the same way?
- Is it as simple as one sensory strategy to help with one sensory input?
- Do sensory strategies always have to match up? For example, feel hungry – eat something, feeling restless – move; or can doing things like eating regularly in the day, getting regular movement breaks help us have a balanced sensory day?
- Do we always know when we are overloaded?
- How can we tell when other people are getting towards sensory overload?
- In the game, five straws led to overload – is it like that in real life? Do different people have different numbers of straws they can carry?
- Can we write five sensory straws that overload us and five strategies we have that can help reduce overload?
- What is the difference between a sensory strategy and a reasonable adjustment or accommodation? (You will need to explain these terms to the group.)

Extension activity: Games for sensory awareness

Having played Jenga, dice, straws, etc., task students with coming up with their own game that aims to educate others about their senses, sensory needs, strategies and wellbeing.

Budgeting our sensory spoons

 An activity that uses "spoon theory" to help students understand how to manage their energy and recognise what depletes them (which may or may not be sensory in origin). This activity is particularly useful for neurodivergent students or those with sensory processing challenges.

 Mainstream and specialist, whole class, small group and 1:1.

 10+.

 30 minutes.

 Packs of disposable wooden tablespoons, enough for five per student. If wooden spoons are a sensory trigger for some people (they are for Alice and Tessa!), normal metal or plastic spoons can also be used or the outline of spoons on paper or card.

Part 1: Explaining spoon theory

Explain to students what 'spoon theory' is. Spoon theory is a metaphor that uses spoons to depict the amount of mental or physical energy a person has and helps recognise that this energy is not in infinite abundance. Originally it was used by Christine Miserandino in her 2003 essay "The Spoon Theory" (https://en.wikipedia.org/wiki/Spoon_theory) to help explain chronic illness, where people with chronic illnesses may not have as many "spoons" available as the general population to carry out daily tasks. It has also been adopted into neurodivergent communities to help explain sensory overwhelm and the cost of invisible disabilities.

Explain that each day someone will have a set number of spoons. They will lose spoons during the day doing things that drain them. In an ideal world, your spoons will reset each day, but for many people they may not be the same every day. We are using spoon theory as a common and very useful analogy to help young people think about bringing more balance to their daily lives. However, it is important to recognise that this is not intended to appropriate or minimise the lived experience of people with chronic illnesses and disabilities. If you are doing this activity with a mainstream group of students, it may be helpful to have a discussion with the class on their thoughts and feelings about bringing 'spoon theory' into mainstream use. You could ask the following question: 'How can we ensure we use spoon theory ethically for wider collective benefit and understanding, yet also to help us understand the experiences of those who are disabled or chronically ill?' For example, it would not be ethical to assume or state that a healthy able-bodied neurotypical person always starts out with the same number of spoons as someone with a chronic illness or disability. It is important to be aware that there are some people who start the day with fewer spoons.

Divide the group into groups of three. Ask students to each take five spoons as their hypothetical allocated amount for this task today. (Remind students they could wake up some mornings after a busy week and it might feel like a 'three spoon day'; or other days, it might feel like a '12 spoon day', it's very individual.)

First, they should go round the group holding their spoons, taking it in turns to share the things that cause their spoon budget to deplete (see the 'Overloaded!' activity on page 182 for ideas). Encourage them to think about their sensory triggers as part of this but it may be wider than that, and for the purposes of this activity that is okay. For each thing they mention, they should put a spoon down until all their spoons are gone.

Ask the group to take one wooden spoon (or a print-out on paper/card); on the front they can draw and write and decorate the spoons with the things that take away a spoon. Use biro or pencil to write as felt tips can bleed into the wood, but felt tips can be used for decoration. Students can keep their decorated spoons as an *aide-mémoire* for spoon theory.

Part 2: Budgeting spoons across the week

There may be some things in our days that deplete us significantly – such as an argument with a friend or parents, coming last in a school test, not having anyone to hang out with at break time and this might have knock-on effects for the amount of spoons we have the next day or over the next week. There also might be things we really want to do like attend a party or concert, take a trip to a theme park. These activities will use up more spoons than the day's allocation, leaving us in spoon deficit so in the days after we are exhausted and need to recover.

So how can we tell (a) what our spoon number is at the start of the day based on how we are feeling? (b) How can we identify whether things in our day are depleting just one spoon or carry a higher charge so are taking more spoons? (c) How can we pace our activities across the week to manage our level of spoons better? (So we don't run out on the first day!) Students could experiment with writing a spoon budget for themselves across a week, writing down the costs of certain activities/situations.

To conclude these activities, ask the students the following questions:

- Be aware of 'false friends' in things that we think may 'boost our spoons' (for example, lots of people use sweets to give them an energy boost, but then there can be a sugar crash afterwards and we feel worse; or lots of people zone out for hours with screens – but find afterwards that they do not feel properly rested and relaxed, so it was deflecting from the issue but not necessarily giving the required boost and may have actually further depleted the spoons). What 'false friends' can you think of?
- Is there any self care you can do to preserve your spoons?
- What actions do we need to take on 'low spoons' days compared to 'high spoons' days?
- Are there activities you are willing to use up more spoons for? What are they? How can you manage your recovery time afterwards?
- How can we support our friends and family manage their spoons?
- Does spoon theory help you understand your needs and think about sensory balance better, or can you think of a different metaphor that works better for you?
- Another way of looking at spoon theory is using jugs – each day, your jug starts out full but empties as the day goes on. People with chronic illnesses may have smaller jugs to start with. Ask students which metaphor they prefer and discuss if they can think of any other metaphor that works for them in terms of thinking about their daily and weekly energy (and sensory) balance.

Sensory scenarios

 A scenario activity that helps students to think about how sensory needs can be balanced in the classroom.

 Mainstream and specialist, whole class, small group and 1:1.

 10+.

 30 minutes.

 Sensory scenarios.

Divide the whole group into groups of 4–6 students. Give each member of the group a scenario to discuss. This can either be from the scenario list or come up with your own based on common issues in your class.

List of Sensory Scenarios
James keeps clicking his pen next to you while you are trying to concentrate. He then starts to chew the end of it loudly. The noise upsets you.
Jade is rocking on two legs of a chair backwards and gets a detention for this as it's the third time this lesson and she has already been told to stop.
Asif is sitting on his feet on the chair, the teacher tells him to sit on his bottom, otherwise everyone will copy.
Amara has used lots of body spray this morning. Finn makes coughing spluttering noises near her.
Lily likes to tap her fingers and rock in her chair but it annoys Joe who is sitting next to her.
Yaz has a time out card and uses this when the class gets too loud. Other students make comments about her abusing this card.
Dot has a slightly different PE kit to everyone else (same logos and similar colours but different fabrics), but she hates it when people ask her about it. A parent complains as her daughter now also wants the different-style uniform and it's not fair.
Nik always hums during individual work on the class activities. His neighbour finds it hard to concentrate when he does this.
Charlie is always a bit too rough in football and has hurt others when playing. He says he never intends to and is genuinely apologetic when he has.
Brian always stands a bit too close when talking to you. He has bad breath.
Own scenario:
Own scenario:

Copyright material from Alice Hoyle and Tessa Hyde (2025), *Becoming a Sensory Aware School*, Routledge

Reflection questions for students

Ask the class to consider the following questions for each scenario:

- What sensory need might be present?
- What might happen next?
- What solutions would you suggest?
- What steps would you put in place to prevent this situation from arising in future?
- Do your solutions or preventative steps follow "Taking care of me, taking care of you, having an equal say and learning as we go"?

Finally, if time allows, students can role play their solutions, if appropriate, to the rest of the group. Remind the group it is important to try and find a balance within the class for all our different sensory needs.

Part 4: Embracing sensory wellbeing for ourselves and others
Sensory me: Strategies, glimmers and triggers

 Creating a keyring of small cards that document individual sensory needs and aversions.

 Mainstream and specialist, whole class, small group and 1:1.

 All ages.

 30 minutes.

 It is a good idea for students to have first completed a version of the 'Sensory Me' activity in this chapter (page 157) so they are familiar with recognising and talking about their own sensory needs. You will need to explain each of the following to the group:

Sensory strategy – something you do to meet your sensory needs. For example, if you are feeling anxious before a test, you sniff your favourite smell (peppermint oil) on a hankie.

Sensory glimmers – these are the things that you can do to spark sensory joy. They are the opposite of triggers. For example, singing in the shower.

Sensory triggers – these are the things that give you the 'sensory ick', the things that set your nerves jangling and you find it tricky to concentrate on anything else when they are present. For example, flickering fluorescent lights.

You can then ask students to fill in and decorate the 'My Sensory Glimmers, Triggers and Strategies Worksheet' found in Chapter 4 on page 68, using visual imagery as well as words to make a highly personal bespoke snapshot of their sensory glimmers, triggers and strategies.

Where students struggle to think independently when presented with blank sheets, you could think about providing visual checklists of common sensory glimmers or triggers for students to select from and come up with their own. You could adapt the 'Sensory checklist' (www.sensorysmarts.com/sensory-checklist.pdf) from the table in Chapter 4 on pages 72–73.

Extension idea: Sensory strategies lanyard cards/keyrings/passports

Students need to be provided with the two sheets on the next page, 'My Sensory Strategies and Glimmers' and 'My Sensory Triggers', printed on card and back-to-back. Students should complete the sheets with their best presentation skills as this will be a reference resource for them and staff working with them to use. You could also laminate the sheets to further protect them if appropriate. When their sheets are complete, they could cut them up into individual prompt cards with one side of each card corresponding to a particular sense with 'the strategies that help me and glimmers' on one side and 'triggers, the things to avoid' on the other side. Punch a hole into the top left-hand corner of each card and attach a keyring. You could attach it to a lanyard and ensure that students feel able to show and share these with staff throughout the school year. You may want to revisit and update this activity on an annual basis as student needs develop and change.

👍 My Sensory Strategies and Glimmers

👍 My sensory strategies for coping with sounds/noises.	👍 My sensory strategies for coping with lights and managing visual distractions.
👍 Glimmers: (Sounds I love)	👍 Glimmers: (Things I love to look at)
👍 My sensory strategies for coping with tastes and smells	👍 My sensory strategies for managing my movement needs
👍 Glimmers: (Tastes and smells I love)	👍 Glimmers: (Moves I love)
👍 My sensory strategies to be aware of what's going on inside my body (interoception)	👍 My sensory strategies for managing my tactile/texture needs
👍 Glimmers: (I love it when I feel…)	👍 Glimmers: (Touches/textures I love)

👎 My Sensory Triggers

👎 My sensory triggers around sounds/noises	👎 My sensory triggers with lights and visual distractions
👎 My sensory triggers around tastes and smells	👎 My sensory movement triggers
👎 My sensory triggers inside my body (interoception)	👎 My sensory triggers with tactile/textures

My personal window of tolerance

 Creative activity exploring the concept of the 'window of tolerance' which develops self awareness and coping strategies through a creative crafting activity.

 Mainstream and specialist, whole class, small group and 1:1.

 10+.

 1 hour.

 Coloured paper or card, markers, coloured pencils or crayons, scissors, glue or tape, magazines or printed images, particularly of windows/houses, craft sticks, string or wool, hole punch, fabric scraps and other craft materials.

Before doing this activity, students should have completed the 'What is the window of Tolerance' activity (see 'Further activities to explore sensory needs and regulation' box in this chapter on page 170). Remind students that it is a metaphor that can help explain coping ability.

Instruct students to create two window-shaped frames using coloured paper or card. They could use collages for this activity using images of different windows. These frames will represent the 'window of tolerance', one for times when they feel regulated (a large window; for example, a wide horizontal picture window) and another for times when they feel dysregulated (a small window; for example, a peephole).

Ask students to decorate the frames using markers, coloured pencils or magazine cutouts. Encourage creativity and personalisation. For example, they could experiment with making just one window but with crafted curtains that move using paper sliders, or using hole punches, wool and fabric scraps to close and narrow their windows, thus making their window of tolerance smaller. There are no right or wrong ways to create their window(s) as it is personal to them. After completing their windows, ask students to reflect on the choices they made in decorating each window. What colours did they use? What symbols or images represent their emotions and coping strategies? Discuss as a group how their crafted windows might change based on different situations and stress levels.

Invite students to share their crafted windows with the rest of the group. Encourage them to explain their choices and the significance behind their designs. Discuss the range of coping strategies and emotions within the group. Emphasise that everyone's window of tolerance is unique and will change in space and time. Depending on the group, you may wish to create a collaborative display in the room showcasing the crafted windows. Remind students that craft and creative activities have been proven to reduce stress levels (and therefore make our window of tolerance bigger!).

My sensory wellbeing toolkit

This activity is adapted from 'Wellbeing Toolkits' found within *Great Relationships and Sex Education: 200+ Activities for Educators Working with Young People* by Alice Hoyle and Ester McGeeney (Routledge, 2019). Shared with permission.

 A creative activity that enables students to begin to create a sensory support box of things that can support them.

 Mainstream and specialist, whole class, small group and 1:1.

 10+.

 Minimum 30 minutes.

 You will need a selection of boxes, plastic jars, a range of fabrics, glue, craft materials, visual list of sensory strategies, etc.

Introduce participants to the 'Five Ways to Mental Wellbeing Model' from the New Economics Foundation (https://neweconomics.org/2008/10/five-ways-to-wellbeing). This suggests that there are five actions that are all equally important for improving our wellbeing:

Connect with people around you and with family, friends and neighbours in your home, community or school. Think of these as the cornerstones of your life and invest time in developing them. These relationships and connections can enrich you every day.

Keep active: Go for a walk or run, dance, garden, play a game. Moving your body makes you feel good. Choose a physical activity that you enjoy and that suits your level of mobility and budget.

Take notice: Be curious. Catch sight of beautiful and unusual things. Notice the changing seasons and savour the moment, whether this is walking to school, eating your lunch or talking to friends. Be aware of the world around you and what you are feeling. Reflecting on your experiences will help you appreciate what matters to you.

Keep learning: Try something new or rediscover a new interest. Fix a bike. Learn to play an instrument or how to cook your favourite food. Set a challenge you will enjoy achieving. Learning new things makes you feel more confident as well as being fun.

Give: Do something nice for a friend or stranger. Say thank you. Smile. Volunteer your time. Join a community group. Look out as well as in. Seeing yourself and your happiness linked to a wider community can be rewarding and creates connections with the world around you.

Task students with writing a version of these with a more sensory focus: 'Five Ways to Sensory Wellbeing', 'Sensory Wellbeing Life Hacks/Top Tips'. Revisit the W.E.L.L.D.O.I.N.G mnemonic on page 75 of Chapter 4 and 'Principles for sensory welldoing' shared on page 124 at the start of this chapter as students may also wish to adapt these models.

Ask participants to work on their own to brainstorm strategies that they use to help them look after their own sensory wellbeing to take care of themselves. Write each strategy on a sticky note. Can the strategies be divided by the eight senses? It doesn't matter if they can't be, but the aim here is to expand our understanding of sensory wellbeing.

Ask the group to consider the answers to the following questions

- What else could I do to look after my sensory wellbeing that I don't do currently?
- What can others do to support me?
- What else do we need to make it possible for us to look after our sensory wellbeing? (For example, support from parents, safe places, enough money.)

Encourage students to jot down any new ideas for how they could support their own sensory wellbeing and any suggestions of organisations and resources that could support them.

To pull these ideas together, ask participants to create their own wellbeing and self care toolkit that they can use as and when they need it. This can take any form they wish. For example:

- A small cardboard box of resources that students can make, find and collect; for example, earplugs, a book, cosy pyjamas, trainers or sports wear, chocolate, an apple, a Pot Noodle, bubble bath, a song list to play.
- A jar filled with useful quotations, instructions to self, or lists of useful websites/ resources. The jar can be decorated with key images and messages.

Sensory wellbeing sprites

 A feel-good task aiming to raise awareness of sensory wellbeing and spread some sensory joy.

 Mainstream and specialist, whole class, small group and 1:1.

 8+

 30 minutes.

 Blank postcards and a range of small treats; for example, herbal tea bags, individually wrapped nut-free sweets, pressed flowers, scratch and sniff perfume samples or moisturiser sachets (beauty counters often have lots of testers like this they will give away).

Task students with spreading the word on what sensory wellbeing is. First, as a group, agree a class definition of sensory wellbeing. On each postcard ask students to write and decorate one side of the postcard with the definition. On the other side of the postcard, they should write and decorate a personalised gift note explaining they wanted to share a particular sensory treat and why. Students should hand out their treats to someone else (for example, a peer, a member of staff, a member of family). Students can also choose to make it for themselves if they prefer, reminding them that self care is important too.

Sensory wellbeing ambassadors

 A long term project working with a group of interested young people to form a working party to develop sensory wellbeing across the school.

 Mainstream and specialist, small group.

 8+

 Minimum one term.

 Audit tools in Chapter 4 and Chapter 7, core messages for sensory wellbeing. Materials for presentation and dissemination (posters, flyers, digital media tools). Meeting space for regular discussions.

Invite students who are interested in wellbeing and advocacy to join you in this project. Try and ensure a diverse group to represent various experiences and perspectives, including students with SEND. You could announce the recruitment through school assemblies and notices at form time. Some schools have let their School Councils lead on this work.

First, you will need to develop the group's understanding of sensory wellbeing using some of the activities from this chapter. From this you could work with students to develop some 'young people friendly' core messages, about sensory awareness, sensory inclusion and sensory wellbeing. A starting point to edit is provided on the next page.

Core messages for sensory awareness, sensory inclusion and sensory wellbeing

- **EIGHT not five:** There are eight senses, not five, and knowing more about each of them and what our sensory preferences are can help us become our best selves.
- **Tune in:** Listening to how your body is feeling and working out where and why you are feeling like that and how you are reacting is a valuable life skill.
- **It's okay to be me:** We are all different with different needs. We should respect each other and our differences and boundaries.
- **Speak out!** We all have the right to articulate our current sensory needs – this isn't always easy to do but gets easier with practice.
- **Enjoy it!** Our lives should be full of sensory welldoing (see W.E.L.L.D.O.I.N.G mnemonic on Chapter 4, page 75) for sensory welldoing.
- **Things change:** Our sensory needs can change in time and space and across a lifetime. Stay open to making new adaptations to cope with these changes and be willing to share these changes.
- **Stay curious:** Experiment with rather than constantly trying to avoid all your sensory triggers – stay open to trying, so you are able to access all life has to offer. You won't know unless you try.
- **Find the balance:** Sometimes we might need a hard boundary (avoid) on some sensory inputs and that is okay (reasonable adjustments). Other boundaries might be softer and depend on what else is going on for us that day or the expectations on us. It is a constant evolution to find the balance in our sensory lives.
- **It's a human need:** Developing sensory lifestyles and sensory wellbeing is vital to live a full life.

Once students are clear about sensory needs and the importance of sensory wellbeing, you will need to train them to use the student versions of the audit tools 'A sensory audit of a school day' on page 178 of this chapter and 'A Student-led School Sensory Survey' on page 217 of Chapter 7, to equip ambassadors with the skills needed to evaluate and report on the sensory environment, identifying potential sensory challenges and areas for improvement. Encourage the ambassadors to also take notes and gather feedback from their peers to ensure comprehensive evaluations.

Based on the audit findings, ambassadors should work together to develop a list of recommendations to submit to the Leadership Team of the school, aimed at addressing the identified sensory challenges. Plans might include rearranging classroom layouts, creating sensory-friendly zones, or organising sensory awareness events. The ambassadors should work with school leadership to implement any action plans and communicate on their progress to the rest of the student body. The ambassadors may also choose to adopt an advocacy role – spreading the word of sensory welldoing for sensory wellbeing amongst the whole student cohort.

At the end of the term, organise a presentation or an assembly where ambassadors can share their achievements and the positive impact of their work on the school's sensory wellbeing, as it is vital to celebrate the efforts and successes of all participants. Make sure you conclude this project with a reflective session where ambassadors can discuss what they've learned and how the project could be expanded or improved in the future. You could consider the possibility of continuing the project for another term with new or returning ambassadors. Offering a student-led project such as this not only enhances the school sensory experience based on student evidence, but also empowers students by giving them a role in shaping their educational experience. It could also develop participants' responsibility, leadership and teamwork.

Reflection questions for Chapter 6

1. Which session ideas will you try with your class?
2. Are there any session ideas you might need more help with?
3. Can you now plan a sensory curriculum for your school?
4. If you have limited time, which activities will you prioritise?
5. Can you think of any wider sensory activities you might like to experiment with?
6. How will you gain student voice from these sessions?

Chapter seven

THE SENSORY AWARE SCHOOL ENVIRONMENT

Thinking about initial school design

Many school buildings are no longer fit for purpose, built in Victorian times with various additional spaces added over the years, creating a real hodge podge of rooms. Where modern schools are now being built, we often see design features such as curved corridors, which improve the flow of moving students, or toilets areas that open onto corridors with shared sinks. These design features may make behaviour management easier, but may have unintended consequences, with certain children no longer feeling safe to use the toilets (see pages 223–225 for more information on school toilets). Where buildings have been specially designed and built for autistic students, they tend to offer dimmable soft lights, lots of natural light, but also neutral coloured opaque blinds to reduce glare. They may have high ceilings and a sense of space, but with built-in acoustic dampers and carpets to mitigate noise. Where design features are an afterthought, such as a Sensory Room with swings and a den, we have seen some spaces created that are not fit for purpose. For example, a 'calm down room' being a small exposed space on the end of the corridor with insufficient space to safely swing.

Therefore, when schools are expanding and building new wings, we would urge you to ensure the architects are aware of the importance of sensory wellbeing and understand how design decisions and consequences, such as lighting, acoustics, spatial layout and the materials used, can all have a significant impact on the people using the space, particularly if they are neurodivergent. We would argue that making building design as neurodivergent-friendly and as physically accessible as possible will bring benefits to everyone using the space and not just the minority. This design approach needs to be adopted from the outset, and the intended users of the space need to be involved in the design development and decision making wherever possible.

> **Reflective questions**
> - Reflect on your current school design – how well does it accommodate different sensory needs?
> - Were any beneficial accommodations by accident or deliberate design?
> - Where features of school design are particularly problematic on a sensory level, can you think of any simple changes that don't require an entire rebuild of the space?
> - Think about any changes or additions planned for school spaces – have sensory wellbeing and physical access been thought about in this planning?

Sensory experiences around the school

Schools can be busy, noisy places where the potential for sensory overwhelm is high. Different spaces across the school and the school day can cause different sensory challenges. The size of the school site and the number of students will also have a considerable impact.

For example, consider the following school spaces and the sensory experience within them:

The dining hall

During breaks and lunchtimes, the dining hall becomes a bustling hub of activity, filled with the clatter and scrape of utensils and the noise of student conversations. The smells of various food combinations can be overwhelming and off putting. Watching other people eat and drink can be very challenging for some students. The space is usually lit with harsh fluorescent light and is busy with colours and movements as the students navigate the space. Proximity to people in food queues and when sitting at tables can cause issues for certain students.

The assembly hall

In the assembly hall, there can be a wide variety of auditory experiences, from announcements, assemblies, performances or presentations. The hard surfaces and wide-open space can amplify sounds, create echoes, making the acoustics more intense. Visual stimuli, such as stage lights or multimedia presentations, can also be overwhelming for some. Having a whole school in one environment can be a challenging experience, particularly if children are sitting on hard floors for extended lengths of time.

Drama/dance studios

These spaces are often windowless with a wide range of lighting options, but often seem to default to 'cold white'. Full-length mirrors can cause the light to bounce around and create discomfort for those who don't want to see themselves. Wall curtains can help soften noises and so improve the acoustics of the space. There is generally more space for students to spread out in these rooms.

The sports hall

These spaces are often poorly heated so they can feel cold and uninviting. They are generally windowless or with low natural light levels and artificially lit. They often smell of sports equipment and sweat. They are loud echoey spaces. Often they are overlooked by a viewing gallery which some students may report makes them feel uncomfortable.

School corridors

At certain times, corridors will be the busiest areas of the school filled with students moving from one class to another. Blockages are common in particular areas, particularly the bottom of stairwells, due to the oppositional flow and direction of students. The sound of footsteps, locker doors slamming and voices echoing off the walls can create disorientation and distress. There is often no natural light and fluorescent strip lighting is used. The narrowness and at times overcrowding of the space can also affect a sense of personal space.

Classrooms

Classrooms are vital spaces to learn in, yet can sometimes be overwhelming, making learning impossible. The hums and flickers from fluorescent lighting and audiovisual equipment, the visually busy wall displays, the constant background noise from other classes, as well as the noise from the class itself such as people talking, the clatter of pens and equipment and the scrape of chairs and tables, might become too much for some students. Subject-specific classrooms such as science or food tech can offer additional sensory challenges such as the smells and smoke from chemical reactions or cooking.

The playground

The playground offers the chance to recover, rest and 'let off steam' after lesson time. However, the sensory mix of outdoor elements like bright sunlight, wind and varying temperatures, combined with the physical activity, noise from play and laughter as well as navigating social expectations can be overwhelming for some. There are significant differences in the way primary and secondary schools use their outdoor spaces, with primary schools much more likely to utilise play for all genders, whereas secondary schools tend towards outdoor socialisation and generally football, which often ends up being 'for the boys'.

School toilets and changing rooms

These spaces often present a unique set of sensory challenges. The echo of hard surfaces, the flush's loud noise and the smell of cleaning products or bodily functions/sweat/feet after PE can be particularly intense in these confined spaces. For more on school toilets, see pages 223–225.

Features to consider in the school environment

We also need to consider the following common features of the school environment to fully understand their potential issues and limitations.

Each of these features contribute to the overall sensory experience of a school environment. This highlights the importance of a sensory aware approach for managing the environment for sensory wellbeing.

Lighting

Whilst often overlooked, the type of lighting in classrooms can significantly affect students' mood and concentration. Harsh fluorescent lights may cause discomfort and strain, potentially impacting the learning experience. Soft, natural light is often more conducive to a relaxed and focused atmosphere, but it's not always feasible in every school setting. Adjusting the colour range of the lighting can help shift the energy in a room. For example, lethargic students in a dimly lit 'warm white light' room may become more alert and engaged if the lighting becomes brighter and like 'cool daylight'.

Visual ambience

The visual ambience of a school, including its colours, decorations and spatial layout of furniture, plays a crucial role in creating an inviting and stimulating learning environment. However, overly stimulating, colourful or cluttered spaces can overwhelm some students, making it harder for them to focus and engage in those rooms.

Sound

Noise levels within schools can vary widely, from the quiet of the school library to the bustling energy of the dining hall. Excessive noise can lead to sensory overload, stress and difficulty in concentrating for both students and teachers. Finding the right balance is key, as some ambient noise, such as soothing music, can be beneficial for learning, providing it's not too distracting.

Temperature

The comfort level of a school's heating system can directly impact students' ability to focus and learn. Too hot, and students may feel lethargic and unmotivated; too cold, and the discomfort can become a distraction. Consistent, moderate temperatures are ideal, yet achieving this can be challenging due to varying individual preferences, the limitations of school heating and ventilation systems and seasonal variation where some rooms in the height of summer can become like 'greenhouses'.

Smell and ventilation

The quality of air in a school can have a significant impact on both students and staff. Poor ventilation may lead to stale and stuffy environments that could harbour allergens, viruses and pollutants impacting on health and wellbeing. Good ventilation leads to a fresh and more pleasant atmosphere, but also potentially improves alertness and therefore may impact on learning.

Your school's unique sensory environment

Take a moment to think again about your school, taking into account the points discussed already in this chapter.

- Can you now identify the spaces that feel boosting to sensory wellbeing?
- What about the spaces that feel challenging and draining on a sensory level?

You will probably be able to recognise and articulate these almost immediately as your body will have an almost visceral reaction when you think about these spaces. Chat with a colleague – see if they have similar findings to you. Now you are ready to start auditing your school sensory space more formally.

Carrying out a whole school sensory audit

In a school it would not be feasible for one person to audit the whole school, and such audits should be undertaken by a small team as different people will spot different things. It is really important also to involve the students. A starting point for carrying out these audits could be running a focus group or questionnaire for students that explore the answers to the following questions:

- How do you feel about your sensory experiences at school?
- What works well for you? What about the school space causes you anxiety or to become dysregulated?
- What improvements to your sensory experience at school can you suggest?

This will give you particular spaces in the school to focus on. You could provide students with a map of the school to colour code Green, Amber and Red according to how they feel in the space. There are also wider activity ideas for involving students in this work in 'A sensory audit of a school day' (Chapter 6, page 178) and 'Sensory wellbeing ambassadors' (Chapter 6, page 199) as well as a 'Student-led School Sensory Survey' on page 217 of Chapter 7.

Spend at least 10 minutes in each space you are considering. The sorts of spaces you are considering are school halls, dining areas and canteens, corridors and stairwells, office spaces, toilets, outdoor areas, playing fields, changing rooms, etc. This audit is for anything that isn't strictly a classroom, as a classroom-specific audit tool is found on page 213. Fill in the audit tables using the prompt questions.

Please use your findings from the whole school sensory audit in conjunction with the classroom audit tool to form a fuller picture of the whole school environment. If you are time limited, we would suggest doing key classrooms and key student-related spaces; for example, school hall, dining hall, corridors, toilets.

Remember that your initial gut feelings on a space count for a lot, that sense of "Is this space too much, just right, or is something missing?" These audits don't need to be detailed or onerous – do as much or as little as works best for you. You can print copies of this audit and use a clipboard, or use the electronic version found in the companion resources to this book found online. One of the easiest ways we have found to complete these audit tools is to use a dictation tool to write up your initial thoughts on the space, using the questions as a prompt, and then copy and paste the paragraphs into the form to be developed and edited later. This way gives the richest responses.

We suggest moving to different points in the space to see if anything changes for you. It might be helpful to consider how the spaces appear for both the students and the teacher – so making sure you also sit at a child's level in the classroom and see it from their perspective. It would also be a good idea to revisit these notes at different points in the day to see if anything changes further; for example, light levels, noise or smells. Remember that environmental conditions vary daily, weekly or seasonally which can also change the way we respond to things at different times. For example, the dining hall is fine to be in 4 days of the week but on "fishy Friday", an individual student might find the smell intolerable; or the winter glare on the board is difficult for 3 months of the year. Therefore, when auditing sensory environments, try to strike a balance as to when the audits happen to get a fuller picture of any variations in the environment.

When you have completed the audit for a particular space, it will be useful to collate and discuss your results with a team as some of you may have noted the same issues or flagged different items. This can help ensure your audit is more robust and less subjective.

Then, as a small group, complete Action Feasibility Assessments (on page 232) for the specific space/classroom to develop your action plans.

School Space Sensory Audit			
Date:		Number of doors and windows to the space:	
Who carried out the audit:		Maximum occupancy of the space:	
Space name and location information:		Approx measurements if relevant (length, width and height):	
Predominant use of the space:		Brief overview of contents of the space (include any soft furnishing such as carpets. curtains):	
Prompt questions These are just questions to help stimulate your thoughts and perceptions of the space; you do not need to answer every question, and this is not an exhaustive list.	Current situation Use the questions but also your own thoughts and feelings about the space. Ensure you note whether this is a strength or weakness of the space		Possible action points to improve sensory experience of this space. Jot any initial thoughts on possible actions to improve the space.
What can you see? (Visual) • What can you see? Is there too much on the walls? Too little? • Does the space feel visually calm or busy? Does this change at different points in the day? • What are the paint and colour choices in the room? • Does this area feel spacious or cramped? • Does it feel like an organised or chaotic space? • How is the lighting? • How much natural light is there? • Are fluorescent lights flickering? • Are projectors using white or purple light? • Is there reflection of light on certain surfaces?			

Prompt questions (cont.)	Current situation (cont.)	Possible action points (cont.)
How can you move around in the space? (Proprioception) • Can children move freely in the space or is it crowded with anyone in? • Are there any obstructions to movement and flow around the room? • What moveable objects/furniture are in the room? • Does this change with different times of the day? • Are there any one-way or queuing systems in place? • Are there different zones for different types of movement?		
What can you hear? (Auditory) • What can you hear? How much does this vary at different points in the day? • Is there a school bell? How does this sound in this space? • Are there any sounds (for example, mains hum) from equipment (for example, servers or air conditioning units) in the space? • When the space is full, how does it sound if everyone is chatting? Is there anything to absorb the noise (for example, curtains, blinds, carpets, ceiling sound dampers) • How are the acoustics in the room? Is there an echo in the room? • Can you hear noises from other areas?		

Prompt questions (cont.)	Current situation (cont.)	Possible action points (cont.)
What can you feel? (Tactile, vestibular and proprioception) (N.B.: School uniform is considered separately on page 244) • When the space is full, does it feel squashed/overcrowded or is there a sense of space? Are students likely to bump into each other? • As students move about the space, are there different textures for them to run their hands along? (for example, wood, carpet, plastic, metal) • What seating is available? Are there various options of varying comfort or movement levels? (for example, cushions/spinning chairs)		
What can you smell? (Olfactory) • How does the space smell? What smells are they (consider food, cleaning products, human scents)? • Do the smells change with the time of day? • Can you make any changes to the smell if you feel it is an issue for the space? • Do the windows open to allow the flow of fresh air? Is there a ventilation system in place for air exchange?		

A classroom audit: Prompt questions

In a school it might not be possible for one person to audit every classroom, but if teachers are allocated particular rooms, it would be useful if they could audit their own classroom as well as a classroom unfamiliar to them and vice versa. Different people will spot different things going on within the classroom so getting a variety of perspectives could be helpful. Involve the students in doing these classroom audits as they will spot things you don't. Perhaps it could be useful to carry out these audits in pairs.

Spend up to 30 minutes in a classroom sitting or standing in at least three different areas of the classroom. Note down any thoughts or observations about the following. Again, it would be a good idea to revisit these notes at different points in the day to see if anything changes; for example, light levels or smells.

Classroom Sensory Audit			
Date:		**Number of doors and windows to the classroom:**	
Who carried out the audit?		**Maximum occupancy of the classroom:**	
Classroom name and location information:		**Approx measurements if relevant (length, width and height):**	
Use of the classroom across the week – full time? Part time?		**Brief overview of contents of the space (include any soft furnishing such as carpets, curtains):**	
Prompt questions These are just questions to help stimulate your thoughts and perceptions of the space; you do not need to answer every question, and this is not an exhaustive list.	**Current situation** Use the questions but also your own thoughts and feelings about the space. Ensure you note whether this is a strength or weakness of the space.		**Possible action points to improve sensory experience of this space. N.B.: Jot down any initial thoughts on possible actions to improve the space.**
What can you see? (Visual) • What can you see? Is there too much on the walls? Too little? • What are the paint and colour choices in the room? • Does the space feel visually calm or busy? Does this change at different points in the day? • Does this area feel spacious or cramped? • Does it feel like an organised or chaotic space? • How is the lighting? • How much natural light is there? Is it a light or dark space? • What is the view out of the window like? • Are fluorescent lights flickering? • Is there a reflection of light on certain surfaces?			

Prompt questions (cont.)	Current situation (cont.)	Possible action points (cont.)
How does the layout in the classroom affect movement and being in the space? • Can children move freely in the classroom or is it crowded with anyone in? • Do children have designated spaces? • Are there any obstructions to movement and flow around the room? • What moveable objects/furniture are there in the room? • Does this change with different times of the day? • Are there any one- way or queuing systems in place? • Are there different zones for maintaining regulation? For example, calm down zone (dark den), activate/wake up/fiddle zone. • Are there alternative seating options such as wobble stools or wobble cushions, or stretchy bands on chair legs to bounce feet on? • Are there different zones children could utilise in the classroom if they need a movement or sensory break? • Is there the option of solo 'workstation' desks at the side of the classroom or desks with pop-up privacy partitions for children who want to focus?		
What can you hear? (Auditory) • What can you hear? How much does this vary at different points in the day? • Is there a school bell? How does this sound in this space? • Are there any sounds (for example, mains hum) from equipment (for example, lights, servers or air conditioning units) in the space?		

Prompt questions (cont.)	Current situation (cont.)	Possible action points (cont.)
• When the classroom is full, how does it sound if everyone is chatting? Is there anything to absorb the noise (for example, curtains, blinds, carpets, ceiling sound dampers)? • What general classroom noises can occur – central heating pipes, fans, creaky chairs, scrape of chairs on floors, drawers/cupboards closing? Can any of them be adjusted if needed (for example, pads on feet of chairs)? • How are the acoustics in the room? Is there an echo in the room? • Can you hear noises from other classrooms or corridors? Does this change significantly if the door is open or closed?		
What can you feel? (Tactile) (N.B.: School uniform is considered separately on page 244) • When the classroom is full, does it feel squashed/overcrowded or is there a sense of space? Are children likely to bump elbows or work when sitting in certain table/chair configurations? • As children move about the space, are there different textures for them to run their hands along (for example, wood, carpet, plastic, metal)? • How do the chairs feel to sit in? Do they have backs? • Are the writing surfaces/tables smooth or rough? Are there opportunities for children to have angled writing surfaces?		
What can you smell? (Olfactory) • How does the classroom smell? What smells are they (consider food, cleaning products, human scents)? • Do the smells change with the time of day? • Can you make any changes to the smell if you feel it is an issue for the space? • Do the windows open to allow fresh air?		

Copyright material from Alice Hoyle and Tessa Hyde (2025), *Becoming a Sensory Aware School*, Routledge

You may want to consider developing a rating tool for each space. We have provided an example one below. It is important to acknowledge there will be limitations on the classroom environment that may be outside of your control, such as the size of the room and budget to change things. However, that shouldn't impact the development of a scoring scale such as the one below.

Sample Sensory Classroom Score

4 – The room still feels calm, light, airy and spacious, even when at capacity. The walls, floors and surfaces are decorated in calm colours, with careful selection of displays. There is a wide variety of sensory seating options and sensory inputs available, ensuring all students can find a comfortable and stimulating learning environment tailored to their needs. Natural light is maximised, and artificial lighting is gentle and non-flickering. Noise levels are consistently managed to minimise distractions. Ambient noise from elsewhere is soothing and not distracting.

3 – The classroom is organised and has some elements of calm and light, but may feel slightly crowded or less spacious at capacity. The decoration includes calming colours, but the balance between stimulating and calming visual inputs isn't always maintained. Sensory seating options are limited, with a few available choices. Natural light and noise control are somewhat addressed, but may not be optimised for sensory needs.

2 – The room has minimal attention to sensory needs. It may feel cramped or overly busy when full, with limited calming colours or sensory-friendly decorations. Sensory seating options and inputs are scarce or not thoughtfully integrated. Lighting is primarily artificial, and there may be occasional issues with noise levels or acoustics, making the environment less conducive to focused learning for sensory-sensitive individuals.

1 – The classroom lacks sensory awareness in its design. It feels crowded and overstimulating when at capacity, with bright or harsh colours and cluttered spaces. There are no specific sensory seating options or sensory inputs provided. Natural lighting is overlooked, and artificial lighting may be harsh or glaring. Noise levels can be distracting, and little effort is made to control acoustics, challenging students with sensory sensitivities.

The bare minimum audit

It is really important that children are involved in the auditing, so we also provide an example of a 'Student-led School Sensory Survey' on the next page which can also help save teacher time. You may find that you do not have the time or capacity to do whole scale audits, so as a minimum for auditing the sensory spaces across the school, you need to be able to answer the following questions:

- How do the children/staff using a particular space feel about that room?
- What improvements to their sensory experience can they suggest?
- List any sensory improvements you can make to the space in order of priority, considering feasibility and budget. Go for the easy quick cheap wins wherever possible.

One easy idea, as mentioned earlier, to do this is to use a map of the school and ask students to colour code the rooms on the map with Red, Amber or Green for how sensory-friendly those spaces are, and use the findings to lead a discussion using the questions above.

A Student-led School Sensory Survey

Give the students copies of the 'Student-led School Sensory Survey' on clipboards if appropriate. Students can either move around the different spaces within the school and record how they feel in those spaces using the table. Alternatively, if that isn't an option, you could lead a group discussion on the sensory spaces around the school and either scribe for the students to capture their key points or task individual students with filling it in themselves.

Student-led School Sensory Survey

School Name:_____

Student Name:_____

Your school needs your help to find out how the different spaces across the school make you feel, and whether they are sensory-friendly or -unfriendly to you and why. You can either fill this sheet in on your own, with a group or get a member of staff to help capture your responses on the table below.

Think about things like lighting, windows, noise and acoustics (the sound qualities in a space; for example, echoey), temperature and airflow, colour, space, furniture, how it feels when full or empty of people.

You can cover the best and worst classrooms, corridors, school hall, entrance hall and reception area, corridors, stairwells, sports halls and so on. You don't need to do every room in the school, just the ones that feel most sensory-friendly or -unfriendly to you.

Please give us as much information as possible to help us understand why they make you feel that way. **Remember to think about how the space affects these main senses – hearing, sight, touch, smell and movement.** (Taste or interoception are not included here because these aren't really relevant to spaces!)

👍 School spaces I like being in and why (Sensory-friendly)	👎 School spaces I don't like being in and why (Sensory-unfriendly)
👍 I like… …because…	👎 I don't like… …because…
👍 I like… …because…	👎 I don't like… …because…

Copyright material from Alice Hoyle and Tessa Hyde (2025), *Becoming a Sensory Aware School*, Routledge

👍 I like…	👎 I don't like…
…because…	…because…
👍 I like…	👎 I don't like…
…because…	…because…
👍 I like…	👎 I don't like…
…because…	…because…

Copyright material from Alice Hoyle and Tessa Hyde (2025), *Becoming a Sensory Aware School*, Routledge

Older students may also quite like be involved in the creation of their own version of a survey with their school-specific prompts to consider. You could also direct students to complete 'A sensory audit of a school day' found in Chapter 6 on page 178 to help give you further insights into critical periods in a school day for your students. The padlet link in 'Further reading and resources' on page 273 also includes some classroom and school audits. Allow students and staff to experiment with the ones they prefer.

Ideas to improve sensory spaces across the school

We know schools can't be knocked to the ground and rebuilt, but we wanted to provide a range of simple practical modifications you can make to improve your school sensory environment. A lot of these suggestions can be implemented at a low cost or are even free.

For example:

Dining halls

- Utilise natural lighting where possible to create a warm, inviting atmosphere. Keep the overhead lights off and the blinds up as much as possible.
- Arrange tables to offer communal eating areas and quieter, more secluded spots for those who may prefer to eat away from others, particularly if they are messy eaters who need more support.
- Consider the use of a classroom for small groups of children who cannot manage the size, noise levels, smells, etc., of the large dining hall.
- Consider playing soft, calming background music to create a relaxing ambience.
- Consider installing acoustic panels to reduce noise levels, making the space more comfortable for everyone.

Assembly halls

- Designate quiet areas with softer lighting and reduced noise for sensory breaks.
- Provide sensory tools such as noise cancelling headphones, fiddle items, wobble cushions, etc., to help manage sensory input during assemblies and performances.
- Offer a variety of seating options, including bean bags and floor cushions, for comfort and choice, or sitting on the end of a row, sitting at the back on a chair/bench.

Drama/dance studios

- Allow your group to choose the preferred lighting for the session, and change it up to change the energy in the room. For example, dim lighting can make some students feel relaxed or even lethargic, but pop on the disco lights and get a mid-lesson energy boost.
- Use curtains to cover up the mirrors when not in use; this has an added bonus of sound dampening in the space too.
- Ensure there's a variety of flexible seating options and clear, defined movement areas. Some students may find comfort in having a personal space marked out on the floor, giving them a sense of security and boundary.

The sports hall

- Rather than spend a whole lesson in a dark cold sports hall, could the warm up or cool down be outside first?
- Regularly clean and ventilate the space to improve the smell and consider investing in high-quality air purifiers.
- Install sound-absorbing materials, such as acoustic panels or foam, on walls and ceilings to help manage the sound. Soft floor mats can also help absorb sound and provide a more comfortable surface for certain exercises.
- Hold small group sessions in a different space if the hall is too overwhelming or if the students have co-ordination difficulties.

Classrooms

- Use adjustable and lamp lighting to mimic natural light and reduce glare.
- Arrange seating for both group work and individual, quiet spaces.
- Set up quiet corners with sensory tools like fidget toys and soft seating, weighted blankets, headphones for sensory breaks.
- Ensure visual displays are clear with calm neutral colours and not overly stimulating to maintain a calm environment.
- Where possible, try to minimise clutter in the room. One strategy for more messy teachers (Alice is one!) is utilising 'DOOM' boxes/drawers/cupboard (Didn't Organise Only Moved) where the surfaces are clear and the chaos is contained in one specific place!
- Install sound-dampening materials to minimise echo and noise – use foam pads on the bottom of chairs and tables and pencil pots to reduce scraping noises.
- Consider if there is any furniture that isn't needed in the classroom that can be moved elsewhere. As much as possible a sense of space really helps.

Corridors

- Implement directional arrows to streamline movement across the school and reduce congestion.
- Use softer lighting to create a more calming environment.
- Incorporate murals or calming colours to provide a visual boost as students move between lessons.
- Consider adding interactive, sensory-friendly wall elements that students can engage with.

Playgrounds

- Create distinct zones for active play, quiet time and sensory engagement with nature.
- Develop sensory gardens with a variety of plants, textures and scents to explore.
- Creating a small woodland or area of tall bushes for outdoor learning spaces offers students different ways of engaging with their learning and with nature.
- Outdoor play equipment and trails for climbing, balancing, hanging from arms or upside down and swinging or spinning. Offering monkey bars for children to hang upside down on safely is particularly useful for those that need vestibular input. While secondary schools don't tend to have play equipment, having a range of walls and benches for seating, and rails for hanging off/leaning on can be beneficial for teenagers. Opening up the school gym at playtimes or lunchtimes can help students who need movement to regulate.

An important note about the school bell

When considering the needs of auditory-sensitive students, the loud and sudden sounds of school bells and fire alarms can be very difficult for some students. It's essential to explore alternatives or adjustments that minimise distress without compromising safety. For school bells, options like visual signals (flashing lights) or softer, gradual sounding alerts can provide a less startling cue for class transitions. Fire alarms, while non-negotiable for safety, can be managed by preparing students with auditory sensitivities through regular drills, using noise cancelling headphones, and having a clear, practised protocol to help them feel more secure and less overwhelmed during an actual alarm.

School toilets

- Use gentle, natural-smelling cleaning products to avoid olfactory discomfort and ensure the space is well-ventilated.
- Provide clear signs and ensure lighting is bright, yet soft.
- Use materials that minimise echoes and reduce noise.
- Install quieter fixtures where possible; for example, install automatic flushes and taps to operate more quietly.
- Offer alternatives to hand driers which are a sensory trigger for many children by offering paper towels or washable fabric roll towels that you pull down. To reduce paper waste, show them the Joe Smith Tedx Talk on 'How to use a paper towel' (on YouTube), which advocates shaking off as much water as possible first, then only using ONE paper towel folded over to thoroughly dry one hand and then the other. Challenge students to only use one paper towel wherever possible.
- Ensure that at least some cubicles in the school have floor to ceiling doors and walls to reduce sounds and increase a sense of privacy and safety. These should be unlockable from the outside in case of emergency.

An important note about school toilets

Toilets are an eternal issue for schools, and many schools do not realise the impact of their poor provision on so many of their pupils, particularly those with sensory needs. Many children and young people, especially those with SEND, will simply not use them and withhold until they get home and this can commonly cause longer-term bladder and bowel issues.

People with issues with interoception often don't feel thirst, so they regularly dehydrate causing constipation or urinary tract infections. These children and young people also often don't feel the urge to use the toilet, causing accidents. Sometimes this lack of urge is caused by them withholding for so long they have damaged the nerves in the bladder and bowel so they no longer have any sensation. It can then be a long and tricky journey back to regaining sensation and continence.

Children and young people with such issues will need to be encouraged and reminded to drink and use the toilet regularly, and should be issued with toilet passes so they can go to the toilet at any point, especially during lessons when it might feel safer and more relaxing for them to go. If toilets are locked during lesson times (a practice we strongly disagree with), these children should have a key.

Toilets often don't feel safe for children to use, and in order to relax the muscles to urinate or defecate, you have to feel safe. If at all possible, schools should offer at least some 'safe home from home'-type cubicles with floor to ceiling walls, containing a toilet, sink, waste paper bin and bin for menstrual products and sufficient ventilation to avoid smells, and facilities to dry hands. These 'safe' toilets should be located in quieter areas of the school (not by Reception, for example) and monitored regularly by staff for cleanliness and behaviour management. These toilets should be available in addition to any disabled toilet provision.

We really like the School Toilet Charter from the Bladder and Bowel Charity ERIC https://eric.org.uk/school-toilet-charter/ and would urge all schools to adopt these principles.

School toilet charter

Access to clean, appropriately stocked toilets whenever the need arises, is a fundamental human right and necessary for good health and wellbeing. This reflects the United Nations Convention on the Rights of the Child (UNCRC), which upholds all children's rights to their best interests being of primary consideration, to healthy development, to participation in decision making, to privacy, to special care and support if they have a disability and to education. This School Toilet Charter is designed to assist schools in meeting these rights.

All schools should provide:

1. Unrestricted access to a toilet, whenever the need arises. This means no school should have a policy of not allowing learners to use the toilet during lesson times.
2. Adequate numbers of facilities for all, which ensure privacy.
3. Dedicated gender-neutral toilets, or female and male toilet cubicles, properly equipped, for users with additional needs. This includes provision of appropriate waste bins and integral washbasins.
4. Properly designed toilet and washroom facilities, suitable for the range of anticipated users, with adequate lighting, ventilation, fixtures and fittings.
5. Hot water, ideally from mixer taps, with adequate provision of soap and hand drying facilities.
6. Toilet tissue dispensers provided at a convenient height, replenished as needed throughout the day.
7. An effective toilet cleaning/inspection regime to ensure adequate standards of hygiene, behaviour and cleanliness, throughout hours of usage.
8. A published school toilet management policy approved by school governors and learners and communicated to all learners, parents/carers and staff.
9. Open access to water throughout the day for all learners, unless inappropriate (e.g. in science labs, computer suites etc)
10. A child friendly comments/complaints/suggestions procedure, for learners, parents/carers and staff to communicate toilet concerns or grievances to the head teacher and/or school governors.

Copyright: Bladder & Bowel UK and ERIC, The Children's Bowel & Bladder Charity (2022), shared with permission.

Considerations for including a School Sensory Room

Designing an effective School Sensory Room involves careful consideration of what the aim is, who will use it, what will be included and how it will be used. The term 'sensory room' covers a myriad of possibilities. Settings often adopt a generic approach with a little of everything; this can lead to a room which does not really meet the needs of any of the children for whom it is being made. Careful discussion, thought and planning at this stage, in conjunction with Occupational Therapists, can help this to be a well-used resource within the school for the benefit of the intended users.

Some basic components could include options for a variety of tactile experiences through differing fabrics and textures, a serene corner with dimmable lights and cosy bean bags, weighted blankets and lap pads for relaxation, and auditory aids like soothing sound headphones. Visual stimuli, such as bubble towers, enhance the room's calming effect. Sensory tents provide private, calming spaces for overstimulated students, while wobble seats, peanut balls and therapy balls encourage movement and concentration through gentle motion. The size and shape of the room will direct the level of equipment that can be included, as it is important to ensure there is enough space in the room without it becoming too full and distracting. All of the sensory resources mentioned previously can be used easily by students with an adult, without the need for specific training but a generic knowledge of the aims of using the room. Clear usage guidelines, and possibly scheduled times, can help manage access, ensuring that every student who needs it can benefit from this space for their sensory regulation. This means schools will need a different room for a 'time out space' for unscheduled drop-in visits. The time out space can also include some resources for sensory regulation, but needs to have a focus on calming and soothing; for example, weighted blankets.

If considering the option of a more complex, therapeutically based School Sensory Room, then this will be more expensive and require considerable advice and planning. Specific sensory equipment such as swings, offering vital vestibular input, require careful risk assessment to ensure structural support for dynamic use and safe use (space to swing without hitting walls/furniture, etc.), with soft impact-absorbing materials on the floor. Conducting regular maintenance is essential. The use of these more specialised rooms will require input from Occupational Therapists and specific staff training and will need careful supervision to avoid misuse.

Creating a School Sensory Room involves selecting a variety of tools and equipment to cater to different sensory needs. Some of the items on the list below could also be used in individual classrooms or across the school depending on need.

Sensory Room resources

This is not an exhaustive list, but covers some of the key items that might be included in a sensory room. More detail on the pros and cons of some of these sensory tools are covered in Chapter 5 on page 106–113:

- **Sensory lighting** – offers variations in colour and intensity
- **Bubble towers** – tall, transparent columns filled with water and colourful, moving bubbles and sometimes plastic fish
- **Fiber optic lights** – lights on narrow fibres that can change colours and intensity
- **Lighting projectors** – display colourful galaxy star systems on walls or ceilings
- Sensory tents/dark dens, enclosed spaces that offer a quiet, dimly lit environment for individuals seeking a break from sensory overload
- **Tactile stations** – interactive areas equipped with various textures and materials to explore
- **Bowl of fidgets** – sometimes known as concentration aids
- **Bean bags** – large, soft, flexible seating options that conform to the body's shape
- **Spinning seats** – chairs designed to spin, providing vestibular stimulation that can help regulate sensory needs
- **Therapy balls** (including peanut balls) – inflatable equipment used for a variety of activities that improve balance, co-ordination and sensory integration
- **Sensory swing** – a swing designed to provide vestibular input
- **Weighted items** – such as blankets, lap pads, vests or shoulder weights that can offer deep pressure input, simulating a calming hug.

When considering sensory resources to add to a sensory room, it's important to balance the sensory benefits with practical considerations such as safety, maintenance and the diverse needs of students.

Reflection questions for a sensory room

If your school has a sensory room	If your school doesn't have a sensory room
• What's in it? • Who designed and developed it? • Which children was it developed for? • What are the rules about using the space? • Is its intended use clear? • If it is used as a 'time out' room, is it available when needed? • Is someone responsible for checking and maintaining equipment?	• If you don't have a sensory room, can you create one? • How will you design it? • What will you include? • Who will you work with to ensure it meets needs? • Is there potential for a bookable room and a room for ad hoc use?

A note about sensory circuits

Sensory circuits are structured sequences of physical activities designed to help students regulate, improve focus and get ready for learning. These circuits typically involve three stages: 'alerting' activities that wake up the body, such as jumping or spinning; 'organising' tasks that demand balance and concentration, like walking on a beam; and 'calming' exercises that help to settle the nervous system, such as deep pressure or stretching. Some schools have painted examples of sensory circuits in their corridors on the walls and floors.

Pros and Cons of Sensory Circuits	
Pros:	**Cons:**
• Supports self regulation • Improves attention and behaviour • Proactive approach to managing sensory processing issues • Better engagement with learning • Effective way to increase engagement with their environment and daily activities	• Requires time, space, and sometimes specific equipment, which may not always be readily available • May not meet unique targeted needs effectively, as often offered as a fixed universal approach • May need ongoing adjustments • Students may not engage with the activities in a way that promotes the desired sensory regulation, if guidance is not given, potentially leading to overstimulation rather than calming

In summary, sensory circuits can be a useful tool for supporting students, but they need thoughtful implementation and ongoing management to be beneficial and mitigate any drawbacks.

Quick wins and planned investment to improve the school sensory environment

Having explored some sensory improvements to school specific spaces, now let's consider more generally features such as light, visual ambience, sound, temperature, smell and ventilation, with tips divided into quick wins that are low cost and easy to implement, alongside longer-term investments that could be considered should funds be available and needs require.

Summary of Possible Improvements to School Sensory Environments		
	Quick Wins	**Longer-Term Investments and Considerations**
Lighting	**Maximise natural light**: Rearrange classroom layouts to ensure desks and activity areas benefit from natural light. Keep windows clear of obstructions, and use light, translucent curtains or blinds to diffuse light without dimming the room. **Upgrade to LED bulbs**: Swap out older, inefficient bulbs for LED options. LEDs offer a brighter, cleaner light and are available in a range of colour temperatures to suit different needs and times of the day. **Introduce task lighting**: Provide individual lamps or task lighting for specific activities or reading areas. **Implement colour temperature variation**: Use warmer lights (lower colour temperature) in relaxation or reading areas to create a calming atmosphere, and cooler lights (higher colour temperature) in areas requiring focus and alertness. **Technology**: Ensuring the colour and typeface of the screen on interactive whiteboards is neurodivergent-friendly.	**Regular maintenance and upgrades:** Establish a maintenance schedule for lighting systems to ensure they remain working effectively and not flickering. Upgrade when possible. **Install dimmable lighting systems:** Investing in dimmable LED lighting systems allows for adjustable light levels throughout the day, catering to different activities and reducing energy use. **Skylights and light tubes:** For areas lacking in natural light, consider installing skylights or light tubes to channel daylight from the roof into interior spaces, brightening them naturally. **Use reflective surfaces wisely:** Position reflective surfaces such as whiteboards to enhance light distribution without causing glare. Light-coloured walls and ceilings can help reflect light more evenly throughout the space.
Visual Ambience	**Clutter-free spaces**: Organise and declutter classrooms to create a more spacious and focused learning environment. Use storage solutions that keep materials accessible but out of sight when not in use. **Natural elements**: Incorporate plants and natural materials to bring a sense of calm and connection to nature into the classroom. Even small tabletop plants or a classroom garden can positively affect mood as well as air quality. **Student art**: Brighten up a space visually using carefully selected student artwork.	**Colour psychology:** Utilise colour psychology to paint walls and decorate spaces. Soothing colours like soft blues, greens and muted tones can enhance concentration and reduce anxiety, while vibrant colours may stimulate energy and creativity in areas like art rooms. **Art:** Collaborate with local artists and the school community to provide artwork, sculptures or installations to provide visual interest across the school

Acoustics	**Soft furnishings and textiles:** Floor and window coverings in classrooms and corridors can help absorb sound. Adding cushions in reading corners or libraries can make a difference. **Door sweeps and seals:** Installing sweeps and seals on classroom doors can help minimise noise leakage from hallways and between rooms. **Quiet zones:** Designate certain areas of the school as 'quiet zones' during specific times. These areas can provide a respite from the busyness of school and are particularly beneficial for students who are sensitive to noise. **Noise rules and signage:** Implement and enforce noise-level rules in certain areas, using signage to remind students and staff of these guidelines. Sometimes, a gentle reminder is all that's needed to maintain a quieter environment.	**Relocation of servers and other noisy equipment to spaces unused by students:** Many schools seem to have their servers in the SEND intervention rooms which can cause a high level of distractibility and distress for staff and students using the room. This equipment needs to be away from working spaces. **Regular maintenance of electronics and plumbing and heating systems:** Noisy infrastructure systems, such as the buzz from a computer fan or the glug of a radiator can contribute significantly to background noise. Regular maintenance and upgrades can reduce these sounds, improving the overall auditory environment. **Acoustic panels:** Mount acoustic panels or foam tiles on walls, especially in areas where echo is a problem, like sports halls or music rooms. These panels are designed to absorb sound and are often easy to install. **Landscaping for noise reduction:** Use outdoor landscaping strategically to block external noise. Trees, shrubs and hedges can act as natural sound barriers, reducing traffic noise and playground sounds. **Soundproofing construction materials:** When renovating or building new spaces, use soundproofing materials in walls, ceilings and floors to prevent sound transmission. **Upgrade windows and doors:** Replace thin, single-pane windows with double- or triple-glazed units to reduce external noise. Similarly, upgrading to solid core doors can help contain noise within or outside a room.
Temperature	**Use fans:** Portable fans can significantly improve air circulation, making rooms feel cooler in warmer months without the need for extensive air conditioning units. **Adjustable window coverings:** Use blinds or curtains to control the amount of sunlight entering a room, reducing heat gain during warmer months and retaining heat during colder ones. **Strategic ventilation:** Open windows in early morning or late afternoon when the outdoor temperature is pleasant to allow fresh air to circulate, reducing the need for mechanical heating or cooling. **Dress code flexibility:** Allow for seasonal adjustments in uniform policy and dress codes, enabling students and staff to wear clothing that is comfortable for the current indoor temperature. **Use of insulating materials:** Simple measures like draft stoppers under doors or insulating films on windows can help maintain consistent temperatures in classrooms without major renovations. **Regular maintenance schedule:** Ensure that all heating and cooling equipment is regularly serviced and maintained to keep it running efficiently and effectively.	**Solar control window films:** Applying solar control films to existing windows can reduce solar heat gain, minimising the need for air conditioning while still allowing natural light. **Window upgrades:** Replacing old windows with double- or triple-glazed units can significantly improve thermal efficiency, keeping the heat in during winter and out during summer. **Automated thermostats:** Smart thermostats can optimise energy use and maintain comfortable temperatures by adjusting settings based on the time of day, occupancy and external weather conditions. **Thermal insulation:** Enhancing wall, floor and ceiling insulation can significantly improve a building's ability to maintain a steady temperature, reducing the need for active heating and cooling. **Green roofing or roof insulation:** Installing a green roof or improving roof insulation can reduce heat absorption in summer and heat loss in winter, leading to more stable indoor temperatures.

Smell and Ventilation	**Regular cleaning:** Implement a regular cleaning schedule that includes the use of non-toxic, fragrance-free cleaning products. This helps minimise odours and ensures indoor air quality is not compromised by harsh chemicals. **Open windows:** Whenever weather and safety permit, open windows to allow fresh air to circulate through classrooms and common areas, naturally diluting and dispersing indoor pollutants and odours. **Indoor plants:** Introduce indoor plants that are known for their air-purifying qualities, such as spider plants, peace lilies and snake plants. They can absorb pollutants and add a fresh, natural scent to the air.	**Install/maintain ventilation systems:** Invest in modern, efficient HVAC systems that monitor air quality and can bring in a continuous supply of filtered fresh air from outside and remove stale air and indoor pollutants while minimising heating loss. Keep the ducts clean to keep them efficient. If designing a new building, ensure ventilation is integrated into the design. **Localised air purifiers:** Place portable air purifiers in areas prone to odours or poor ventilation, such as bathrooms, locker rooms and kitchens. These can help filter out pollutants and improve air quality. **Green roof or living walls:** Consider installing a green roof or living walls within the school. These features not only improve air quality, but also add to the aesthetic appeal and can serve as educational tools for students. **Sustainable building materials:** When renovating or building new spaces, opt for low-VOC (volatile organic compound) and non-toxic materials for paint, flooring and furniture. This reduces off-gassing and improves overall air quality.

By balancing these quick wins with strategic longer-term investments, schools can create environments that are not only healthier, more energy-efficient and sustainable, but also more pleasant, comfortable and conducive to learning. This will support students' and teachers' sensory needs and enhance the overalleducational experience. Remember, the key is to maintain flexibility and adaptability to accommodate the diverse needs of all school occupants.

Action Feasibility Assessment

Sample Action Feasibility Assessment from Sensory Audit of Classroom or other School Spaces	
Possible action from the Audits:	Wall displays are too busy and cluttered.
Possible costs?	New calmer backing paper £10 and reduce the number of display boards in the classroom.
How long will this action take?	An afternoon.
Who will carry out this action?	Teaching Assistant/Teacher (possible caretaker help with removal of boards).
How easy is this change to make? 1 – Easy; 2 – Achievable with some effort; 3 – Difficult	2
How beneficial is this change for the majority of the users of the space? 1 – Very beneficial; 2 – Some benefit; 3 – Not very beneficial	2
What are the possible unintended negative consequences to making this change on the space?	Children becoming unsettled at the change? Concern from teaching staff about where to locate key visual content.
How can these possible consequences be mitigated?	Work with children to choose backing paper and what they want in displays. Teachers considering alternative display options (for example, back of cupboard door or key visuals saved on desktop to show on screen when needed).
Rank the action based on previous answers. 1 – Do this action within the next half term; 2 – Keep action under review if time or funds permit; 3 – Don't do this action	1
Any other relevant information:	Consider implications for school corridors too.

Blank Action Feasibility Assessment from Sensory Audit of Classroom or other School Spaces

Possible action from the Audit:	
Possible costs?	
How long will this action take?	
Who will carry out this action?	
How easy is this change to make? 1 – Easy; 2 – Achievable with some effort; 3 – Difficult	
How beneficial is this change for the majority of the users of the space? 1 – Very beneficial; 2 – Some benefit; 3 – Not very beneficial	
What are the possible unintended negative consequences to making this change on the space?	
How can these possible consequences be mitigated?	
Rank the action based on previous answers. 1 – Do this action within the next half term; 2 – Keep action under review if time or funds permit; 3 – Don't do this action	
Any other relevant information:	

Evaluate your action feasibility assessments for those that provide the maximum benefit for the least effort and cost, then implement those ones first. Revisit these every half term for the next cycle of sensory changes you wish to make.

Use the information provided in this chapter as well as the audit tools to start to think about your overall action plan for making sensory improvements to your school environment. The blank action plan on page 271 of Chapter 9 can also help you with this. Prioritise the quick wins and make a longer-term plan for sustained improvement and investment on further sensory environment changes to benefit all.

> **Reflection questions for Chapter 7**
>
> 1. Was there anything that surprised you in this chapter about the school environment?
> 2. Have you had a realisation about a particular room in your school from this chapter?
> 3. What are your quick wins/bare minimum approaches you can take after reading this chapter?
> 4. Do you have a plan to start this process?
> 5. Will you involve your student voice as part of this process?

Chapter eight

WHOLE SCHOOL APPROACH TO BECOMING A SENSORY AWARE SCHOOL

The importance of a whole school approach

Adopting a whole school approach to sensory wellbeing is essential because it ensures that our unique sensory preferences are recognised, and our sensory environment considered (**sensory awareness**) leading to our needs being better supported (**sensory inclusion**), and thus develops our **sensory wellbeing**, integrating it across every aspect of school life. By including sensory-friendly practices into the school's culture, policies and everyday routines, this creates inclusive and supportive environments for learning and overall wellbeing. A whole school approach involves all stakeholders in the school community – teachers, staff, students and parents, working together to acknowledge and support diverse sensory needs.

It may help to consider the diagram on the next page where all the crucial elements for a whole school approach for Sensory Aware Schools are noted.

A WHOLE SCHOOL APPROACH FOR SENSORY AWARE SCHOOLS

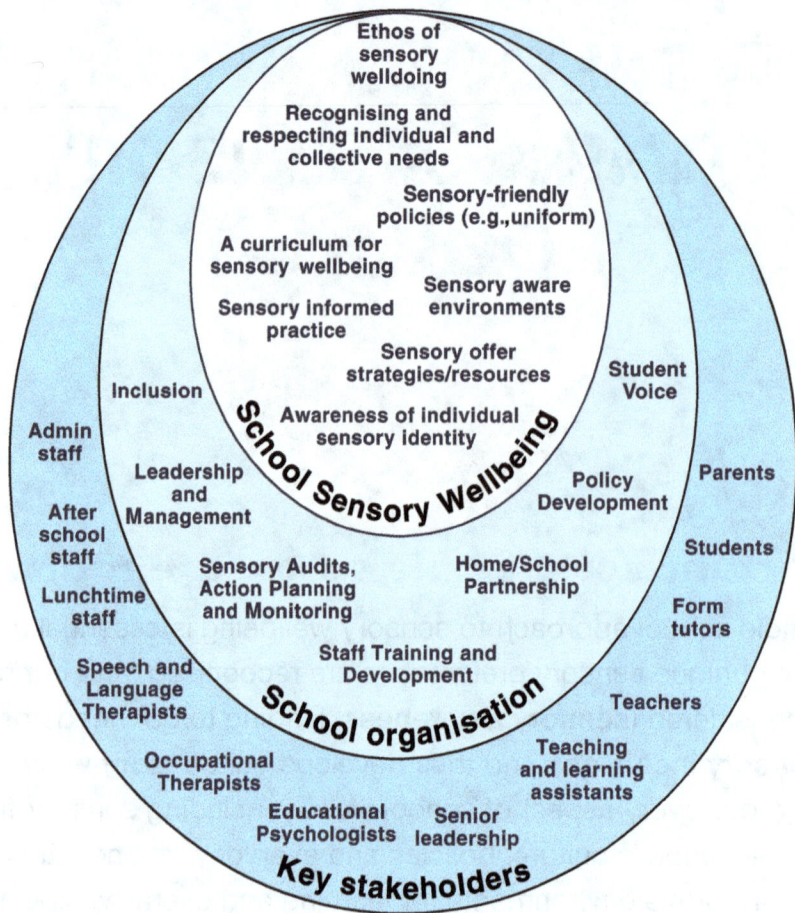

Case study: Sensory inclusion at The Springfields Academy

At The Springfields Academy, a large all-through special school for children with Autism and speech, language and communication needs, the commitment to creating a sensory-friendly environment is evident across the school site and school day. Recognised for its inclusive approach to sensory wellbeing, the academy has developed its learning spaces to cater to the diverse needs of its students. The academy operates on a 'Therapy First' principle and has its own unique Therapy House which children can access throughout the day. Classrooms undergo regular monitoring by the Head of Therapy who checks that the environment is conducive to learning and Autism-friendly. The light and airy classrooms have carefully selected minimal displays and offer a wide range of sensory aids, such as wobble stools and cushions, pods and ball chairs and concentrators. Fidget toys are referred to as 'concentrators' by the school because they feel these tools are often misunderstood due to negative connotations with their name, implying they are distracting. The school recognises that sensory stimulation and feedback can enhance learners' focus, hence they call them 'concentrators' to emphasise their role in aiding concentration in the classroom.

The Springfields Academy has also integrated multisensory learning across its curriculum. In particular, staff use concrete resources or manipulatives to help support abstract concepts. Activities such as sensory bags and funky fingers to develop fine motor skills and hand eye co-ordination are incorporated into the timetable. To reinforce the importance of a focus on sensory as part of a healthy lifestyle, The Springfields Academy has reimagined its physical education curriculum to become dedicated Physical and Sensory lessons. These are led by a specialist team of PE teachers and supported by an OT. The school even has their sports hall named the "Physical and Sensory Department" in large letters outside the building to really reinforce the importance of sensory. These sessions are timetabled and are designed to promote physical health and development. Activities, such as rebound therapy and sensory circuits, are tailored to engage different senses and support motor skills development, providing a holistic approach to student physical and sensory wellbeing. In addition, the school offers a sensory-friendly uniform by offering adaptations to its uniform to meet each student's individual sensory profile. Through these approaches, The Springfields Academy is clear about the value of sensory inclusion in education and how it enables students to thrive.

Reflection questions

- How could your school adopt a 'Therapy First' approach?
- How far is your school from The Springfields Academy approach?
- Are any of these ideas adaptable to mainstream schools?
- Are there any ideas in this case study you would like to adopt for your school?

Revisiting the Self Assessment Tool

The rest of this chapter will focus in more detail on the key areas mentioned within the Self Assessment Tool (pages 19–23 of Chapter 2) that haven't already been covered in detail elsewhere in the book, including:

- School values and ethos
- Leadership and management
- Policy development
- Budgeting and resourcing
- The school day
- Uniform
- Staff role and responsibilities
- Behavioural approaches
- Staff training and development needs
- Supporting staff sensory needs
- Student voice
- Parents and carers
- Wider partnerships.

Any remaining key areas from the Self Assessment Tool are covered in the following locations:

- Planning and implementation (Chapter 9)
- Reasonable adjustments and supporting student sensory needs (Chapter 5)
- Curriculum and learning opportunities (Chapter 6)
- Sensory audits of the environment and a sensory-friendly school environment (Chapter 7)
- Sensory audits of the staff and students (Chapter 4).

The Self Assessment Tool is a vital starting point to adopting a whole school approach as it sets out the Core and Quality Standards schools must adopt in order to become a Sensory Aware School. We recommend you revisit this tool before reading this chapter.

School values and ethos

A whole school approach means having sensory wellbeing embedded across the school culture, so it can be helpful to highlight this commitment to sensory wellbeing in the school's ethos and values statements, as these statements say a lot about the setting and its approach. This will help truly embed sensory wellbeing across all aspects of school culture. Some examples of sensory school ethos statements are included below and can be adapted and personalised according to need:

- At our school, we embrace an inclusive learning environment where every student's sensory experiences are acknowledged and valued.
- We are committed to ensuring that sensory welldoing is at the heart of our educational approach, enabling every child to have their needs met and enhance their sensory wellbeing to enable them to fully access their learning.
- We are dedicated to creating a supportive environment that accommodates sensory differences, ensuring every student feels safe, respected and included.
- We are a Sensory Aware School/Sensory Inclusive School which means we aim to remove barriers and create equitable opportunities for all students, meeting their diverse sensory needs.
- We adopt common sensory approaches to meet the sensory needs of all students in our care.

You can also look at the Charter from page 14 of Chapter 2 or the Sensory Informed People and Practice box in Chapter 9, page 265 and The 12 Principles for Sensory Aware Schools box on page 269 of Chapter 9.

Leadership and management for Sensory Aware Schools

School leaders are absolutely crucial for developing a Sensory Aware School. This work can only succeed with a commitment from the top to prioritise sensory wellbeing as a fundamental aspect of the school's ethos, values and approach, and to ensure that all stakeholders are adopting sensory informed practice.

Leaders who show they recognise the importance of Sensory Aware Schools would aim to create a high-profile (ideally paid) role such as a "Sensory Wellbeing Champion". This position would not only reinforce the importance the school places on sensory wellbeing, but also provides a dedicated person for implementing strategies, training staff and serving as a point of contact for students, parents and wider professionals. The Sensory Wellbeing Champion could lead by example, advocating for sensory-friendly initiatives, and ensure that these practices are consistently applied across all levels of the school.

Schools should also establish a working group focused on sensory wellbeing consisting of key stakeholders. This could involve parents and carers, students, teaching assistants, SENDCOs and any staff with a keen interest in sensory wellbeing. In addition, there should be a school governor allocated an oversight role for scrutinising the implementation of sensory wellbeing approaches.

With strong leadership and a clear dedication to sensory awareness, schools can transform their schools into safe and calm sensory spaces where individuals are able to thrive and learn effectively, improving their wellbeing and educational attainment.

Policy development

It is important that schools consider adopting a Sensory Aware School Policy to document their commitment to sensory awareness and wellbeing. Ideally this should be developed by a working party of key stakeholders including, as a minimum, the Sensory Wellbeing Champion, the designated lead governor and the school SENDCO. You may wish to invite selected pupils and parents to be part of this development process as well. Revisit the Sensory Aware Schools Charter on page 14 of Chapter 2 as this may also help you develop your policy.

Here are some sample headings and points to help you develop you Sensory Aware School Policy:

Developing your Sensory Aware School Policy
Rationale: What is sensory wellbeing?

- Define what your school means by sensory wellbeing and why this policy is important.
- Add aims and objectives of what you are trying to do and why. For example: *"Sensory wellbeing refers to the state of feeling comfortable and balanced in relation to our school sensory environment. This is achieved through sensory welldoing – a deliberate and conscious effort to actively use personalised sensory strategies. This school aims to enhance sensory wellbeing through adjustments to the environment, offering individualised approaches and strategies and supporting an ethos of mutual respect for all sensory needs. Through embracing sensory wellbeing for everyone in our school we will create safer and calmer sensory-friendly spaces that enhance overall wellbeing ability to learn and attainment."*

Overview of sensory approaches at [School name]

- Set out some of the key strategies you have identified and implemented following your comprehensive audits of your school's sensory environment.

For example: *"We have identified and implemented strategies to make our classrooms, uniforms, routines, and overall school culture as sensory-friendly as possible. Key initiatives include:*
- *Using low-arousal visual displays in certain classrooms.*
- *Offering a variety of seating options to accommodate different sensory needs.*
- *Providing skin-kind uniform alternatives.*
- *Issuing sensory passports for students with specific needs.*
- *Implementing structured opportunities for movement/learning breaks.*
- *Strategically addressing stress points in the school day, such as staggered break times and the provision of movement break cards."*
- [Edit and add points specific to your school].

Ensuring sensory informed practice

Set out how your staff will adopt sensory informed practice.
Include information on:

- **Training and professional development:** List the training available to staff and how the policy ensures ongoing support and professional development in sensory awareness.
- **Roles and responsibilities in supporting students' sensory needs:** List the titles of the staff with responsibility for leading on sensory informed practice and how they will support students; for example, *"We have a Sensory Wellbeing Champion who is responsible for sensory wellbeing across the school and a SEND Sensory Specialist Key Worker who ensures that the students on the SEND register with sensory needs have these fully understood and met."*
- **Behaviour and reasonable adjustment:** State how you consider that behaviour arises as both a reaction to the environment and communication, and that staff are open to the possibility that there may be a sensory root for some behaviours; for example, *"We consider the possible sensory causes for overt behaviours and note these in behaviour logs to help improve and refine sensory supports for our students. Sensory accommodations are never treated as 'rewards' but as essential adjustments to facilitate curriculum access."*
- **Implementing strategies:** This policy should also consider how to balance the sensory needs across the entire school community. For example, *"Discreet fidget tools may be used during lessons, while more distracting*

items are reserved for designated break times, ensuring a conducive learning environment for all."
- **Staff sensory wellbeing:** Set out how your policy also supports staff sensory wellbeing; for example, *"We support our staff with their own sensory preferences by supporting room choices where possible, a sensory-friendly staff dress code, optional display and furniture layout and adaptations (for example, felt pads on chair legs), adaptive lighting options."*

Appendices: Audits and action plans

Include detailed appendices with classroom and whole school audit reports from Chapter 7, and the associated action plans and areas for development. The Policy could include:

- Findings from the audit tools in the section 'Your school's unique sensory environment', Chapter 7 (pages 207–220)
- Action Feasibility Assessment from Sensory Audit of Classroom or Other School Spaces from Chapter 7 (page 232)
- The Assess Plan Do Review Cycle action plan from Chapter 9 (page 271).

Resources and budget

Summarise the resources available to staff and how further resourcing and budgeting can be requested and implemented. Set out how the Sensory Aware School's budget is managed.

Integration with other policies

Set out how this policy integrates with other school policies. For example, *"This Sensory Aware School Policy is to be followed in conjunction with other key policies, including the SEND, Behaviour, and Mental Health and Wellbeing policies, ensuring a holistic approach to student support."*

Monitoring and evaluation

Set out how this policy is going to be monitored and evaluated. For example, *"This policy is subject to annual review by [Designated Person/Committee], incorporating feedback from the Sensory Aware Schools Working Group, which includes school leaders, parents and student representatives."*

Date

Date of next review [Insert date].

Budgeting and resourcing

It is important to think carefully about resource and budget allocation to your Sensory Aware School. Schools can often get carried away into purchasing lots of different and expensive physical sensory resources without thinking properly through their use and need. Your most valuable asset is your people, so prioritising investment in training and support for staff will go a long way to helping them to support students more effectively without as much need for physical resourcing. Budget- friendly options could be using some of the training ideas later on in this chapter for a twilight continuing professional development (CPD) session and supporting staff to carry out some of the Sensory Me activities from Chapter 4 (under 'Assessing your own sensory identity in more detail') and develop your sensory curriculum using some of the ideas in Chapter 6. You could purchase a range of professional publications about sensory needs for a staff library (see 'Further reading and resources' for a suggested list).

It's essential to strike a balance between immediate, cost-effective solutions and long-term investments that promote a sustainable sensory-friendly environment. Chapter 7 went into detail on some of these short- and longer-term options. Your starting point should always be the audits of both people and place and if you can't find a financial budget, then the resource of 'time' to staff to carry out these audits and research possible interventions will be beneficial. Where your budget allows, one key offer schools should consider investing in is Sensory Inclusive Schools membership (www.sensoryinclusiveschools.org) which offers online training and ongoing support for schools working on their sensory inclusion.

The school day

Sensory awareness should be considered throughout the whole school day including break times, lunchtimes, assemblies and student movement across the school. We need to think beyond the classroom experience and explore how the whole school day unfolds for each student (see the 'bottle of pop' example on page 44 of Chapter 3).

Consider the following:

- How are timetables planned and lessons paced to enable sensory balance across the day? (For example, a balance of stimulating and calmer activities.)
- Are natural movement breaks included to help regulate sensory needs? (For example, moving between different classrooms or collecting different equipment, including a 'learning break' or 'brain break' between activities.)

- How can the transition times between classes be optimised to reduce sensory overload? (For example, by staggering bell times or offering quieter, alternative routes through the school, or some students getting passes to leave lessons a few minutes early.)
- Can students opt into specific activities that help regulate their sensory needs, such as quiet reading or movement exercises? (For example, offering a movement break card.)
- Can students be given jobs such as handing out books, taking things to the office, helping to get out lunch trolleys, etc,, enabling their sensory needs to be met in a positive manner?
- Is there a full range of activities available for students at break and lunchtimes to meet different sensory needs? (For example, balancing on beams, trim trail and hanging from monkey bars for vestibular input; sensory gardens for tactile and olfactory input; opportunities to push/pull for proprioception.)
- Do lunch and break times offer opportunities for sensory engagement or decompression? (For example, through the introduction of designated quiet areas, indoor or outdoor sensory spaces, play equipment such as trim trails, adventure play equipment, forest school areas and Scrapstore PlayPods.)
- Do children have to attend for a whole day, or are part day, or flexi-schooling across the week options available? The ability to manage a whole school day will vary. Where a child is struggling to attend school, then it is important to support sensory needs to enable them to manage within the school environment for some of the time. Research and experience tell us that once out of school, it can be hard to get back in, so offering child-led flexible timetabling or flexi-schooling opportunities may help to manage this.

The aim is to embed these sensory aware practices throughout the whole school day, ensuring balance through regular opportunities for sensory regulation, thereby enabling all students and staff to have their sensory wellbeing supported and nurtured across the school day.

Uniform

Uniforms are a perennial issue for schools, but in many cases, schools have not considered the sensory implications of their uniform choices, instead focusing on appearance (smart) or cost effectiveness or easy laundry care. Common sensory issues with uniform include:

- Itchy fabrics such as woollen jumpers or woollen blazers
- Static-inducing fabrics like shiny nylon PE kits or skirts and trousers

- Collars and ties causing sensory issues around the neck
- Linings in items like blazers or sports trousers causing two fabric layers to rub against each other when worn, which is intolerable for some
- Itchy labels or name tags sewn into necklines or waistbands
- Issues caused by seams, zips, velcro or other fastenings
- Expecting shoes to be hard leather and more narrow and constricting than wide soft barefoot style shoes
- Constriction feeling of arms and upper torso when wearing a jumper plus a blazer
- Tights, socks, underwear such as bras, vests, pants can be problematic for some
- How students are expected to wear their hair; for example, ponytails or loose hair
- Rules around when blazers are allowed to be taken off in the heat of summer
- Rules around hoods never being up in PE kits which include a hoodie!

Students cannot learn effectively when the clothes they wear are a constant source of niggling discomfort.

A Sensory Aware School uniform would include:

- A range of uniform options for students to pick and mix their uniform look according to needs
- Fabrics chosen carefully to be skin kind, not itchy or static-inducing, with options for embroidering the school logo onto an alternative fabric of the same colour if a student still can't cope with the chosen fabric
- Minimal seams where possible
- Options on fastenings where needed
- Options to wear black leggings instead of tights
- Option of clip-on ties rather than full-length ties or ties being entirely optional
- Offering a range of shoe options that meet a wide variety of sensory needs
- Labels that are printed onto the fabric including space to write a name and the sizing so that information doesn't get lost when labels are cut
- Option to wear PE kit (generally more comfortable) for some students if they are having a particular bad sensory day
- Students are allowed to remove jumpers and blazers as needed to regulate their own temperature and according to sensory preference
- Permission to wear hair according to sensory preference, and where hair must be tied up for health and safety (for example, PE or science) then a range of comfortable options available
- Permission to keep hoods up if needed (see 'Thinking point' on the next page).

Schools should offer a 'reasonable adjustment to uniform card' which details the exact adjustment for students to reduce the likelihood of embarrassment or conflict during uniform checks. It is important that this is not then considered a matter for detention, causing additional and unnecessary stress for the student and family.

> ### Thinking point: Hoodies are an excellent sensory-friendly uniform item
>
> Many schools we work in hate them, but from a sensory point of view, hoodies offer ways for children and young people to reduce the sensory inputs into their world. They can help mute sounds and block out peripheral vision. Having the option to block a bit of the world out when it all gets too much can also be a useful way to signal to others to give them a bit of space. The kangaroo pocket also allows individuals to be able to store their fidgets and use them more discreetly. If your uniform offers a PE hoodie, is there scope for some students to be allowed to wear their hoodie on the days they need to?

> ### Reflection questions for thinking about school uniforms
>
> - How do all elements of the uniform feel to wear for a range of students (especially those with sensory issues)? How do you know? Do you consult a wide range of students (and not just those on the School Council!) for their views on their uniform?
> - Can students wear compression skins (long-sleeved undergarments) underneath their uniform to help mitigate some issues caused by the current uniform?
> - Can a wider range of options be provided so students can choose what they can cope with; for example, leggings or tights, jumper or blazer?
> - Who gets to decide the reasonable adjustment to uniform? The parent/child? The form tutor? The pastoral lead? The SENDCO? The Senior Leadership Team? Will they require evidence from an Occupational Therapist/Educational Psychologist, GP or other professional to authorise the request?

Case study: A specialist school develops a sensory-friendly uniform

A sensory aware school uniform was developed in conjunction with students at a new specialist school for autistic students. Fabrics were carefully chosen with comfort in mind, with no uncomfortable blazers or ties but a shirt and a jumper with black trousers or skirt. Reasonable adjustments are made with velcro swapped for buttons or zips depending on sensory preferences; some children prefer baggy clothes, others slim fitting – all preferences can be accommodated. Having designed the uniform, students are also permitted to choose whether to wear their uniform or their PE kit to school (even if it is not a PE day), as the PE kit offers further comfort to some students with sensory needs and has the option of a hood.

Reflection questions

- How can you work with students to develop a sensory aware school uniform?
- Which is more important to your school – consistency of appearance or sensory comfort? Can a balance be struck between the two?
- If a complete uniform overhaul isn't possible in your setting, what small adjustments can you make to your school uniform policy to improve the sensory element?

Case study: A mainstream primary school adjusts uniform for an undiagnosed student

Daisy is in Year 4 in a mainstream primary school. She does not have any diagnosis of any additional need, but is highly sensory. She cannot tolerate wearing socks or any underwear, and her clothing is generally limited to a pair of loose jersey grey knee-length shorts of a very particular fabric and style (with no pants) that is unfortunately no longer available (and alternatives unacceptable), pull-on canvas shoes or Crocs with no socks and either a school polo shirt and on good days a school jumper. She wears this even in the depths of winter. She will not wear a coat. Her hair is always worn long and never tied up. Daisy does not cope well with transitions including getting dressed and getting to school. Her sensory needs increase if she is having a bad day, hasn't slept, has had a friendship issue, etc. Daisy also struggles when she grows out of clothes or shoes and has to transition to the next size up. She is often in items that are slightly too small, partly because this gives her compression which helps her to regulate, and also because she cannot cope with change. New larger clothing in the right size doesn't feel 'right' so she often refuses to wear it.

The priority for Daisy is for her to access her education and be able to get dressed and come to school. School permits her to wear what she needs to in order to access school, and Daisy is allowed to come in a little later, after the first rush, for a calmer start to school. On particularly cold days, she is permitted to stay inside if she wants to, but she doesn't seem to feel the cold. When peers question Daisy or staff about why she is wearing something different to what is generally allowed, staff remind students of the school values around celebrating difference and that Daisy is sensitive to certain fabrics. Students are happy with that explanation because they are familiar with the individual needs of students being met in different ways. Reasonable adjustments across the school are regularly agreed with evidence from home or professionals as to why they are necessary.

School and family work closely together to support Daisy's needs. They are starting to explore diagnosis as they are aware that the transition to secondary school and new uniform requirements are going to cause issues. Also, puberty and menstruation mean Daisy will start to need to wear pants. They enlist the help of an Occupational Therapist for further advice.

Reflection questions

- Can you think of a student who is highly sensory like Daisy?
- What does your school do well to support them?
- What could they do better?
- How could you support Daisy in different seasons?
- How could you support Daisy when other things going on for her are increasing her sensory needs?
- How would you support Daisy with the secondary transition?
- How would you support other students to understand Daisy's need for an adjusted uniform?
- Do you think students need a diagnosis in order to have reasonable adjustments to uniform?

Case study: A mainstream secondary school adjusts PE kit for a diagnosed student transitioning into Year 7

Arjun is autistic, dyslexic and has ADHD and as part of that profile has some significant sensory needs. Arjun has an EHCP which states "reasonable adjustments to uniform to be agreed between home and school". Arjun is about to start at a secondary school with a very strict uniform policy. At primary school, Arjun had a thing about wearing odd bamboo socks, which he was permitted to do as one of his 'quirks' and initially Arjun wanted to continue this practice at secondary school.

As part of the transition plan in Year 6, Arjun was visited by the local Autism Support Service who liaise with Arjun and his parents about the uniform. Arjun tried on the uniform and while mum initially thought the blazer and jumper would be impossible (and thought she would have to pay a tailor to line the blazer with soft cotton jersey rather than the shiny satiny fabric). To their surprise, Arjun really liked and could cope with the main school uniform, mainly because he really liked all the blazer pockets he could keep all his treasures in and the additional weight of the blazer appeared to provide some sensory comfort. However, the PE kit was another story. This was two-layered PE trousers which were absolutely intolerable in the way the fabrics rubbed over each other, and a shiny nylon PE T-shirt with seams that ran down the chest and itched, especially on sensitive tissue like nipples. The local Autism Support Service wrote to the school to request that the PE kit be adjusted and the SENDCO agreed with the parents that they would get the school PE logo embroidered onto a black cotton polo shirt and a black pair of cotton joggers. Arjun's new school had a post-COVID policy of wearing PE kit all day to school on PE days which meant that at least twice a week Arjun would be in PE kit all day.

However, the Senior Leadership Team initially tried to suggest that Arjun could wear a sensory-friendly base layer under the uniform, but mum pointed out that Arjun has interoception issues, meaning he cannot tell when he is too hot and gets dysregulated as a result (often wearing a hoodie in the height of summer) so a base layer plus uniform plus physical exercise would not work. The Senior Leadership Team then simply ignored the paperwork from the Autism Support Service and so the SENDCO suggested to the parents that they also get Arjun's Occupational Therapist to write a letter specifying the reasonable adjustments to uniform. Over the summer Arjun's parents purchased their own version of the PE kit, and in order to arrange the embroidery, the SENDCO had to write a letter to the Uniform Outfitters giving permission for this embroidery. The parents also had to work closely with the seamstress to ensure that the backing used on the embroidery wasn't going to cause further sensory issue, and the logos were located on the pockets of the trousers and initially on the hip area of the T-shirt until a suitable backing was found so that Arjun could tolerate the PE kit logo in the same place as everyone else – the chest. Arjun's mum also purchased multiple pairs of black bamboo socks and some with a discreet pattern hidden on the sole so Arjun could continue with his preference for odd socks whilst also following the uniform policy.

When Arjun started the school in September, unfortunately the 'reasonable adjustment to uniform' card he was promised was not ready and then Arjun was too shy to use it. Arjun's parents had to coach Arjun into saying, "I have permission" when he kept getting challenged about his slightly different (but still complementary to the main PE kit) uniform. Arjun's friends also stepped up to support him when peers were commenting on the difference, but there were a few home meltdowns about the different uniform and how difficult it was. Over time, people got used to Arjun's different PE kit, but when there was a cover PE teacher, or senior leaders were on the prowl, Arjun would still occasionally be challenged so his parents had to be vigilant about addressing it with the school and really trying to encourage Arjun to show his 'reasonable adjustment card' that showed the permissions. Certain sports in PE also became challenging; for example, sports where a gum shield was required were particularly difficult (Arjun already was finding it incredibly hard to cope with braces) and the knee-high sport socks that are traditionally used to support shin pads were intolerable, so Arjun had to wear knee-high black cotton socks over the shin pads (as bamboo knee-high socks were too loose).

Reflection questions

- What did the school do well? What could they have done better?
- How could the school have made Arjun not feel different and more comfortable to wear his adjusted uniform?
- What wider sensory aspects of PE need to be considered?
- If you had a child like Arjun in your school, how would your current policies and practices support him? What needs to change?

> ### Reflection questions for all three case studies
> - Is there a difference between primary and secondary school approaches to sensory adjustments to uniform and uniform policies generally?
> - Where there are fluctuations in sensory needs (for example, due to tiredness, demands, hunger, friendship issues) how can schools work with children to accommodate this?
> - How can seasonal changes to uniforms be thought about to also support sensory needs?
> - Some children prefer clothing that is extra loose or extra tight – does the uniform policy take this into account to be accepted without challenge?
> - How can schools support children as they grow and change and there are resultant uniform issues from 'next size up'?
> - What could different settings (primary/mainstream/special) learn from each other about sensory-friendly uniforms and policies?

Staff role and responsibilities

The role of staff is vital in the success of a whole school approach to sensory awareness. Adopting sensory informed practice is key. Staff need to be aware of the possible sensory base for behaviours, and be open to adjusting environments and using a variety of strategies to support the sensory wellbeing of their students. Chapter 4 helped staff identify their own sensory needs, Chapter 5 covered teaching and support staff roles and responsibilities for integrating sensory aware strategies into their lesson plans and classroom management. Chapter 6 covered a huge range of learning opportunities for teachers to deliver to students. Chapter 7 supports staff to audit spaces for the benefit of the whole school's sensory wellbeing. This book has mainly focused on the role and responsibilities of teaching and support staff with an emphasis on continuing professional development on sensory awareness.

However, every staff member, regardless of their specific role, is responsible for modelling sensory informed practices. For example, lunchtime supervisors and site staff play an important role in maintaining a sensory-friendly environment, from the dining hall to the playground. We strongly believe that through collective understanding and implementation of sensory aware approaches, across the whole staff team, this will mean everyone can work together to create more supportive and inclusive sensory-friendly educational environments.

Behavioural approaches

Chapter 5 went into more detail on how staff can recognise and respond to sensory needs. It is important to note that staff should be mindful of the possibility of environmental and/or sensory reasons or triggers for observed behaviours (remember "**See behaviour – consider sensory**" page 82). Remember to consider that '**all behaviour is communication**' and "**children do well when they can**" (a phrase first coined by Dr Ross Greene) . It would also be useful if recorded behaviour incidents offered opportunities to record any possible sensory reasons or triggers for the episode, to establish any patterns and develop pre-emptive sensory strategies.

This approach shifts the focus from merely reacting to behaviours to understanding and addressing any possible sensory-based origins. Interventions such as movement breaks, quiet/time out areas or the use of fidget items are therefore implemented not as afterthoughts, but as a core strand of the school's behaviour policy. This sensory informed practice not only promotes positive behaviour by directly addressing the root causes, but also empowers students to develop their self regulation skills, enhancing their wellbeing and educational experience.

Staff training and development

Below we have included some of the main ways staff can develop their sensory informed practice as a range of CPD activities. This will help to upskill the workforce to advocate for sensory awareness, sensory inclusion and sensory wellbeing.

- Design a fun sensory awareness twilight training session by utilising some of the fun activities in the 'Quickfire sensory education activity ideas' box (Chapter 6, page 130) as well as the 'Activities to help explain our proprioception and vestibular senses' box (Chapter 6, page 138). Many of these have been tried and tested with staff and work well to start to build sensory awareness and understanding.
- Encourage all staff to use Chapter 4 to identify their own sensory profiles. Where appropriate, they could share elements of their sensory profiles with their team to establish understanding of the similarities and differences and recognise and support each other's differing needs.
- Ask each department to designate a Sensory Champion whose role it is to lead on sensory informed practice across their department. This group could do a thought experiment where they fill in a sensory snapshot imagining a

hypothetical student in hypothetical situations. For example, in PE outside on a rainy day, in a science lesson with the bunsen burners going, everyone singing in assembly, queuing up in the canteen. You could work with students to help develop these situations (they will likely produce ones they struggle with). This will give you rich data about different sensory experiences across the school. Use that data to feed back to the school's Sensory Wellbeing Champion and/or the Sensory Wellbeing Working Party.

- Use an INSET day to get a sensory practitioner, such as an Occupational Therapist or a trainer/educator with lived expertise of sensory needs or a SEND parent/carer, in to train all staff. As part of this day, aim to come up with a list of Sensory Informed Practice Principles that staff will aim to follow.
- SENDCOs and teaching assistants could be tasked with writing a sensory profile of a particular student and comparing it with the student's own sensory profile. Consider where the similarities and differences are and why. This activity may give you new insights which will help your relationship with the student.
- Pastoral leads and form tutors could play 'sensory detectives' (see page 82), where they take time to think back and reflect on a particular behaviour exhibited by a student. They should consider what were the possible reasons for the behaviour and whether there was any sensory cause ("See behaviour – consider sensory"). Remember to consider that 'all behaviour is communication' and "children do well when they can" (Dr Ross Greene).
- All staff can use the following discussion scenarios to help build their sensory informed practice.

Teacher A has significant light sensitivity. For her period 6 class on a Friday, she is timetabled in a brightly fluorescently lit room with minimal windows. As a result, she needs to teach with the lights off. Many of her students are lethargic and sleepy in her lessons, probably as a result of the time of day and the very low lighting levels. She is frustrated with their concentration levels in her class.
- What mitigations could Teacher A put in place to manage her own needs on light levels but also to boost her classes awareness?

Teacher B is a form tutor to an autistic student. This boy often gets dysregulated particularly before lunch and after sessions such as PE, drama and art.
- How could Teacher B get to the bottom of what is going on for this student? Would a focus on sensory needs help? How could Teacher B support the teachers of this student to meet his needs better so the episodes of dysregulation reduce?

Teacher C has a girl with ADHD in her class who is constantly moving and unfocused. She lets her sit on an office chair at the back of the class so she can spin gently while working, and notices a significant improvement in her concentration. However, other children in the class find it unfair that she gets special treatment.
- How could Teacher C handle this so she continues to meet the child with ADHD's needs without the rest of the class becoming resentful?

Teacher D is a pastoral lead for a year group. He is constantly checking and battling with uniform issues as per school policy, but students are allowed reasonable adjustments. He has his own sensory issues so personally never wears a tie or a jacket, preferring shirt and trousers and a jumper if cold. Students are starting to complain when he makes them wear their blazers.
- How can Teacher D navigate this double standard?

Teacher E has a student who is constantly chewing his cuffs or pens or bits of paper. The school has a no chewing gum policy. He does not disrupt other students and this appears to help him concentrate, but he is shredding his blazer and the teacher finds it challenging as she keeps thinking he is chewing gum. He reacts badly when challenged for chewing, as he is never chewing gum.
- How can teacher E discuss with parents and students to find an alternative which is mutually agreeable but provides the chewing sensory input that enables concentration?

Teacher F teaches a student for music last thing in the day after he has just had PE followed by science. On days where there have been practical science experiments, this student will walk out if the music lesson is also a practical lesson and not a theory lesson.
- What should Teacher F do to support this student?
- Can Teacher F liaise with his other teachers to support his needs better on these days of lots of practicals (think of the bottle of pop analogy)?

The **playground supervisor** has noticed a little girl who constantly plays by herself and does not join in, spending most break times rotating herself upside down on the handrails (which are not part of the playground equipment). The supervisor is concerned she may injure herself.
- What should the playground supervisor do?
- Are there alternative equipment options to provide the same sensory input?

The **dining hall supervisor** is concerned about a boy who is always slow to eat, last to finish and spends much of the lunch hour with his hands over his ears.
- What should the dining hall supervisor do?
- What reasonable adjustments could be put in place to support this child?

Supporting staff sensory needs – staff sensory wellbeing

We hope since reading this book, especially Chapter 4, that you have more of an idea of your own sensory profile. Make sure you revisit the W.E.L.L.D.O.I.N.G mnemonic in Chapter 4 on page 75 and make sure you are building sensory joy into your life. We recognise that schools can be sensorily overwhelming places at times, so we wanted to provide you with some of our favourite sensory strategies and top tips for those working in schools. Remember, **you cannot pour from an empty cup;** meeting your own sensory needs and embracing your own sensory wellbeing through sensory welldoing will open up your window of tolerance and enable you to have more capacity to more effectively meet your students' needs.

Top tips for your sensory-friendly clothing

- Life is too short to wear uncomfortable clothing. Get rid of anything in your wardrobe that is itchy or uncomfortable to wear.
- If you find comfortable and smart workwear that doesn't cause sensory issues, some people like to buy the same item in all the different colours/patterns available. This ensures you are comfortable and don't have decision fatigue in the mornings when getting ready.
- Long-sleeved vests and leggings worn as a base layer (sometimes called skins) can help with compression or as a sensory barrier. If the shiny lycra feel causes issues, you can look for cotton jersey or bamboo which tends to be softer. Seamfree bamboo socks and tights feel great for some people.
- Look for brands and stockists that offer "skin kind" or "sensory" or "sensory smart" items.
- Keep a 'quick unpick' seam ripper sewing tool near your clothes storage for safely removing itchy labels without causing damage.

> **Reflection question**
> - How does school policy on staff appearance differ from expectations on uniform? Do they need any changes to become more sensory-friendly?

Top tips for your sensory-friendly work environment

- How can you reduce visual clutter in your classroom? If your room is due a repaint, choose a calming colour and think carefully about the colour of backing paper you choose for display boards. If you are not the tidiest person, adopt D.O.O.M boxes (Didn't Organise Only Moved) under your desk to keep your desk clear. Can you enlist students to help you keep a calm environment?
- You may be in one room or several across the week. If there are particular rooms that you find sensorily tricky, think how you could manage that – tinted glasses or ear plugs to help reduce the impact of the lights or noise? Can you engineer room swaps (ask your timetabler for a list of rooms free at the same time to see if there is a better room to swap to)?
- Ask for help – can you flag with students that you are struggling and ask them to do things to help you like move their chairs quietly, or ask the site team for pads under the chairs to reduce the noise? If tech is noisy, get IT staff on the case – sometimes these noises have a simple fix like cleaning a fan. Can tech be orientated so the projector glare doesn't catch you right in the eyes when you are trying to teach? Can you add more plug-in lighting to reduce the glare from overhead lights or blinds to reduce sun glare. See Chapter 7 for more detail on adapting environments to be more sensory-friendly.

Student voice

It is so important that student voice is included in Sensory Aware Schools. Supporting children and young people to be their best sensory selves cannot happen as an adult-led, top down approach. We have to engage with young people to find out what their sensory issues are in school, in order to make effective changes. Many of the activities in Chapter 6 can be used to generate student voice, but especially 'A sensory audit of a school day' (page 178) and 'Sensory wellbeing ambassadors' (page 199). In Chapter 7, 'Carrying out a whole school sensory audit' on page 208 involves student consultation including using colour coded school maps or try a version of the 'Student-led School Sensory Survey' on page 217. You will need to make sure students are already clear about what sensory needs are and the importance of sensory wellbeing so that they can successfully identify potential sensory challenges and areas for improvement. You should encourage the ambassadors to also take notes and gather feedback from their peers to ensure comprehensive evaluations. Involving students in this way will help encourage their self advocacy and sensory management skills. Through working with student sensory wellbeing ambassadors, this will help increase awareness amongst peers and increase sensory inclusion and understanding across the whole student body.

Parents and carers

Schools should always work in partnership with their parent community for the best outcomes for the children and young people. Parents can be the best advocates for their children's needs, but sometimes relationships between home and school can become tricky and hostile to navigate, especially where parents feel that their child's sensory needs are not being met appropriately in school. This can be particularly apparent when a child has an Education, Health and Care Plan (EHCP), or when a child heavily masks at school but is very dysregulated at home due to the sensory overwhelm from school; because this is just not evident in school, therefore the school does not know to make any adjustments for the child.

We would advise having a section on the school website explaining about sensory needs and how your school works to accommodate a range of needs. This should also signpost useful reading and support for parents. Schools that have parent/carer groups for SEND students (including those with significant sensory needs) enable parents to feel better supported with appropriate forums for communication. One supportive approach could be to offer a menu of supportive webinars for parents across the year, ensuring at least one of those is on sensory awareness. Could the school also offer a lending library of useful parenting books including ones on sensory needs such as those listed in 'Further reading and resources' on page 273?

Another way of getting parents and carers involved would be to complete a Home/School Partnership Form (on the next page) or a communication book for meeting a particular child's needs. This way both home and school know across a day/week where the sensory stress points are occurring. It is also really important to have an open and honest conversation about masking. It is really common for children and young people to display very different behaviours between home and school.

A Home/School Partnership for Meeting [Student name]'s Sensory Needs

Form completed by _____(Home) and _____(School)

(include relationship to child)

Date completed: | Review due:

An overview of the sensory needs

The things that help _____ to regulate:

The things that cause _____ to become dysregulated:

Strategies employed at home to support meeting these sensory needs:	Strategies employed at school to support meeting these sensory needs:
Daily:	Daily:
Weekly:	Weekly:

Action points for school *(include details of any passes that need to be issued, how staff will be informed, who is responsible for monitoring, etc.)*

> **Recommended reading for parents**: One of our favourite books for parents is *Sensory Processing Explained: A Handbook for Parents and Educators* by Heather Greutman and Sharla Kostelyk (CreateSpace Independent Publishing Platform, 2018). It has lots of simple practical strategies for parents to trial at home but also a wide range for educators too. It's a nice easy read, not too 'jargony' and very helpful.

Reminder: Please don't forget about the siblings!

Where children have significant sensory needs, it is often their siblings who will bear the brunt of the meltdowns at home. These children may also have their own sensory needs (genetics has a role) but often these can get overlooked for the sake of the sibling with more overt needs. Schools can have a role to play here in ensuring that siblings get appropriate additional pastoral support and being open and curious about meeting any possible sibling sensory needs. Supporting siblings to understand their own sensory needs and that of their sibling will help home life, so it's well worth doing. In some cases, referring siblings to Young Carer Groups may be an appropriate course of action so siblings can access safe spaces to vent away from their siblings.

Wider partnerships

Occupational Therapists

An Occupational Therapist plays an important role in a school setting, helping to observe, assess and clarify the needs of students facing sensory and motor skills challenges. In the context of sensory processing, they may use formal sensory questionnaires (see table of 'Wider Sensory Questionnaires/Checklists Available', Chapter 4, page 72), observation and discussion with parents and teachers, alongside motor co-ordination assessments where needed, to help identify specific challenges. They will then suggest strategies and lifestyle changes aimed at helping children engage in daily tasks with increased ease, from improving handwriting skills to engaging in playtime or PE. Some children will be offered regular therapy sessions either individually or in a group to help develop and refine these skills. Occupational Therapists may also provide training in further understanding of sensory needs to parents and/or teachers. Occupational Therapists help children and young people grow, learn, have fun, socialise and play – so they can develop, thrive and reach their full potential.

Speech and Language Therapists (SaLTs)

As well as working with receptive or expressive language delays/differences, SaLTs may also have a focus on the mechanics of eating and drinking, and so they can support with oro-motor work, for those who are not able to swallow safely or those with limited and restricted diets due to sensory differences. This may include children with a history of reflux who have a negative experience of eating orally, or autistic population members who may have a diet that is so restrictive it impacts on their physical health. Other sensory input tends to be in collaboration with OTs around supporting regulation using a multidisciplinary approach.

Educational Psychologists

Educational Psychologists work to improve the learning and wellbeing of all children. Alongside their role in reporting on cognition and behaviour, they may also help identify sensory impacts on children's learning and behaviour. They may make recommendations based on their observations and assessments, including the use of checklists, to compile information from other practitioners such as Occupational Therapists into their reports. Their reports are a legal requirement of an Education, Health and Care Plan and therefore often this advice becomes embedded into a plan. Therefore, Educational Psychologists can have a key role in identifying sensory needs and effecting change to benefit students. They work closely with parents/carers, educational setting staff and other professionals involved.

School Nurses

School nurses can offer firstline support for children's health issues; for example, issues with feeding, continence or other issues which may have a sensory element. They can provide initial support and assessment for children and parents as well as referrals to appropriate specialists for further evaluation. They can have a role in educating staff and parents about the implications of related sensory needs, advocating for accommodations that help manage or alleviate symptoms, like dietary modifications or scheduled toilet breaks.

Paediatricians

Paediatricians are doctors who are trained to assess the health, wellbeing and development of children from birth to late adolescence. They are generally the ones who will diagnose neurodevelopmental conditions such as Autism or ADHD, in conjunction with other professionals. They can also offer diagnosis, management and treatment, including medication, for a wide variety of conditions that affect children. Some of these conditions may have a sensory basis (for example, chronic constipation with soiling is very common in autistic children who struggle with their interoception and so have difficulties feeling thirsty, or recognising when they need a poo). Paediatricians can support by writing letters to schools setting out the students' diagnosed conditions and management and what the school should be doing to meet needs.

Mental health practitioners

A variety of mental health professionals may be involved with students and offer advice for wider professionals working with the student. They may work therapeutically with the child to support their understanding of regulation and dysregulation for their mental health and wellbeing. They may work in partnership with parents, schools and other professionals for the benefit of the child.

Local Authority: Local Offer

Local authorities play a crucial role in supporting children with Special Educational Needs and Disabilities (SEND) through their Local Offer. This details the support and resources available within the community for children and young people with SEND and their families. The Local Offer serves several key purposes: it informs families about how to access vital services, what they can expect from different services, and how decisions are made about who can receive specific types of support. It also outlines the process for assessing children's needs and the criteria for getting an EHCP. Increasingly, local authorities are improving their Local Offer around sensory needs. For example, Derbyshire County Council offers a toolkit for professionals about sensory processing needs (www.localoffer.derbyshire.gov.uk/education-and-learning/derbyshire-area-sensory-processing-needs/derbyshire-area-sensory-processing-needs.aspx).

Local Autism Support Services

Lots of local authorities have Autism Support Services which may be managed under health or education teams. They may have at least one person as part of that team who specialises in sensory needs and can offer support to autistic students in schools with sensory needs.

National support

The national recognised body for sensory awareness and sensory informed practice is Sensory Integration Education (www.sensoryintegrationeducation.com/) which is a well-respected not for profit organisation offering sensory integration training for professionals. They also offer Sensory Inclusive Schools www.sensoryinclusiveschools.org/ which offers online training and ongoing support for schools working on their sensory inclusion for an annual fee, as well as free support for parents via Sensory Help Now (www.sensoryhelpnow.org/).

It is also important to work in partnership with other schools to develop and share best practice to develop your confident, skilled workforce.

> ### Reflection questions for Chapter 8
> 1. How will you work in partnership with your key stakeholders (including students, parents and wider professionals)?
> 2. What is your staff development plan for training?
> 3. How will you support staff to meet their sensory needs?
> 4. Can you consider further uniform adjustments?
> 5. How will you advocate for sensory wellbeing across the school (who are your allies, what changes are needed to environment, policy and practice)?

Chapter nine

CONCLUSION AND NEXT STEPS

This book has aimed to give you a firm understanding of what a Sensory Aware School could look like, and given you practical ideas for how to deliver on a vision of sensory wellbeing in your school. We hope we have provided you with new understandings of our eight sensory systems and how they impact on our wellbeing and ability to learn. We have shared key elements of recognising and responding to sensory needs as well as adaptations that can be made to the school ecosystem for the benefit of all students and stakeholders in the school. We have also offered you a wide range of sensory wellbeing education ideas, audit tools and reflective and discussion questions to raise your sensory awareness and develop your understanding about sensory wellbeing as applicable to your school.

Live a life of sensory welldoing

Teachers can often be guilty of putting the wellbeing of others before their own. This can come at a mental and physical cost, so at this point we wanted to stress that **there is more to life than teaching!** We absolutely do not want this book to become another millstone around your neck of "things you should be doing for your school". We hope we have written it in such a way that you can pick and mix the bits you have time, energy and capacity for. If nothing else, if your sole takeaway from this book is that embracing sensory welldoing in your own life may have an impact on your stress and anxiety levels, and boost your overall wellbeing, then we would be delighted by that!

You may find it useful to revisit the W.E.L.L.D.O.I.N.G mnemonic on page 75 of Chapter 4 and embrace those tips while recording the difference it makes to your life. If you can be seen as a role model in meeting your own sensory needs, this will help the students who have sensory needs feel 'seen'. It also helps students to build empathy and, we hope, feel able to ask for help to get their own needs met. For an easy whole school approach, you could revisit the draft core messages from the Sensory Wellbeing Ambassadors activity on page 199 of Chapter 6 and adapt them into your own version that suits your needs and those of your school. Perhaps display them in posters around the school and on the back of toilet doors to get people talking and thinking about sensory awareness, sensory inclusion, sensory wellbeing.

Now you have read the book: What is your action plan?

If we revisit our self assessment from pages 19–23, Chapter 2, it is time to start thinking in more detail about how your school is going to fully become sensory aware and include everyone to support sensory wellbeing.

Where are you currently in the Assess Plan Do Review Cycle and where do you want to get to? The end of this chapter on page 271 has an Action Planning Sheet you can start to make notes on.

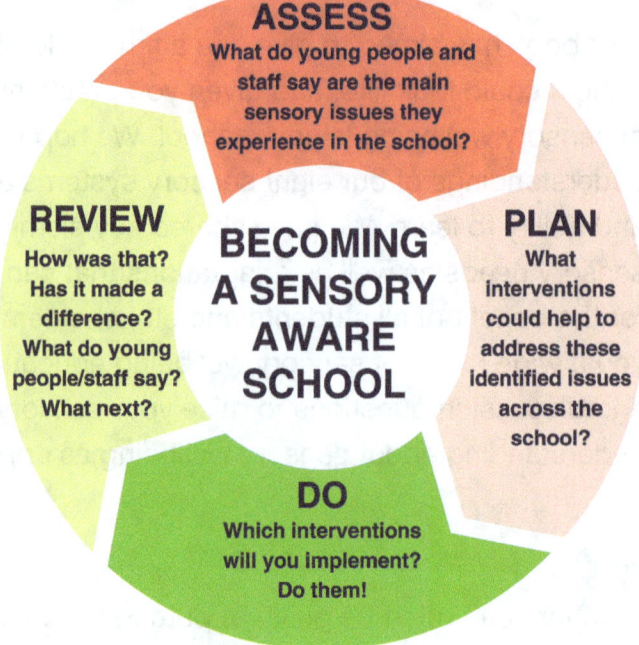

To help you with this, we have formulated some reflection questions to assist the development of your action plan under the six pillars of Sensory Aware Schools:

- People
- Place
- Policy
- Practice
- Provision
- Participation.

To help you with this, we have formulated some reflection questions to assist the development of your action plan under the six pillars of Sensory Aware Schools (see pages 266 and 267).

You can use these questions to help you develop statements of best practice such as the example on the opposite page.

Sensory Informed People and Practice

A Sensory Aware School is one where…

…the individual…
…recognises that each and every one of us has sensory needs
…respects that we all have different levels of sensory needs
…feels able to ask for reasonable adjustments to support specific sensory needs
…understands that the space and humans in the space are not perfect, but we all aim to support each other's sensory needs, balancing the needs of the group as a whole.

…the school…
…has a whole school approach and policy on sensory awareness led by a designated champion
…regularly audits and works to improve the school sensory environment
…provides specific spaces for sensory regulation (including alerting and calming options)
…funds the purchase of required sensory resources
…offers regular training and support for all staff on sensory awareness.

…the staff…
…understand the impact of sensory needs on behaviour
…are vigilant to the sensory needs of the individuals in their environment
…offers sensory adjustments where they feel a student is understimulated or overstimulated in the environment
…supports the Sensory Aware School Policy.

…the student…
…understands the impact of sensory needs on their own behaviour
…is open to learning more about their sensory needs and developing their sensory wellbeing
…is willing to trial reasonable sensory suggestions made by staff
…takes responsibility for managing their own sensory needs wherever possible.

…the parents…
…recognise that their child/ren have different levels of sensory needs and understand the impact of these on their child's behaviour
…support the school and staff in their sensory aware approaches
…work with the school to identify any additional reasonable adjustments needed for their child.

…external professionals…
…understand they are working in a sensory aware environment and follow school policy
…understand the impact of sensory needs on behaviour
…offer sensory adjustments where possible.

THE SIX PILLARS OF SENSORY AWARE SCHOOLS

POLICY: Sensory aware leadership. School values and ethos and school policies that are sensory inclusive and support sensory wellbeing.

PROVISION: Funding, resources and reasonable adjustments provided to support sensory wellbeing.

PRACTICE: Adopting sensory informed approaches. Education, training and support for students and staff.

PARTICIPATION: Engagement between people to support each others' sensory needs. Interactions between people and place.

PEOPLE: Individual sensory needs. Actively engaging with sensory welldoing for sensory wellbeing.

PLACE: The physical features of the school spaces. Fluctuations in the sensory environment (daily/ weekly/ seasonal).

Place	• How do the physical features of the school environment (for example, light, space and acoustics) impact sensory experiences, and what quick wins can be made for sensory wellbeing? • How can longer-term and more expensive changes be planned into the review cycle to maximise benefit to the school community while offering value for money? • How are fluctuations in the sensory environment, (for example, temperature, lighting and season) considered and managed?
People	• How are unique sensory profiles identified? • How are individual needs accommodated for staff and students? • What opportunities are in place to educate staff and students about sensory awareness and wellbeing? • Who is leading on sensory wellbeing across the school? • How are all the key stakeholders included?
Participation	• How are students and staff encouraged to embrace sensory welldoing? • What mechanisms are in place for ensuring staff and student voice is heard in decision making on sensory awareness? • Which key stakeholders will you work with for sensory wellbeing in your school? Is this a representative cross-section of the whole school community? • How can you encourage wider participation around sensory awareness, sensory inclusion and sensory wellbeing.
Practice	• Are staff trained in sensory informed practice? • Are there opportunities for students to learn about sensory wellbeing? • Are staff and students advocating for sensory wellbeing and supporting each other in this? • How are school policies enacted in practice?
Provision	• Are reasonable adjustments discussed and offered? • What resources are provided to support sensory needs? • Is there a ring-fenced budget for the sensory offer? • Who gets the resources? (Do teachers get to give these out, or direct to students or open access?) • How does the school ensure fair access to sensory resources?
Policy	• Have you got a Sensory Aware School Policy? • What wider policies support a sensory aware approach within the school? • How do the school's values and ethos reflect understanding of and accommodations for meeting diverse sensory needs?

Copyright material from Alice Hoyle and Tessa Hyde (2025), *Becoming a Sensory Aware School*, Routledge

ROADMAP FOR BECOMING A SENSORY AWARE SCHOOL

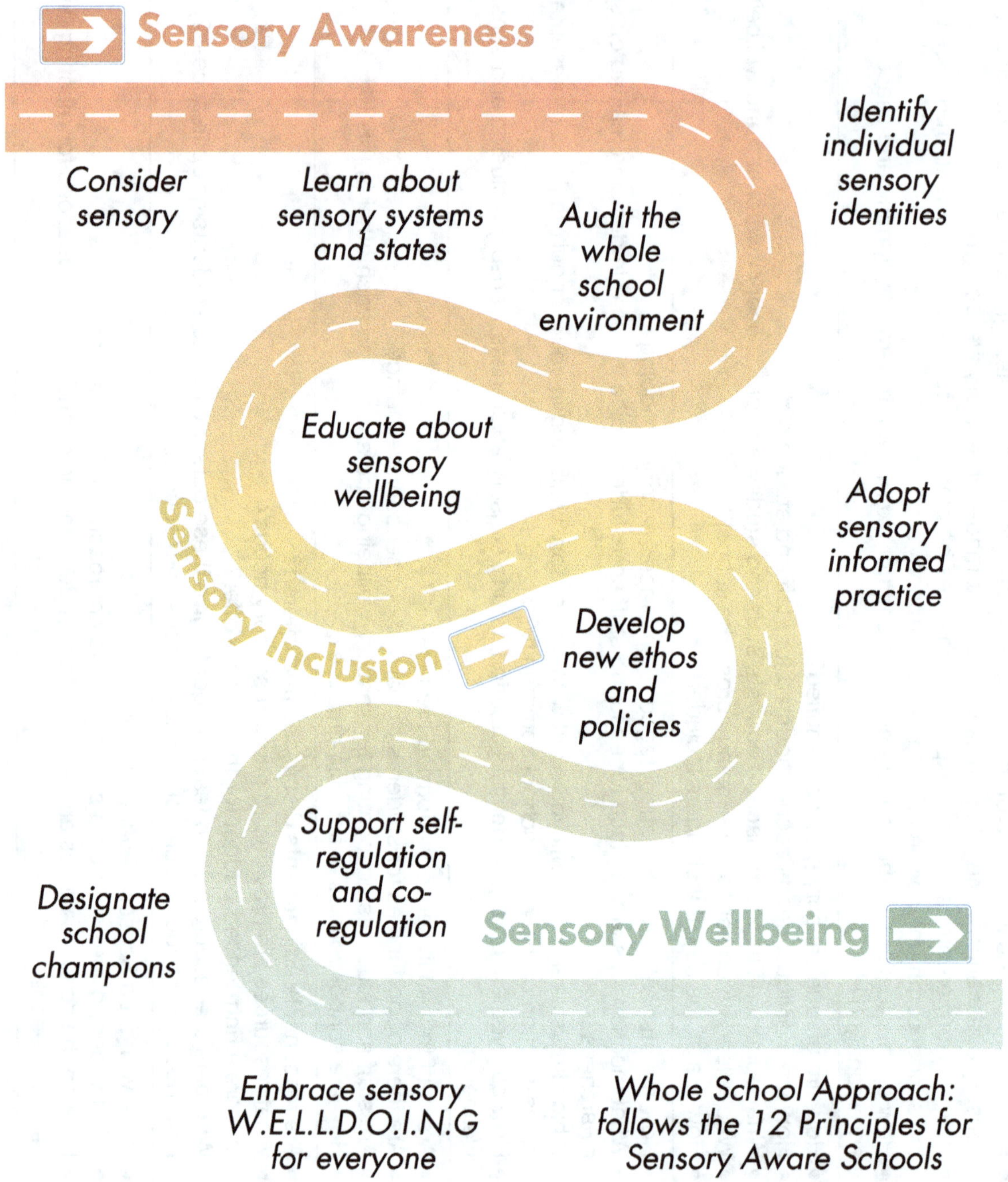

➡️ **Sensory Awareness**

- Consider sensory
- Learn about sensory systems and states
- Audit the whole school environment
- Identify individual sensory identities
- Educate about sensory wellbeing

Sensory Inclusion ➡️

- Develop new ethos and policies
- Adopt sensory informed practice
- Support self-regulation and co-regulation
- Designate school champions

Sensory Wellbeing ➡️

- Embrace sensory W.E.L.L.D.O.I.N.G for everyone
- Whole School Approach: follows the 12 Principles for Sensory Aware Schools

This roadmap shows the journey that schools can take as they become a Sensory Aware School. This is a journey that starts with becoming **sensory aware** but also builds on that to become **sensory inclusive** (where sensory needs are fully understood and met) and on to achieving **sensory wellbeing** as a whole school approach through adopting the 12 Principles of Sensory Aware Schools.

The 12 Principles of Sensory Aware Schools

Our school is committed to being sensory aware, which means we are:

1. **Inclusive** – everyone in our school community has a **unique sensory profile** and we listen to student and staff voice about their sensory needs, **including those with special educational needs**, to better enable us to meet needs.

2. Actively promoting **sensory wellbeing through sensory W.E.L.L.D.O.I.N.G** for all.

3. **Collaborative** – we work together to support our own and each other's sensory needs across our school community and bring in external support when needed. We work in partnership with parents and carers to support their children.

4. Clear about our **school ethos, values, policy and practice** in relation to sensory wellbeing.

5. Led by a designated **Sensory Wellbeing Champion** who advocates for sensory awareness and sensory wellbeing across the school in conjunction with a Sensory Wellbeing Working Party which includes the Senior Leadership Team, lead governor, staff, students and parents and wider relevant professionals.

6. Providing **continuing professional development** to develop a sensory skilled workforce.

7. We use a **common sensory approach** in implementing sensory informed practice.

8. **Curious** – we 'See behaviour – consider sensory'. We are open to the possibilities that sensory wellbeing can bring.

9. Developing the **school environment** so that more spaces are sensory-friendly.

10. Offering **sensory wellbeing education** as an identifiable part of our curriculum, with planned, timetabled lessons across all the Key Stages.

11. **Flexible** to suit the sensory needs of the individual and groups and dependent on time and space available.

12. **Reflective** – which enables growth, learning and development of self and practice for learning to live life well.

Action planning for Sensory Aware Schools

To help you to start to take action from all the learning from this chapter, and the book as a whole, we have provided you with an action plan on the next page. You can use this action plan in conjunction with the action feasilbility assessments on page 232. Print out your own copies to make notes on. Note down relevant page numbers in this book on the action plan that you may want to revisit to help you deliver your action plan.

ACTION PLAN
Our Sensory Aware School Review Cycle

School Name: _____

Assess...
What are the current issues?

Plan...
What interventions/resources/change are needed?

Do...
What are the priorities to do now?

Review...
How was that? What next?

Final words

We hope you have found this book a useful addition to build on your sensory informed practice. We wish you all the best with your journey to become a Sensory Aware School. Remember this is **nothing new, different or difficult**. We want you to prioritise **progress over perfection**. It's impossible to meet all sensory needs for everyone, all of the time, but through adopting a sensory aware approach, over the course of the school day, week, term and year, sensory regulation on the whole will broadly improve across the school. It is easiest if you **start with the quick wins**. Small changes can have a big impact, so start there. We want you to **embrace change** – we need a cultural shift in understanding sensory needs and a willingness to make physical changes to improve environments and changes to our practice that may initially feel out of our comfort zone.

Finally, remember to **stay curious, always be willing to learn and adapt, embrace new ideas and strategies to support sensory needs and remain open to possibilities.**

We hope you will see the value in adopting sensory aware approaches and the massive difference it can make in the lives of children and young people. We would love to hear how you get on!

Alice and Tessa

FURTHER READING AND RESOURCES

This section provides some further reading and a padlet link for wider resources.

We have created a padlet of resources (https://padlet.com/Drestermcgeeney/SensoryAwareSchools) for you to use that accompanies this book and includes many of the links and books below.

Sensory Inclusive Schools membership (www.sensoryinclusiveschools.org) offers online training and ongoing support for schools working on their sensory inclusion.

Caudwell Children offers free sensory packs to eligible families: www.caudwellchildren.com/changing-lives/how-we-can-help/autism-services/autism-sensory-packs/

Books

Answers to Questions Teachers Ask about Sensory Integration (Including Sensory Processing Disorder): Forms, Checklists, and Practical Tools for Teachers and Parents (2001) by Carol Stock Kranowitz, Deanna Iris Sava, Elizabeth Haber, Lynn Balzer-Martin and Stacey Szklut. Sensory Resources LLC.

Building Bridges through Sensory Integration: Therapy for Children with Autism and Other Pervasive Developmental Disorders (2015) by Paula Aquilla, Ellen Yack and Shirley Sutton. Future Horizons.

Creating Sensory Smart Classrooms (2021) by Jamie Chaves and Ashley Taylor, Routledge.

Diary of a Young Naturalist (2020) by Dara McAnulty. Little Toller Books.

Everyday Games for Sensory Processing Disorder: 100 Playful Activities to Empower Children with Sensory Differences (2016) by Barbara Sher. Althea Press.

From Wellbeing to Welldoing: How to Think, Learn and Be Well (2023) by Abby Osborne, Karen Angus-Cole and Loti Venables. Sage Publications Limited.

How to Support Pupils with Sensory Processing Needs (2016) by Lois Addy. Hyde.

Interoception: How I Feel: Sensing My World from the Inside Out (2018) by Cara N. Koscinski. PocketBooks for Special Needs.

Further reading and resources

The Interoception Curriculum: A Step-by-Step Framework for Developing Mindful Self-Regulation (2019) by Kelly Mahler. Hershey.

Living Sensationally: Understanding Your Senses (2007) by Winnie Dunn. Jessica Kingsley.

The Out-Of-Sync Child: Recognizing and Coping with Sensory Processing Differences (2022, 3rd edition) by Carol Stock Kranowitz. Penguin Publishing Group.

The Out-Of-Sync Child has Fun: Activities for Kids with Sensory Processing Disorder (2006) by Carol Stock Kranowitz. Perigee Books.

Raising a Sensory Smart Child: The Definitive Handbook for Helping Your Child with Sensory Processing (2005, 2009, 2018 and beyond) by Lindsey Biel and Nancy Peske. Penguin Publishing Group.

The Reason I Jump: One Boy's Voice from the Silence of Autism (2021) by Naoki Higashida. Sceptre.

Sensational Kids: Hope and Help for Children with Sensory Processing Disorder (SPD) (2014) by Lucy Jane Miller. Penguin Group.

Sensory Circuits: A Sensory Motor Skills Programme for Children (2009) by Jane Horwood. LDA.

Sensory Modulation Resource Manual (2018) by Julie O'Sullivan and Carolyn Fitzgibbon. Sensory Modulation Brisbane.

Sensory Processing Explained: A Handbook for Parents and Educators (2018) by Sharla Kostelyk and Heather Greutman. CreateSpace Independent Publishing Platform.

Sensory Solutions in the Classroom: The Teacher's Guide to Fidgeting, Inattention and Restlessness (2021) by Monique Thoonsen and Carmen Lamp. Jessica Kingsley Publishers.

The Sensory Team Handbook: A Hands-On Tool to Help Young People Make Sense of Their Senses and Take Charge of Their Sensory Processing (2009) by Nancy Mucklow. Michael Grass House.

Untypical: How the World Isn't Built for Autistic People and What We Should All Do about It (2023) by Pete Wharmby. Mudlark.

The Zones of Regulation: A Curriculum Designed to Foster Self-Regulation and Emotional Control (2011) by Leah Kuypers. Social Thinking Publishing.

100 Ideas for Primary Teachers: Sensory Processing Differences (2021) by Kim Griffin. Bloomsbury Publishing.

For Product Safety Concerns and Information please contact our EU
representative GPSR@taylorandfrancis.com
Taylor & Francis Verlag GmbH, Kaufingerstraße 24, 80331 München, Germany

www.ingramcontent.com/pod-product-compliance
Lightning Source LLC
Chambersburg PA
CBHW080849010526
44115CB00016B/2776